ENGRAVER
ENGRAVING
VISITING CARDS
CUMINGE
COMMINGS
EXCHANGE
&

The First One Hundred and Fifty Years

End papers, front and back, show Charles Wiley's office at 3 Wall Street in 1814

JOHN WILEY

THE FIRST ONE HUNDRED

A History of John Wiley and Sons, Incorporated

1807 - 1957

AND FIFTY YEARS

New York · John Wiley & Sons, Inc.

Library of Congress Catalog Card Number: 57-7626
Printed in the United States of America

Contributors

To the men and women,

past and present,

the many loyal and faithful members of our staff,

who have contributed so much to our progress

Preface

When the idea of a history of the firm was first discussed, we, of course, went immediately to our so-called archives to see what information we had available. For a long time we had known that material on our past was inadequate; but not until we had given it a careful examination did we realize how sparse indeed our records were. We had nothing of the Charles Wiley period (1807–1826) except a few old newspapers of the time advertising some Wiley imports or soliciting help in a want advertisement for compositors. Thus we had to depend on intensive research to come upon any data whatsoever. Charles Wiley left no files of his correspondence with Gulian C. Verplanck, James Fenimore Cooper, Washington Irving, Fitz-Greene Halleck, William Cullen Bryant, and others. If they ever were kept, they long ago had been destroyed as "useless stuff cluttering up the premises." Despite the fact that Charles Wiley was a founder and a respected member of the Bread and Cheese Club, and was in friendly intercourse with at least seven portrait painters in the group, including the famous S. F. B. Morse, no portrait of him is known to have been painted. Consequently, in displaying portraits of the men who have guided the destinies of this company throughout a century and a half, we have had to begin with John Wiley. Because John Wiley lived a long life and was known to several persons still living, there are many more data about him than about his father. John Wiley, too, had a genius for anonymity, and disposed of his records regularly. Much of our information about him comes from the record of his partner (1838–1848), George Palmer Putnam, his direct opposite, who seems never to have destroyed any copies of his letters. In all fairness, we must confess that this inclination to get rid of all sorts of paper still persists at Wiley's, and those of us who have been with the firm some two decades or more must admit to the same failing. Perhaps it is another indication that we as individuals and as a group are more concerned with the present than with the past. However laudable such a trait may be, the fact remains that for the researcher who must dig out these buried facts the problems are numerous and complex.

When Charles Wiley opened his shop for business in 1807, the new nation had been in existence only thirty-one years. It had essentially an agricultural economy, but, after the second war with England, manufacturing began to assume more importance. Thus we like to think that our firm, founded in this early industrial period, grew with the country and published books to meet new needs. This industrial growth was to be the theme of the Wiley History, and we envisioned a book that would trace briefly the background of a science or technology, with our publications placed in their proper historical perspective. It soon became clear that because of the diversity of subject matter covered by our books no one person could be expected to write an authoritative history of the firm. The task would require specialists in each area of knowledge, particularly those with an expertness in the bibliography of the subject. In most instances, we turned to our own authors who knew something of us and the things that we try to do in publishing. The results have been even better than we had anticipated. For the writers of some chapters, it was not an easy undertaking, since certain subjects had little historical background to fill in, with the result that the major portion of the article had to be devoted to the story of Wiley books. A number of our good friends even thought it an excellent opportunity to write a testimonial. These we restrained as much as possible and with much use of the editorial pencil. We still feel unhappy about many fine books not mentioned by our writers—

books that for one reason or another have been among our favorites for years. To these authors and to their descendants we offer our apologies. Obviously, all our books could not be mentioned by name; had they been, this history might have developed into nothing more than a complete catalogue of Wiley books, 1807–1957. In the chapter, "Of This and That," we have attempted to mention a number of titles of some importance not part of a specific area. Even that chapter is incomplete, as we have attempted to touch only the high spots in areas not covered by a special chapter.

We realize that this is an informal history of our company. It is not exactly the kind of history that we would have preferred to publish. In our opinion it would have been more interesting to tell many anecdotes, to quote from letters of our forebears in crises in the firm's history that would give us a more precise idea of the kind of people responsible for our past publishing ventures, some conception of the problems they faced and how near they came to realizing their publishing ambitions. Of one thing we are certain—none of our early predecessors, particularly Charles and John, both modest men, had any idea that their firm had more than a passing importance; they struggled only in the current scene and never suspected that years later there would be a demand for a formal history of their efforts and those of their descendants.

The conception and the execution of the plan for this history were carried out over a period of several years by Martin Matheson, senior vice president and secretary of our company. It was he who did the original research so necessary to determine what information was available, and from his findings came the framework around which this book has been developed.

As we view the struggles and achievements of our predecessors in this business, we have a feeling of humility and great respect. They accomplished more than they knew. Each of the men in charge of the firm's destinies, however they differed in temperament and in capabilities, passed on to his successors a point of view, a philosophy that, though difficult to express, has dominated throughout these years our way of doing business. We owe them much, and we hope that our admiration for them is reflected in the pages of this book.

EDWARD P. HAMILTON — *Chairman of the Board*

W. BRADFORD WILEY — *President*

August 29, 1956

Acknowledgments

THE LIST IS LONG of those who have in one way or another helped in the development of this book, either as advisers or as critics; to these many friends we are indeed grateful. We are glad to acknowledge specifically the assistance of Nelson F. Adkins, P. L. Alger, E. S. Ault, Ralph M. Barnes, Virginia Bartow, Robert F. Beach, James F. Beard, M. L. Begeman, Louis H. Bolander, Orlan W. Boston, H. L. Bowman, Margaret S. Bryant, Colin Carmichael, Samuel T. Carpenter, H. E. Carter, William Charvat, Austin H. Church, I. Bernard Cohen, E. J. Crane, Winterton C. Curtis, V. L. Doughtie, Rolf Eliassen, Liberata Emmerich, Katherine Esau, Gordon M. Fair, Richard F. Flint, R. G. Folsom, Joseph S. Fruton, Billy E. Goetz, A. T. Granger, Truman S. Gray, Jesse L. Greenstein, L. E. Grinter, George A. Hawkins, Harold L. Hazen, John B. Heffernan, N. S. Hibshman, O. A. Hougen, Eugene B. Jackson, Lyman E. Jackson, L. R. Jackson, T. W. Johnson, Jr., Joseph H. Keenan, Paul J. Kiefer, Richard S. Kirby, Philip G. Laurson, Helen R. LeBaron, Robert S. Lewis, Chester R. Longwell, J. F. McDermott, Donald H. McLaughlin, Arthur J. McNair, C. C. MacDuffee, Edgar MacNaughton,

C. H. Mathewson, Frederic G. Melcher, Raymond P. Morris, William J. Morton, Jr., Hugh C. Muldoon, Wilbur G. Nelson, Clarkson H. Oglesby, Austin M. Patterson, Courtland D. Perkins, A. A. Potter, Miles O. Price, James R. Robbins, Hunter Rouse, Henry S. Saylor, Dorothy Scott, F. B. Seely, Walter A. Shewhart, Frank T. Sisco, Harold R. Sleeper, C. Richard Soderberg, H. L. Solberg, R. W. Sorenson, George A. Stetson, D. B. Steinman, W. H. Timbie, Parker D. Trask, F. J. Van Antwerpen, John K. Vennard, Ernst Weber, Virginia Lee Wilcox, R. L. Wilder, Curtis L. Wilson, and Reginald D. Wood.

It is a pleasure to acknowledge our indebtedness to Kendall B. Taft, who not only wrote the first two chapters, but also had a share in the general editing of the book and was of invaluable assistance to us on matters concerning style, illustrations, and format.

Contents

Illustrations

. . . there is a charm about that little spot of earth, that beautiful city and its environs, that has a perfect spell over my imagination. . . . I thank God for my having been born in so beautiful a place among such beautiful scenery.

WASHINGTON IRVING to HENRY BREVOORT, *December 11, 1824.*

Charles Wiley's New York

ONLY A FEW MONTHS before the day, in 1807, that Charles Wiley opened his printing shop and bookstore on Reade Street, Stephen Carpenter brought his *Monthly Register and Review* from Charleston, South Carolina, to New York City. He had come to Manhattan, said Carpenter, that he might "stand at the confluence of the greatest number of the streams of knowledge."

Thus early in the formative years of the republic was there testimony to the increasing prestige of New York as a cultural center. Despite keen rivalry from other towns along the Atlantic seaboard, the importance of New York as a trading port and a commercial center was already established. In the very year that Wiley began his bookselling career, a local patriot named Samuel Latham Mitchill brought out his "Picture of New-York; or, The Traveller's Guide through the Commercial Metropolis of the United States," a self-assured account of the wonders of the author's home town. That Mitchill's complacent air and pedestrian style made his book a ready target for the town wits probably did not bother him greatly; he was content if his

"Traveller's Guide" had helped to publicize the Commercial Metropolis of the United States.

Even the town wits who ridiculed Mitchill's book were aware of the restless energy, the shifting social patterns, the potential greatness of New York. Only an awareness that they were addressing a relatively sophisticated, cosmopolitan audience could have induced Washington Irving and his co-authors to assure the public in the first issue of *Salmagundi* (January 24, 1807) that it was their intention "simply to instruct the young, reform the old, correct the town, and castigate the age."

The city that witnessed the birth of *Salmagundi*, in 1807, had gone through many changes since the close of the Revolution. As William Cullen Bryant put it, many years later:

> When *Salmagundi* appeared, the quaint old Dutch town in which Irving was born had become transformed to a comparatively gay metropolis. Its population of twenty thousand souls had enlarged to more than eighty thousand, although its aristocratic class yet had their residences in what seems now to us the narrow space between the Battery and Wall Street. The modes and fashions of Europe were imported fresh and fresh. *Salmagundi* speaks of leather breeches as all the rage for a morning dress, and flesh-colored smalls for an evening party. Gay equipages dashed through the streets. A new theatre had risen in Park Row, on the boards of which Cooper, one of the finest declaimers, was performing to crowded houses. The churches had multiplied faster than the places of amusement; other public buildings of a magnificence hitherto unknown, including our present City Hall, had been erected; Tammany Hall, fresh from the hands of the builder, overlooked the Park. We began to affect a taste for pictures, and the rooms of Michael Paff, the famous German picture dealer in Broadway, were a favorite lounge for such connoisseurs as we then had, who amused themselves with making him talk of Michael Angelo. Ballston Springs were the great fashionable watering-place of the country, to which resorted the planters of the South with splendid equipages and troops of shining blacks in livery.*

Late in November, 1807, the English visitor John Lambert arrived in New York City. His first-hand observations, eventually recorded in one of the many travel books of the period, present a picture of the town as it could have been seen by Charles Wiley and his contemporaries. Having noted

* William Cullen Bryant, *A Discourse on the Life, Character and Genius of Washington Irving* (New York: G. P. Putnam, 1860), pp. 14–15.

that New York was already "the first city of the United States for wealth, commerce, and population," and that it was also "the finest and most agreeable for its situation and buildings," Lambert went on to say:

> It has neither the narrow and confined irregularity of Boston, nor the monotonous regularity of Philadelphia, but a happy medium between both. [A remark that must have pleased the Gothamites.] When the intended improvements are completed, it will be a very elegant and commodious town, and worthy of becoming the capital of the United States, for it seems that Washington is by no means calculated for a metropolitan city. New York has rapidly improved within the last twenty years; and land which then sold in that city for fifty dollars is now worth 1,500.
>
> The Broadway and Bowery Road are the two finest avenues in the city, and nearly of the same width as Oxford street in London. . . . Much of the intermediate spaces between these large streets, and from thence to the Hudson and East rivers, is yet unbuilt upon, or consists only of unfinished streets and detached buildings.
>
> The houses in the Broadway are lofty and well built. They are constructed in the English style, and differ but little from those of London at the west end of the town; except that they are universally built of red brick. In the vicinity of the Battery, and for some distance up the Broadway, they are nearly all private houses, and occupied by the principal merchants and gentry of New York; after which the Broadway is lined with large commodious shops of every description, well stocked with European and India goods, and exhibiting as splendid and varied a show in their windows as can be met with in London. There are several extensive book stores, print-shops, music shops, jewellers, and silversmiths; hatters, linen-drapers, milliners, pastry-cooks, coach-makers, hotels, and coffee-houses. The street is well paved, and the foot-paths are chiefly bricked.*

As both Bryant and Lambert indicate, the built-up part of New York in 1807 was mainly on the narrow lower tip of Manhattan Island. The house of John Pintard on Duane Street, just above Rhinelander's Ship Yard, stood beyond the busier and more thickly settled thoroughfares. Greenwich Village was still a rustic settlement where some of the wealthier families had country estates, and a potter's field occupied the land that a few years later was to become fashionable Washington Square.

* I. N. Phelps Stokes, *The Iconography of Manhattan Island* (6 volumes. New York: Robert H. Dodd, 1915–1928), V, 1475.

Within their narrow confines, however, the varied thousands of the growing city went their separate and communal ways, pursued their dreams, worked and played.

A century and a half ago, as now, a major practical interest of many New Yorkers was commerce. In the post-Revolutionary effort to develop American trade and to stabilize the national economy, the port of New York had played, and was continuing to play, a major role. Until the Embargo Act of December 22, 1807, began to take effect, the wharves and the business district of the city were scenes of continuous, bustling enterprise. When he arrived in New York in November, John Lambert observed that

> . . . the port was filled with shipping and the wharfs were crowded with commodities of every description. Bales of cotton, wool, and merchandize; barrels of pot-ash, rice, flour, and salt provisions; hogsheads of sugar, chests of tea, puncheons of rum, and pipes of wine; boxes, cases, packs and packages of all sizes and denominations, were strewed upon the wharfs and landing-places, or upon the decks of the shipping. All was noise and bustle. The carters were driving in every direction; and the sailors and labourers upon the wharfs, and on board the vessels, were moving their ponderous burthens from place to place. The merchants and their clerks were busily engaged in their counting-houses, or upon the piers. The Tontine coffee-house was filled with underwriters, brokers, merchants, traders, and politicians; selling, purchasing, trafficking, or insuring; some reading, others eagerly inquiring the news. The steps and balcony of the coffee-house were crowded with people bidding, or listening to the several auctioneers, who had elevated themselves upon a hogshead of sugar, a puncheon of rum, or a bale of cotton. . . . The coffee-house slip, and the corners of Wall and Pearl-streets, were jammed with carts, drays, and wheel-barrows; horses and men were huddled promiscuously together, leaving little or no room for passengers to pass. . . . Every thing was in motion; all was life, bustle and activity. The people were scampering in all directions to trade with each other, and to ship off their purchases for the European, Asian, African, and West Indian markets. Every thought, word, look, and action of the multitude seemed to be absorbed by commerce; the welkin rang with its busy hum, and all were eager in the pursuit of its riches.

The following April, Lambert thought that the same scene presented a "melancholy appearance," for, because of the embargo, most of the shipping and trade had been suspended. Other hard times were to accompany the War of 1812, and further economic crises were to be met. On the whole,

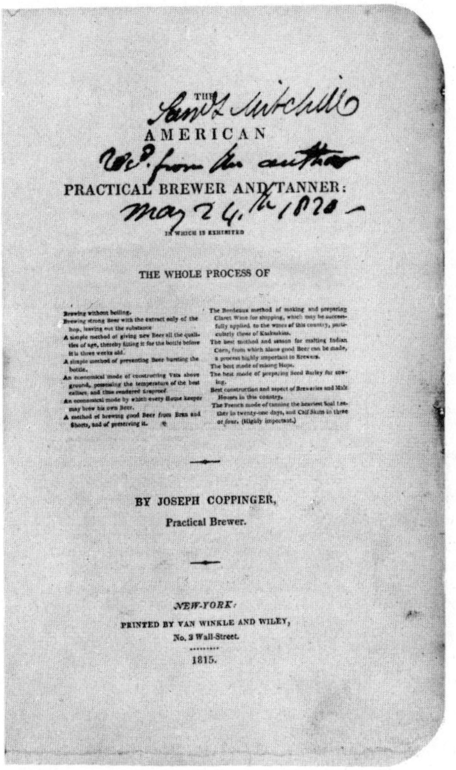

Saml. L. Mitchill
Recd. from the author
May 24th 1820

THE
AMERICAN
PRACTICAL BREWER AND TANNER:
IN WHICH IS EXHIBITED
THE WHOLE PROCESS OF

Brewing without boiling.
Brewing strong Beer with the extract only of the hop, leaving out the substance
A simple method of giving new Beer all the qualities of age, thereby fitting it for the bottle before it is three weeks old.
A simple method of preventing Beer bursting the bottle.
An economical mode of constructing Vats above ground, possessing the temperature of the best cellars, and thus rendered fireproof.
An economical mode by which every House keeper may brew his own Beer.
A method of brewing good Beer from Bran and Shorts, and of preserving it.
The Bordeaux method of making and preparing Claret Wine for shipping, which may be successfully applied to the wines of this country, particularly those of Kaskaskias.
The best method and season for malting Indian Corn, from which alone good Beer can be made, a process highly important to Brewers.
The best mode of mixing Hops.
The best mode of preparing Seed Barley for sowing.
Best construction and aspect of Breweries and Malt Houses in this country.
The French mode of tanning the heaviest Soal Leather in twenty-one days, and Calf Skins in three or four. (Highly important.)

BY JOSEPH COPPINGER,
Practical Brewer.

NEW-YORK:
PRINTED BY VAN WINKLE AND WILEY,
No. 3 Wall-Street.
1815.

Earliest technical book published under the Wiley imprint

however, during the years that Charles Wiley conducted his bookstore, New York was a growing, thriving community.

Such a community was almost certain to have a brisk political life. In 1807, though temporarily displaced as mayor of the city, DeWitt Clinton was the recognized leader of "reform" forces in local and state politics. (Later, as governor of the state, he was chief sponsor for the construction of the Erie Canal, completed in 1825.) The local Federalists—party of the landed gentry and the propertied classes generally—who since the turn of the century had often been outmaneuvered by their Republican (that is, Democratic) adversaries, made gains in 1807 by waging a "nativist" campaign and relabeling themselves the American Party. During the next few years mercantile resentment of the Embargo Act and the success of the Washington Benevolent Society in combating Tammany consolidated these gains, but party shifts and realignments were frequent. Eventually the Federalists lost their identity in the anti-Jackson grouping that, from 1833, was called the Whig Party. From 1807 on, the Democrats, though split by factionalism and occasionally losing elections, increased in numbers and influence, particularly as the suffrage was extended.

Closely related to both commerce and politics was journalism. Of the eight daily newspapers available to New York readers in 1807, four or five were frankly partisan: the *Commercial Advertiser* and the *Evening Post* were Federalist organs, whereas the *American Citizen* supported the Clintonian Republicans, and the *Morning Chronicle*, for a time, defended the devious political career of Aaron Burr. Other papers, such as the *Daily Advertiser* and the *Public Advertiser*, were devoted primarily to mercantile news, and, as their titles imply, advertising. A dozen triweekly or semiweekly and weekly newspapers also appeared, as did several magazines and periodical essays. The *Monthly Register and Review* and the irregularly issued *Salmagundi* have already been mentioned. Among their contemporaries were such variously titled publications as the *Christian's Magazine*, the *Lady's Weekly Miscellany*, the *Medical Repository*, the *New York Weekly Museum*, and the *Weekly Inspector*. Within the next two decades, of course, many other newspapers and magazines came into being.

In their lighter hours, away from the cares of business and politics, Wiley and his fellow citizens did not lack entertainment. *Salmagundi* testifies to, and ridicules, the fondness for dancing—"this dancing mania, which prevails chiefly throughout the winter." (In passing, it may be noted that the Salmagundians also satirized the feminine fashions of the day: "Picnic silk stockings, with lace clocks, flesh-colored are most fashionable, as they have the appearance of bare legs—*nudity* being all the rage.") Also popular were picnics, and dinner and supper parties, as well as formal banquets, at some of which the menus were, by present-day standards, truly staggering. One could, if he wished, spend an evening at Savage's Museum, 166 Greenwich Street, where he might witness "a new exhibition of Philosophical Experiments, shewing the great use of the Electric Fluid to the human body." Or, if he preferred, he could go to Brevoort's, 26 Chatham Street, and see "Spottee," the African horse, said to have been of "four rich and distinct colours, arranged like those of a leopard, and with a tail resembling that of an elephant"—a horse who could "add, subtract, multiply and divide, tell the hour of the day by a watch, and also count the number of buttons on a gentleman's coat." If one had a taste for music, he could attend concerts at the Mechanics' Hall or the City Hotel. In the summertime, Vauxhall Gardens, about two miles north of the old City Hall, offered refreshments along with "Fireworks and Illuminations," as well as occasional concerts and plays. Other summer gardens, such as Ranelagh and Columbia, also tempted the amusement seeker.

The Park Theatre, having had its interior extensively remodeled in the summer of 1807, was admiringly described by a local journalist as uniting "more of taste, grandeur, room, convenience and elegance" than any other playhouse in the country. Certainly it was roomy enough, for the same reporter declared that it contained 2,372 seats. Here, during the 1807–1808 season, were to be seen the celebrated Thomas Abthorpe Cooper (currently also the manager), Mr. and Mrs. John Darley, William Twaits, John Harwood, and many other performers. Here, too, besides a varied repertoire of popular comedy, farce, and melodrama, were presented "Hamlet," "Macbeth," "King Lear," "Othello," "Henry IV," and "The Merchant of Venice."

Despite all the opportunities for amusement, many New Yorkers attended on the Sabbath places of worship, of which, John Lambert tells us, there were thirty-three in 1807. Of these, nine were Episcopal and six Presbyterian; but adherents to the Dutch Reformed, Lutheran, Roman Catholic, Baptist, Methodist, and Jewish faiths also had their meeting houses, as did the Moravians and the Society of Friends. On weekdays, one might exercise his bent for spiritual, humanitarian, or other reform by taking part in the activities of one or more of the many charitable institutions and societies. That not all who called New York their home were devoted to lives of faith and good works is suggested by the petition to the mayor made by one Samuel Stillwell on November 5, 1807, in regard to "violences and insults committed by rowdies and crowds on Sunday against the Methodist churches." Nor was the treatment of the Catholics—many of whom were Irish—all that might have been hoped for in a town that boasted of its tolerance and its love of liberty.

On the other hand, as the city grew, it was making steady progress in providing for the physical, social, and educational needs of its citizens. Recurring epidemics of influenza, smallpox, and yellow fever in the late eighteenth century led to the establishment of a Board of Health Commissioners. Although the diseases named, and others, continued to claim victims for many years, by 1807 there was at least an organized effort to improve health conditions in New York. The Marine Hospital (for quarantine purposes) was in operation, as were the City Hospital, Bellevue Hospital (for contagious diseases), the Lying-in Hospital, and the New York Dispensary (for medical relief to the poor). Both private and public funds helped to support most of these institutions. Among agencies active in the relief of social distress were the Almshouse, the New York Orphan Asylum, the Humane Society (to aid imprisoned debtors), and the Howard Association, a forerunner of the Legal Aid Society.

The concern for public health was supplemented by a lively interest in the advancement of medical science and the other natural sciences. When the New York College of Physicians and Surgeons received its charter in 1807, two other medical schools were already in existence: the medical department of Columbia College and Dr. Nicholas Romayne's New Medical Institution. Dr. Romayne became president of the College of Physicians and Surgeons, and among other faculty members were Drs. David Hosack, Archibald Bruce, and Samuel Latham Mitchill. Something of the unspecialized character of early nineteenth century science is reflected in the fact that each of these medical men was an "authority" in several fields. Romayne was an ethnologist and classical scholar; Bruce, a mineralogist and geologist, and editor of the *American Mineralogical Journal;* Hosack, a botanist, and founder in 1801 of the Elgin Botanic Garden, first of its kind in the United States; Mitchill, one of the most famous physicians and surgeons of his day and an extraordinarily versatile figure who not only founded and helped edit the *Medical Repository*, but also made contributions to the literature of medicine, chemistry, zoology, botany, geology, ethnology, and ichthyology. Such men, and others, encyclopedic though they were, added measurably to the stock of scientific knowledge.

In 1807, although the idea of tax-supported free public schools was making slow headway, New York children had a better than average chance of getting at least an elementary education. Those whose parents could afford it went to one or another of the several denominationally or privately controlled schools. Some of the church schools received state grants for charity scholars, but for poorer children a much better opportunity was offered by the newly established New York Free School, maintained from 1806 for a number of years by a Free School Society, of which DeWitt Clinton was president and guiding spirit. The Lancastrian monitorial system of instruction, introduced at the same time, also worked toward bringing more students into the schools. The cause of higher learning in New York City was served almost exclusively at this time by Columbia College, located between Barclay and Murray streets. A small faculty instructed young men in classical languages, mathematics, rhetoric, philosophy, and other subjects. The graduating class of 1807 had twenty-two members.

Relatively little industrial activity contributed to the wealth or polluted the air of New York in 1807. There were nevertheless many craftsmen in the city: coppersmiths, silversmiths, potters, leather workers and shoemakers, cabinetmakers, hatmakers, and shipbuilders, to name only a few. The "age of steam" had not yet fully arrived, but all sorts of experiments were in progress. Locally, John Stevens and Robert Fulton were working on the development of the steamboat. Fulton's *Clermont* made its first trip up the Hudson on August 17, 1807, and later that year began a regular run between New York and Albany. The following year Stevens launched the *Phoenix*, first steamboat of entirely American manufacture. The aging Christopher Colles was still trying his hand, as one historian has said, "at everything from mouse traps to steam engines." Elsewhere in the United States and, of course, in Europe, there were many other signs of the encroaching industrial revolution—a revolution that was to transform the ways of life for millions of people. But for the moment New York was predominantly a city of commerce and handicrafts.

It also had its artists. In 1807 Archibald and Alexander Robertson were conducting their art school, the Columbia Academy of Painting, at Number 79 Liberty Street, only a few doors from the shop of the well-known engraver, Peter Rushton Maverick. At Number 3 Cedar Street, John Wesley Jarvis and Joseph Wood had their studio of portrait and miniature painting. William Dunlap, veteran playwright and theatrical manager, also was carrying on his career as a painter. During the year both Thomas Sully and

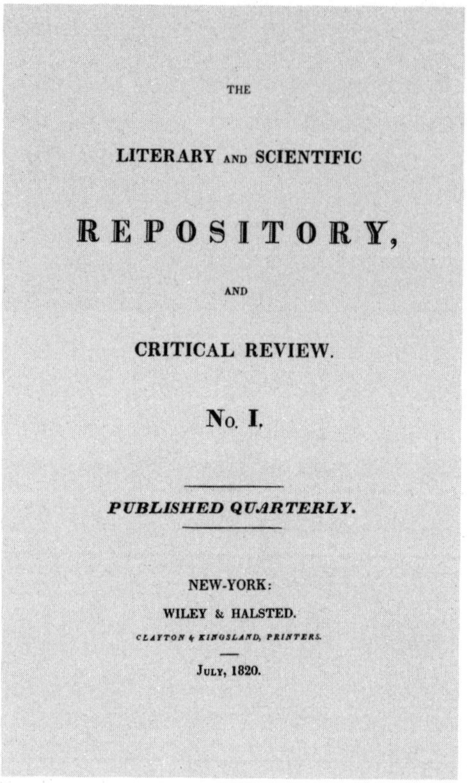

THE

LITERARY AND SCIENTIFIC

REPOSITORY,

AND

CRITICAL REVIEW.

No. I.

PUBLISHED QUARTERLY.

NEW-YORK:

WILEY & HALSTED.

CLAYTON & KINGSLAND, PRINTERS.

JULY, 1820.

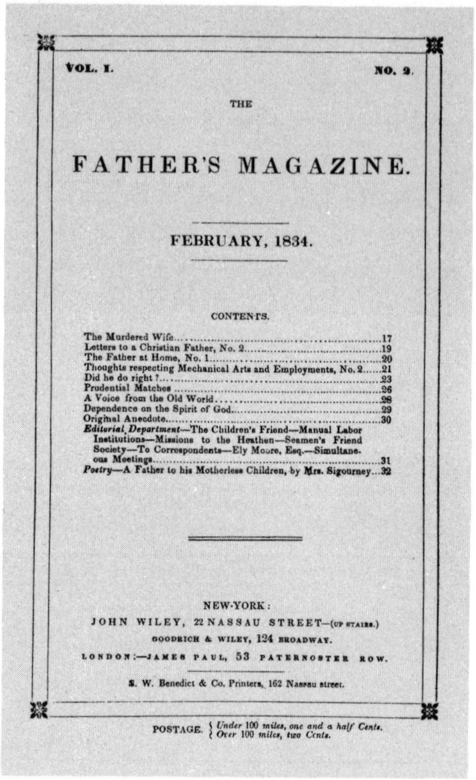

VOL. I. NO. 2.

THE

FATHER'S MAGAZINE.

FEBRUARY, 1834.

CONTENTS.

The Murdered Wife....17
Letters to a Christian Father, No. 2....19
The Father at Home, No. 1....20
Thoughts respecting Mechanical Arts and Employments, No. 2....21
Did he do right?....23
Prudential Matches....26
A Voice from the Old World....28
Dependence on the Spirit of God....29
Original Anecdote....30
Editorial Department—The Children's Friend—Manual Labor Institutions—Missions to the Heathen—Seamen's Friend Society—To Correspondents—Ely Moore, Esq.—Simultaneous Meetings....31
Poetry—A Father to his Motherless Children, by Mrs. Sigourney....32

NEW-YORK:

JOHN WILEY, 22 NASSAU STREET—(UP STAIRS.)

GOODRICH & WILEY, 124 BROADWAY.

LONDON:—JAMES PAUL, 53 PATERNOSTER ROW.

S. W. Benedict & Co. Printers, 162 Nassau street.

POSTAGE. { *Under 100 miles, one and a half Cents.* / *Over 100 miles, two Cents.* }

Wiley magazines of 1820 and 1834

Colonel John Trumbull were living and working in the city. Dr. Alexander Anderson, who has been called "New York's own master of wood-engraving," was active, as were the portraitists James Bailie, Caleb Boyle, and James Martin. At his museum on Greenwich Street, Edward Savage let it be known that he was skilled in the execution of historical paintings. Temporarily quiescent, the New York Academy of Fine Arts, established in 1802, was about to re-open its exhibits in new quarters at the Government House under the new name, American Academy of the Fine Arts. New York had no Copley, no Benjamin West, no Washington Allston. But it did have a group of practicing artists, some of them men of substantial talent.

When Charles Wiley went into business, a hundred and fifty years ago, the

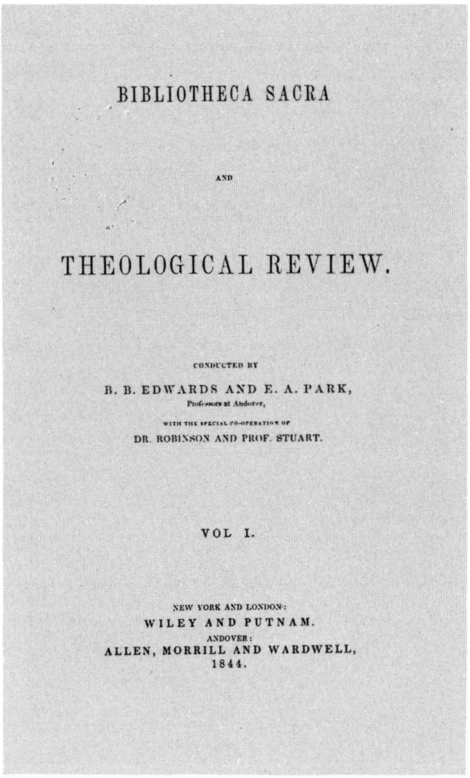

BIBLIOTHECA SACRA

AND

THEOLOGICAL REVIEW.

CONDUCTED BY

B. B. EDWARDS AND E. A. PARK,

Professors at Andover,

WITH THE SPECIAL CO-OPERATION OF

DR. ROBINSON AND PROF. STUART.

VOL I.

NEW YORK AND LONDON:

WILEY AND PUTNAM.

ANDOVER:

ALLEN, MORRILL AND WARDWELL,

1844.

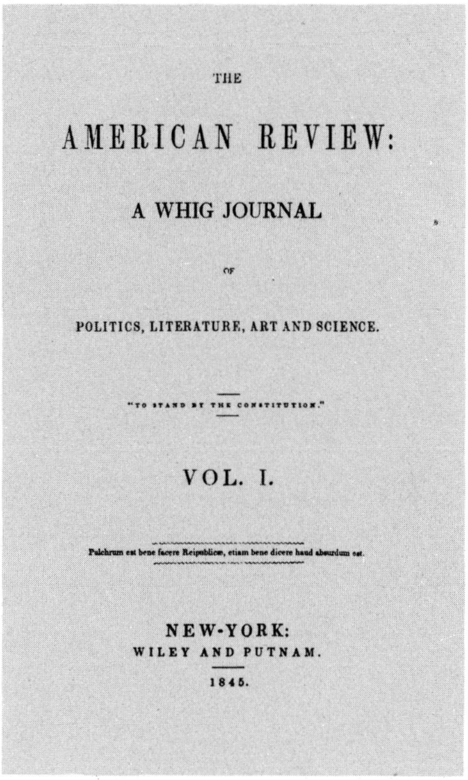

THE

AMERICAN REVIEW:

A WHIG JOURNAL

OF

POLITICS, LITERATURE, ART AND SCIENCE.

"TO STAND BY THE CONSTITUTION."

VOL. I.

Pulchrum est bene facere Reipublicæ, etiam bene dicere haud absurdum est.

NEW-YORK:

WILEY AND PUTNAM.

1845.

Wiley magazines of 1844 and 1845

functions of bookseller, printer, and publisher were virtually inseparable. In early city directories Wiley is listed variously as "printer," "bookseller," and "printer and bookseller." The term "publisher," as it is generally understood today, was not used until some years later. In Charles Wiley's time the risks of publication might be taken by author, printer, or bookseller. Frequently the relationship between writer and printer-bookseller was very close, as it certainly was between Wiley and some of the American authors whose books he brought out.

The New York book trade in 1807 was already highly competitive, for there were dozens of booksellers and scores of printers and bookbinders in the city. Although, as we shall see, Charles Wiley enjoyed the friendship of several notable authors, it is unlikely that his services to them ever brought him much financial reward. He lived a full, useful, and, let us hope, happy life in the long-gone days when New York was young. It remained for his successors, in a new stage of development in city and in nation, to create a real publishing firm.

KENDALL B. TAFT

Wiley's Literary Books

By 1815 Charles Wiley had moved his bookstore to Number 3 Wall Street. Here came into being his famous "back room," The Den, for some years a favorite gathering place for men of letters, artists, and others. From the friendships formed in The Den grew, about 1822, the Bread and Cheese Club, or "Cooper's Lunch," of which Wiley was a member. The same friendships stimulated Wiley's interest in fostering native American literature, an interest that was to be carried on by John Wiley.

Like other American publishers of his day, Charles Wiley realized that it was usually more profitable to bring out books of European, especially English, authorship. Of some sixty titles issued under his imprint, nevertheless, about a third were by American writers—ample evidence of his devotion to the cause of national letters.

Between 1814 and 1819 Wiley reprinted and marketed a number of books by well-known European writers, such as Lady Morgan's *O'Donnel*, Thomas Campbell's *Poems*, James Hogg's *The Pilgrims of the Sun*, Henry Kirke White's *Remains*, Lord Byron's *Manfred*, Thomas Moore's *Lalla Rookh*, and works by

Chateaubriand, Fénelon, Goethe, Scott, and Southey. With the publication, in 1819, of Fitz-Greene Halleck's satirical poem, *Fanny*, Wiley turned more and more to the sponsorship of American authors.

Fanny was issued, in wrappers, on December 27, 1819, and retailed at fifty cents a copy. It was so much in demand that the edition was soon exhausted. Wiley offered Halleck five hundred dollars for a continuation of the poem. Halleck obligingly wrote fifty more stanzas, and a second edition was published in 1821. The success of this venture possibly had something to do with Wiley's willingness to undertake the publication of a novel by the author of an ill-starred tale entitled "Precaution." The new book was, of course, James Fenimore Cooper's *The Spy* (1821), which succeeded beyond all expectations. As Henry W. Boynton tells us, Cooper retained his own copyrights, but Wiley continued as his publisher, and brought out *The Pioneers* (1823), *Tales for Fifteen* [two short stories for girls, written under the pseudonym "Jane Morgan" (1823)], *The Pilot* (1824), and *Lionel Lincoln* (1825). Wiley was thus instrumental in launching the career of the first important American novelist.

During the same period he met the elder Richard Henry Dana, and for a time in 1821–1822 published Dana's short-lived periodical, *The Idle Man*. His imprint also appeared on three works by Washington Irving's old friend and collaborator in *Salmagundi*, James Kirke Paulding. These were *A Sketch of Old England by a New-England Man* (1822), *Koningsmarke, The Long Finne* (Paulding's first novel, 1823), and *John Bull in America; or, The New Munchausen* (1825). The last-named book was a vigorous satire on the numerous books in which British travelers ridiculed and—many thought—misrepresented American life and institutions.

Among other American authors published by Charles Wiley were Henry Whiting (*Ontwa, The Son of the Forest*, 1822), James Gates Percival (*Poems*, 1823), Gulian C. Verplanck (*Essay on the . . . Evidences of Revealed Religion*, 1824), and David Porter (*Journal of a Cruise Made to the Pacific Ocean*, a reprint, 1822). Porter's *Journal* was to provide some of the background material that went into Herman Melville's *Typee* and "The Encantadas."

Charles Wiley died early in 1826. Shortly thereafter, his son John took over the family business of bookselling and publishing under his own and varying firm names: John Wiley, Wiley and Long, Wiley and Putnam, and eventually John Wiley and Sons. Until the company turned to the publication of primarily scientific and technical books, it continued to carry an extensive list of literary works. As has been said, John Wiley inherited much of his father's vital interest in the furtherance of American literature. Under his direction the firm was to publish the work of some of the most significant native writers of the pre-Civil War period.

Books of American history, travel, and exploration occupied a prominent place among John Wiley's earlier publications. Some of these were Samuel L. Knapp's *Life of Aaron Burr* (1835), Edwin Williams' *Narrative of the Recent Voyage of Captain Ross to the Arctic Regions* (1835), George W. Montgomery's *Narrative of a Journey to Guatemala in 1838* (1839), Catharine R. A. Williams' *Biography of Revolutionary Heroes* (1839), Abigail Adams' *Journals and Correspondence* (1841–1842), and John Trumbull's *Autobiography* (1841).

Widespread popular interest in the opening of the West was also reflected in the Wiley books, particularly in the eighteen-forties. The bitterly contested Oregon question produced *Memoirs of the Northwest Coast of North America* (1840), the work of Robert Greenhow, a translator in the United States State Department. This study, based to a large extent on first-hand accounts and originally published as a government report, was later revised and re-issued as *The History of Oregon and California.* Very much in the public eye at this time and for some years thereafter was the brilliant, impetuous explorer and military leader, John Charles Frémont. His *Report of the Exploring Expedition to the Rocky Mountains in the Year 1842 and to Oregon and Northern California in the Years 1843–1844,* first issued, like Greenhow's work, as a government report, was reprinted by several publishers, including Wiley in New York. Two other volumes that helped to satisfy the public appetite for accounts of the West and the Southwest, on the verge of the Mexican War, were Alfred Robinson's *Life in California* (1846) and Waddy Thompson's *Recollections of Mexico* (1846). A woman's view of life on the frontier was given by Caroline Kirkland in a collection of tales entitled *Western Clearings*, published by Wiley in 1845.

Another topic that received attention as Americans became more aware of the unparalleled variety, the vastness and grandeur of their homeland, was the Indian. By the forties, some of Cooper's novels, a few plays and tales by other writers, and such factual narratives as Heckewelder's "Account of the

. . . Indian Nations" had portrayed the Indian as, for better or worse, a part of the national culture. In 1841 Wiley published Alexander W. Bradford's *American Antiquities and Researches into the Origin and History of the Red Race*, a pioneer study in the ethnology of the Indian. In the same year the firm issued William Leete Stone's *The Life and Times of Red Jacket*, an informal biography of the Seneca chief Sagoyewatha. Another item on the Wiley list was Henry Rowe Schoolcraft's *Oneóta, or . . . The Red Race of America*, brought out in eight parts in 1844 and 1845. This book and Mary H. Eastman's *Dahcotah*, published by Wiley in 1849, supplied Longfellow with some of the Indian lore, not always accurate, that went into "The Song of Hiawatha." George H. Colton's poem, *Tecumseh* (1842), and James Hall's collection of tales and verse, *The Wilderness and War Path* (1846), were further additions in these years to the literary treatment of the Indian.

During the period of John Wiley's and George Palmer Putnam's partnership (1837–1848) the firm devoted much of its energy to building a strong list of literary books. While Putnam conducted a branch of the business in London and acted as English representative, Wiley looked after New York bookselling and publishing activities. In this period many of the books that appeared under the Wiley and Putnam imprint belonged to a series of reasonably priced books called "The Library of Choice Reading." With the aid of Evert A. Duyckinck as literary adviser (or editor), Wiley now began a companion series, "The Library of American Books," advertised as "an appeal for the literature of America—such a one as it has the right to make in its own behalf, with the expectation of a hearty response."

The first title in "The Library of American Books" was the *Journal of an African Cruiser*, published in 1845. This was a factual narrative based on the manuscripts of Horatio Bridge. Its principal literary interest probably derives from the fact that Bridge's manuscripts were edited by his friend and college classmate, Nathaniel Hawthorne. "I have remodelled the style, where it seemed necessary," Hawthorne told Duyckinck, "and have developed Bridge's ideas, where he failed to do it himself, and have put on occasional patches of sentimental embroidery." The following year Hawthorne was represented in the "Library" by a much more important title, *Mosses from an Old Manse*, issued in two volumes and presenting for the first time, in collected form, "Roger Malvin's Burial" and "Young Goodman Brown."

The second title in "The Library of American Books" was by another writer who has since achieved at least his share of fame. The author, this time, was Edgar Allan Poe, and the book was *Tales*, issued in June, 1845. Before the end of the year, some fifteen hundred copies of the *Tales* had been sold, with a royalty to Poe of eight cents a copy. Later in the same year Wiley brought out a companion volume, *The Raven and Other Poems*. Thereafter the two books were sometimes sold separately, in wrappers, and sometimes bound together, in cloth.

In the summer of 1845 Duyckinck tried to interest Ralph Waldo Emerson in adding a collection of his poems to the "Library." Duyckinck's offer called for a paper-bound book to retail at thirty-one cents a copy, on which Emerson was to receive a royalty of six cents. But the New Englander felt that he would do better to keep control of the copyright himself, and he eventually arranged with a Boston firm to publish his book of verse.

With William Gilmore Simms, Duyckinck proved to be more persuasive. For the Southern journalist and romancer, Wiley published, in two parts, a collection of tales called *The Wigwam and the Cabin* (1845). Among them was "Murder Will Out," which Poe once called the "best ghost story" he had ever read. Also included in the "Library" was a two-volume gathering of Simms's essays, *Views and Reviews in American Literature, History and Fiction*, published in 1846–1847.

In England, early in 1846, Putnam saw the proofsheets of a book that was about to be published by John Murray, and thought that it would be a valuable addition to the "American Library." Consequently, in March of that year Wiley brought out a narrative entitled *Typee: A Peep at Polynesian Life*, the first book of a young seafaring man named Herman Melville. *Typee* sold for seventy-five cents a copy paper-bound, and a dollar, in cloth. The first edition of two thousand copies was succeeded in the fall of 1846 by a revised—and, it may be added, considerably expurgated—edition. By the time the Harpers took over the rights to *Typee*, in 1849, nearly six thousand copies of the book had been disposed of, with author and publisher sharing equally in the profits.

As may be supposed, various other native writers appeared in "The Library of American Books." One was the redoubtable and, in many ways, remarkable Margaret Fuller, whose *Papers on Literature and Art* was published

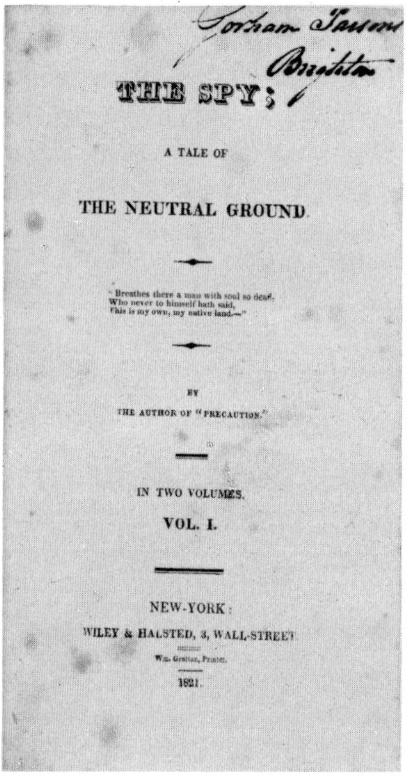
THE SPY;

A TALE OF

THE NEUTRAL GROUND.

"Breathes there a man with soul so dead,
Who never to himself hath said,
This is my own, my native land.—"

BY

THE AUTHOR OF "PRECAUTION."

IN TWO VOLUMES.

VOL. I.

NEW-YORK:

WILEY & HALSTED, 3, WALL-STREET.

Wm. Grattan, Printer.

1821.

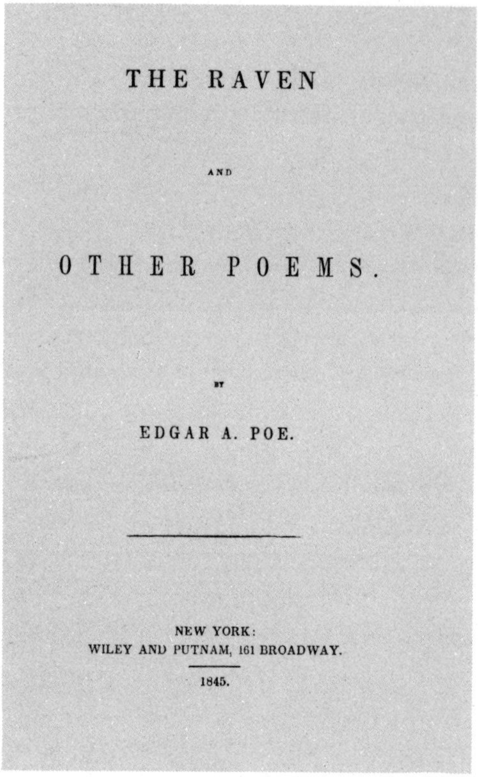
THE RAVEN

AND

OTHER POEMS.

BY

EDGAR A. POE.

NEW YORK:
WILEY AND PUTNAM, 161 BROADWAY.

1845.

The illustrations on this and the opposite page show four notable American books published under the Wiley imprint. The author of The Spy *is, of course, James Fenimore Cooper.*

in 1846. Another was Bayard Taylor, who was just beginning his spectacular career when the first of his many travel books, *Views a-Foot* (1847), was added to the "Library." The more sedate personality of John Greenleaf Whittier was represented by *The Supernaturalism of New England* (1847). And there were such now almost completely forgotten figures as George B. Cheever, with his *Pilgrim in the Shadow of Mont Blanc and the Jungfrau* (1845) and his *Journal of the Pilgrims at Plymouth* (1848); and Joel T. Headley, author of *Letters from Italy* (1845) and *The Alps and the Rhine* (1846). A complete history of the "Library" would tell much more than has been told here about the literary tastes and the cultural strivings in an important decade of American life.

It should not be thought that Wiley and Putnam neglected trans-Atlantic literature. Throughout the period of their association, they reprinted the work of a great many European writers. In "The Library of Choice Reading" books of many kinds appeared, often very shortly after the date of their original (that is, foreign) publication, although older books were also included in the series.

J. C. Derby, during the forties a bookseller in Auburn, New York, writes in his autobiography of buying from Wiley and Putnam a thousand copies of Alexander W. Kinglake's *Eothen, or, Traces of Travel Brought Home from the East* (1845). Kinglake's book, a minor classic of travel writing, seems to have been in wide demand among American readers, and was clearly a success for the publishers. The taste for travel literature and books of somewhat

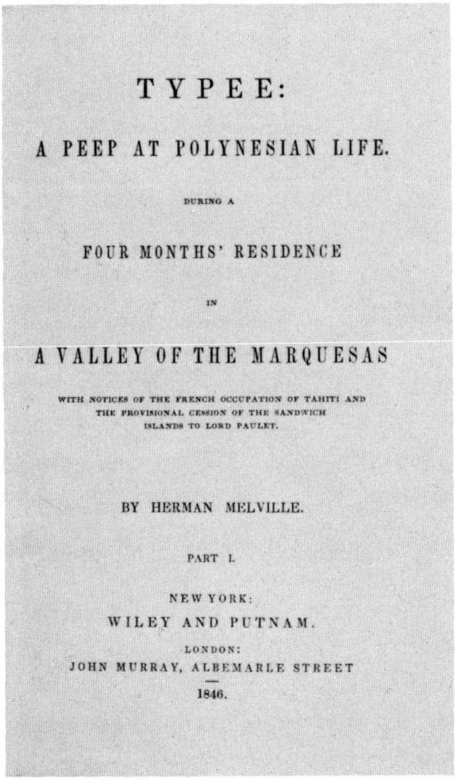
TYPEE:
A PEEP AT POLYNESIAN LIFE.
DURING A
FOUR MONTHS' RESIDENCE
IN
A VALLEY OF THE MARQUESAS
WITH NOTICES OF THE FRENCH OCCUPATION OF TAHITI AND THE PROVISIONAL CESSION OF THE SANDWICH ISLANDS TO LORD PAULET.
BY HERMAN MELVILLE.
PART I.
NEW YORK:
WILEY AND PUTNAM.
LONDON:
JOHN MURRAY, ALBEMARLE STREET
1846.

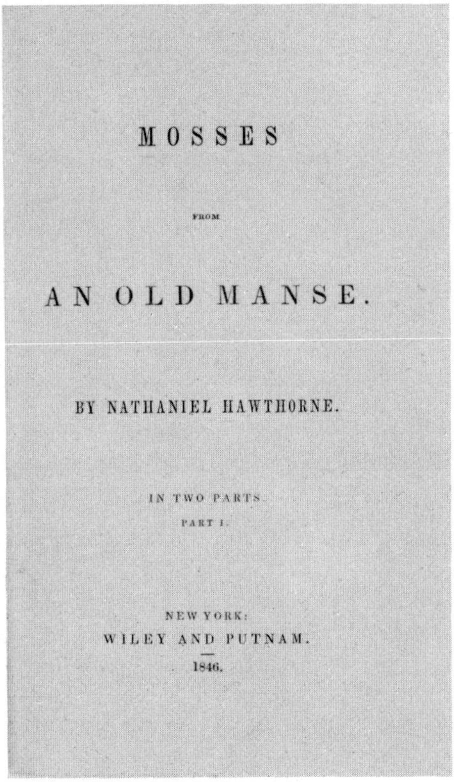
MOSSES
FROM
AN OLD MANSE.
BY NATHANIEL HAWTHORNE.
IN TWO PARTS
PART I.
NEW YORK:
WILEY AND PUTNAM.
1846.

exotic flavor is also reflected in such titles as George Borrow's *The Zincali, or . . . the Gypsies of Spain* (1842), Victor Hugo's *Tour on the Rhine* (1845), and William Makepeace Thackeray's *Notes of a Journey from Cornhill to Grand Cairo* (1846).

Although not among the principal American publishers of Charles Dickens' books, Wiley and Putnam responded to the current enthusiasm—almost a mania—for "Boz" by issuing *Pictures from Italy*, *The Cricket on the Hearth*, *The Battle of Life*, *Dombey and Son*, *David Copperfield*, and a collection called *Christmas Stories*.

Two other well-known English writers extensively represented on their list were William Hazlitt and Leigh Hunt: Hazlitt, by *Characters of Shakespeare's Plays*, *Lectures on the English Poets*, *Lectures on the English Comic Writers*, *Lectures on the Dramatic Literature of the Age of Elizabeth*, *Table-Talk*, *The Spirit of the Age*, and *Life of Napoleon Buonaparte;* and Hunt, by *Imagination and Fancy*, *The Diary of Lady Willoughby*, *The Indicator and the Companion*, and other titles. Charles Lamb also was represented by *Essays of Elia* and *Specimens of the English Dramatic Poets*, as was Samuel Taylor Coleridge, by *Biographia Literaria*, and Thomas Love Peacock, by *Headlong Hall and Nightmare Abbey*.

The wide range of "The Library of Choice Reading" is further suggested by the inclusion in its lists of such diverse writings as Thomas Carlyle's *History of the French Revolution* and *Heroes and Hero Worship*, Schiller's *Works*, A. W. Schlegel's *Lectures on Dramatic Literature*, and Goethe's *Autobiography*. The last of these books was Parke Godwin's edition, published in four parts in 1846–1847.

For some years after the dissolution of the Wiley and Putnam partnership, although Putnam took over many of the titles they had jointly published, Wiley continued to carry a list of literary books. He added few new authors, but he had a special enthusiasm for bringing out the successive works of John Ruskin. As early as 1847, Wiley and Putnam had issued one part of *Modern Painters*, and another part was published in 1848. The following year Wiley brought out *The Seven Lamps of Architecture*, and, in 1851, *Pre-Raphaelitism* and *The Stones of Venice*. During the next thirty-five years he published some fifty additional Ruskin titles.

Throughout much of the nineteenth century Wiley in its several individual entities provided literary fare for an incalculable number of American readers.

Probably the largest contributions were made by Charles Wiley in encouraging native writers when American literature was still in its infancy, and by John Wiley in supplying the public, long before the days of mass production, with varied and reasonably priced "libraries" of books by both American and European authors. That some of these books were of slight permanent interest or value is hardly to be questioned. But it is also true that among them were books of the highest quality—victors in the quenchless feud, as the author of *Typee* phrased it, between Time and the sons of Men.

It is singularly fitting that one of the few literary books published by John Wiley and Sons in the present century should have been Henry Walcott Boynton's *Annals of American Bookselling* (1932). In this sprightly narrative by the distinguished biographer of Irving, Bret Harte, and Cooper, full recognition is given to the parts played by Charles and John Wiley and by many of the others who had a share in the early shaping of the American book trade. The motto Mr. Boynton chose for the title page of his *Annals*, a quotation from the English printer and bibliographer John Nichols, is well worth repeating here: "If asked Why Printers and Booksellers, I answer, they are a valuable class of the community—the friendly assistants at least if not the patrons of literature."

KENDALL B. TAFT

Wiley and Putnam

At the close of the preceding chapter, reference is made to Annals of American Bookselling, 1638–1850, *by Henry Walcott Boynton (1869–1947). In that book, published by John Wiley and Sons in 1932, on the occasion of its one hundred and twenty-fifth anniversary, Boynton gave a systematic and lively account of the development of the American book trade from its beginnings until the middle of the nineteenth century. Since two chapters of the book contain many comments on Charles and John Wiley and on the historical background of the firm of Wiley, it has seemed appropriate to reprint them in this book. They are here presented in a sparingly edited version.*

WILEY HAS DONE BUSINESS under the same name for more than a century. It was founded in 1807, and therefore celebrates this year [1932] its 125th anniversary. Irving's *Salmagundi* appeared in that year, and no doubt was on sale at Charles Wiley's bookshop in Reade Street. That was 'way down town, but so was all of the New York that mattered, in those days. Charles Wiley had been born and brought up in the neighborhood. His father John Wiley was a New Yorker of note. He lived on a large plot of land leased from old Trinity, lying between the church and the river. His house was just behind the rear wall of the churchyard; his distillery was nearer the river. There he made a fortune in the approved pre-Revolutionary manner, owning a fleet of brigs and schooners which plied profitably in the rum-slaves-and-molasses trade that was also enriching Puritan New England. Early in the Revolution he equipped a company for active service, became its captain, and later a major actively serving in the Revolutionary army. He was a useful citizen and an ardent Whig, was of the party that tore down the statue of George III in the Bowling Green in 1781. He once bore a challenge to Alexander Hamilton from the Colonel Oswald who had fought with Matthew Carey. Major John Wiley was a bluff and crusty citizen of the old school, loved his quarrel and would have his way. On the authority of one of his descendants, "his wife once refused to sign a deed which he wished to have executed, and he threatened to hold his finger in the flame of a lighted candle until she consented. He did so and for the rest of his life had a crooked finger; but my grandmother signed the deed. . . . He was well educated, vastly more patriotic than amiable, loved his friends devotedly, hated his enemies fervently, used a great deal of bad language and old Jamaica. He was an honest man, a brave soldier, a true patriot."

Charles Wiley was twenty-five when he began as a bookseller. He seems to have been at school or at leisure during the age when most of his contemporaries in the book trade were serving as shop-boys or apprentices. Certainly his clients recognized him as a man of education and taste. No doubt his father the Major started him in business when he was ready for it. He was primarily a bookseller, though he owned a printing press at some time during the early years; and would later become publisher of some of the earliest American books of high literary quality.

Up to 1815 or even later American imprints are confusing. "Published by" seems to have been used casually as an equivalent of "printed for." Often (as in eighteenth century England) a book was issued as "printed for" a number of booksellers, who presumably shared the risks of publication. Till about 1830 most of the Harper books bore on the title-page merely "printed by J. and J. Harper"; soon after, without apparent consciousness of radical change, the Harper imprints read "published by" or "printed and published by." The Harpers were primarily printers. A bookseller sponsoring a new publication was naturally more likely to call himself publisher on the imprint. But the general usage was haphazard. One of the earliest books to bear the Wiley name was a *Life of Wellington*, issued in 1814 with the imprint: "Printed and Published by Van Winkle and Wiley, Wall and New Streets, New York." But *Travels in Egypt*, a year later, was "published by Jacob Gillet, Van Winkle and Wiley, Printers." Van Winkle was a printer by trade, Wiley, primarily a bookseller. These two had some sort of partnership for a few years. But in 1819, when Fitz-Greene Halleck's *Fanny* was "published by C. Wiley and Co.," Van Winkle can hardly have been the "Co."; for that year Irving's "Sketch Book" was "printed by C. S. Van Winkle" alone. Wiley probably gave the work to Van Winkle and was its unnamed publisher; a letter of Halleck's supplies the evidence. Halleck was one of the reading and writing men (*literati* was the word) who already found a pleasant gathering-place at Wiley's bookshop. Charles Wiley was the sort of bookseller that makes his clients feel at home and shares their interest in bookish matters. Halleck was among the New Yorkers exiled by the yellow fever epidemic of 1819, and whiled away his days in the country by writing a string of satirical verses called *Fanny*. He would naturally have mentioned them to his friend Wiley, on his return to the city; and at the end of the year wrote to his sister: "I have spun out the poem which I repeated to you last summer into a book of fifty pages. . . . I had no intention of publishing it, but the bookseller who brought out Irving's 'Sketch Book' offering to publish *Fanny* in a style similar to that work, I consented to his doing so. . . . The bookseller stated to me that I was the only writer in America, Irving excepted, whose work he would risk publishing." The opinion was founded partly on his judgment of *Fanny* and partly on the popularity of the "Croaker Papers," which had just been issued in an unauthorized edition, and were as popular as Irving's *Salmagundi* had been a dozen years before.

Charles Wiley presently published *Fanny*, and was clearly the bookseller mentioned as having "brought out" the "Sketch Book." There is a clue to his connection with it in Pierre Irving's "Life"; though the biographer does not see the meaning of his own evidence. Here and elsewhere (like Lounsbury and others) he confounds Charles Wiley and his son John. The numbers of the "Sketch Book," of course, were written in England. From London, Irving wrote to his friend Brevoort asking him to arrange for the publication of the sketches here. Irving had been acting as a sort of agent in London for Moses Thomas, the Philadelphia bookseller. Thomas seems to have been unable to meet certain obligations incurred for him, and Irving did not now feel like turning the "Sketch Book" over to him as publisher, though he wished him to have preference as a bookseller. "I wish," he wrote Brevoort, "the copyright secured for me, and the work printed and then sold to one or more booksellers, who will take the whole impression at a fair discount, and give cash or good notes for it. This makes short work of it, and is more profitable to the author than selling the copyright." Brevoort apparently turned the matter over to Wiley, and Wiley placed the book with his friend Van Winkle. Irving was much pleased with Van Winkle's work, and "Bracebridge Hall" went to him also, though Irving again had thoughts of Moses Thomas as publisher. Whatever his temporary delinquency may have been, Thomas was a respectable and successful man, and Irving and he were life-long friends.

If chance failed to set Charles Wiley's name on the title-page of the "Sketch Book," chance or merit very soon associated him with an equally famous author and work. Traveling on his ordinary business through western New York in 1820, Wiley made an agreeable acquaintance, a country gentleman named Cooper whose family hailed from up-state, though he was then living at Mamaroneck. Cooper had already published a book, his early stunt-novel "Precaution." But it had been issued anonymously, and Wiley knew nothing of its authorship. When Cooper presently wrote *The Spy*, he naturally offered it to the New York bookseller with whom he had passed some pleasant hours on the road, and whose shop he had very likely visited after their meeting. Wiley was receptive, he would print the book and put his name to it; but he would not pay cash for the copyright. It was the only time any publisher ever got the chance to buy a Fenimore Cooper novel. For *The Spy* succeeded beyond hope, and Cooper thereafter, like Irving, chose to keep his copyrights in his own hands. Cooper indeed had the habit of attending to the actual manufacture of his books. He bought the paper, hired the printer, saw his book through the press, and showed a general distrust of professional publishers. As against selling outright, or accepting a percentage of the profits, he preferred taking the whole risk of profit and loss. Copyright for *The Spy* and its successors was recorded in Wiley's name, but this simply to preserve the anonymity of "the author of 'Precaution.'" The imprint of *The Spy* reads: "New York: Wiley and Halsted, 3 Wall-Street. William Grattan, Printer." Oliver Halsted was probably the "Co." of the *Fanny* imprint. Charles Wiley's mother was a Halsted, and the several Halsteds associated with the Wiley firm at intervals for many years were cousins or connections. The second and enlarged edition of Halleck's *Fanny* had the Wiley and Halsted imprint. Cooper's *Pioneers*, *Pilot*, and *Lionel Lincoln* bore the name of Charles Wiley alone, with various printers.

The Spy was an experiment; no wonder Charles Wiley failed to jump at it. The "Waverley Novels" were just then at the top of their popularity. What chance did American materials offer an American romancer? Cooper himself had little faith in the book, and left the first volume lying about for some time before he began the second. Its printing began before the end was in sight, and Charles Wiley, as the copy rolled in, was troubled lest the book run altogether beyond reasonable limits; whereupon Cooper supplied a closing chapter which was at once printed and paged, leaving the romancer to fit his tale into the intervening space as best he might. Cooper, living in the country, had no chance to read the proofs. Even an author who camped next door to his printer must correct his proofs piecemeal, without chance of revision, since the chapters were printed and the type broken up as the book went on. His only recourse from gross errors was the list of errata—a clumsy afterthought.

A letter to Cooper from Charles Wiley, when *The Spy* came out, throws light on their friendly relations, as well as on the small scale by which success was measured at that time. "*The Spy* has succeeded over and beyond my expectations, and they were not easily to be exceeded. We have sold 100 to M. Carey and Lea, 100 to Lockwood, each at six months, 50 to Gilley at three months, besides 24 copies to several others. We have also retailed a very considerable number ourselves. A number of copies have been sold or sent on commission to the principal towns in different States. We have sold and sent off on commission about 600 copies, and think it probable the whole edition will be sold in three months." Wiley goes on to give some of the opinions he has had of *The Spy*, mainly approving; Halleck was especially delighted with it. And a postscript indicates that Charles Wiley's father, the Major, was still very much alive: "I forgot to mention that my father read *The Spy*, and is so delighted that he proposes, on your arrival in 'The Mamaroneck' [the stagecoach of that name] to take off the horses and with assistance of others to drag you throughout the city."

Wiley's guess fell short. The first small edition was followed within four months by two others of three and five thousand copies. The American novel was on its way. England could not long delay recognition though the great John Murray refused *The Spy*, as he had refused the "Sketch Book," till others had taken the risk of their first publication in England. Later on, England was disposed to claim that Cooper had been first encouraged there, which Cooper himself stoutly denied. American rights in England, at that time, had to be guarded by the same uncertain methods used for English books in America. Early sheets, simultaneous publication, "author's editions," strove for the crumbs that fell from the table. England, to be sure, was ready for a square deal some half-century before America would meet her with the necessary legislation.

During the early 1820's Wiley's bookshop became a rendezvous for bookish people, the Mermaid Tavern or the Old Corner of its place and time. There was a back room known as The Den, where the writing gentry of the city forgathered. Charles Wiley was host; Fenimore Cooper, now living in town, was the nerve-centre of the group. In The Den the "Bread and Cheese Club," or "Cooper's," came into being. Wiley habitués, with Wiley himself, were its charter members. To it belonged sooner or later Fitz-Greene Halleck and J. K. Paulding and Verplanck and Percival, and later the Yankees S. F. B. Morse, the painter, and Bryant, the poet, and a young lawyer named Dana. It was a literary-convivial club noted for its dinners and its rational jollity, if there is such a thing. It met on stated evenings. By day Wiley's shop was still the gathering-place. One summer Cooper sailed almost daily from Hallett's Cove to the city, in his sloop *Van Tromp*, and often took his daughter Susan with him, "resting until the turn of the tide at Mr. Wiley's bookstore" (Cooper, "Pages and Pictures").

Working as apprentice or clerk in Charles Wiley's bookshop at that time was his oldest son John. Born in 1808, the boy had been well schooled up to the college age, and had then gone into his father's business. He grew up in the atmosphere of The Den, and never forgot the remarkable group that frequented it. He never forgot, it may be, that some of these genial gentlemen with their scribbling had cost his father a pretty penny. Charles Wiley seems to have been more successful as a host than as a man of business. His publishing, certainly, brought him no fortune. Though *The Spy*, *The Pioneers*, and *The Pilot* were famous successes, there was no vast profit in them, and the author was astute enough to bag most of what there was. Cooper's fourth novel, *Lionel Lincoln*, was a failure. About then Charles Wiley's health was failing too, and by 1825 Cooper had to look elsewhere for a publisher. For Wiley's sake as well as his own, Cooper arranged with the Philadelphia Careys to take over his forthcoming book, "The Last of the Mohicans." Charles Wiley died, we know, in 1826, just as the "Mohicans" was being issued under the imprint of H. C. Carey and I. Lea.

Soon after Wiley's death we find his son John, then just a man by law, fairly launched as a bookseller under his own name. By 1828 he had made an excellent connection as agent for Carey and Lea, who thus far held their advantage as general publishers over the oncoming Harpers of New York. John Wiley was New York agent also for Thomas Wardle of Philadelphia, by all odds the leading importer of English and foreign books for the American market. In 1832 John Wiley formed a partnership with George Long (another bookseller's son), and Wiley and Long did business together for a few years. In 1834 Fenimore Cooper's provocative *Letter to His Countrymen* appeared under the imprint of John Wiley alone. According to the preliminary "advertisement" the author has "presented it to the son of his old and much-esteemed publisher, Charles Wiley, who has given it its present form for purposes connected with his own convenience." Osborn and Buckingham were the printers; John Wiley (unlike Charles) does not seem to have been a printer at any time. The *Letter* cannot have been a valuable gift in a money way; it is of interest as the first book that bore Fenimore Cooper's name on the title-page. John Wiley's was there with it.

Wiley and Long were associated for some years as booksellers, publishers, and distributors for the Philadelphia firms of Carey, Lea and Blanchard and Carey and Hart. With them, by 1833, was a young man of a name fated to become mighty in the publishing field. In 1840 Long withdrew, and a new firm came into being, Wiley and Putnam. For more than a decade the records of the Wileys and Putnams are inextricable.

John Wiley, the senior member of the firm, was a man of good sense, conservative by nature and inclined to play safe in a business that had proved treacherous for his father's sanguine temper. Young George Palmer Putnam, with no such background of experience, was full of ideas and ambitions. Born at Brunswick, Maine, in 1814, at eleven he was living prentice-fashion in the house of a Boston uncle who had a carpet-store. Detesting carpets and the rigor of a Puritan household, he headed for New York at fifteen and found a job in a little bookshop on Broadway near Maiden Lane, at $25.00 a year and board. The master of the shop, G. W. Bleecker, published one of the flimsy, pretentious periodicals of the time, *The Euterpiad, an Album of Music, Poetry and Prose*. "An apprenticeship of a year or two," says Putnam in an autobiographical fragment, "in this little mart of school-books, Andover theology, albums, stationery, and cheap pictures, was not a severe ordeal." He read the best stuff he could get hold of. After his year or two with Bleecker he made a better connection as general clerk for Jonathan Leavitt. Theological and religious books were still a leading branch of the book trade, and Leavitt specialized in them. He was a Yankee bookbinder who had come to New York to look out for the book department of Mr. Daniel Appleton, a dry-goods merchant. They were brothers-in-law. The book department flourished, but for some reason Leavitt chose, after a year or so, to set up for himself.

We have a sweeping view of the American book trade in the 1830's in the fragment of autobiography left by the original Putnam:

> At this time (1832–1833) the chief publishers of the land were these: In Boston, Lincoln and Edmunds (succeeded by Gould and Lincoln), devoted especially to the views of the Baptists; Crocker and Brewster, the leading orthodox Congregationalist publishers; Cummings and Hilliard, afterwards Hilliard, Gray and Co., chiefly engaged in schoolbooks; Lilly, Wait and Co., reprinters of foreign reviews, etc.; R. P. and C. Williams, respectably rusty in the general trade; Allen and Ticknor, predecessors of the present firm of Ticknor and Fields; Little, Brown. . . .
>
> In New York T. and J. Swords, the ancient Episcopal booksellers in Broadway, whose imprint may be found dated as early as 1792; Evert Duyckinck, an

estimable man, father of the well-known authors E. A. and G. L. Duyckinck; S. Wood and Sons (the sons worthily continuing) and J. B. Collins in the school-book and jobbing trade; Elam Bliss, the gentlemanly and popular caterer on Broadway, whose elegant little *Talisman*, edited by Bryant, Verplanck, and Robert C. Sands, was the father of American "annuals," and a good deal better than some of the children; G. and C. Carvill, the English successors of the still more famous Eastburn, on the corner of Wall Street and Broadway, the most exclusive dealers in general literature and, like Bliss's opposite, the lounging place of the *literati;* George Dearborn, then a new star, issuing double column Byrons, Johnsons, Burkes, besides *The American Monthly*, *The Republic of Letters*, and *The New York Review*, Jonathan Leavitt taking charge especially of the department of theology; and the brothers Harper were holding up their gigantic business of producing general literature, then consisting chiefly of reprints of English authors.

In Philadelphia this main branch of the trade was then largely in control of Carey and Lea, successors of the famous Matthew Carey, in the premises still occupied by Blanchard and Lea, the leading medical publishers. Carey and Hart, in the same "corner of Fourth and Chesnut," rivaled the Harpers in their dispensation of new novels, and also in more solid literature. . . .

In Andover, Mass., Mr. Flagg printed the learned works of Moses Stuart and Leonard Woods. In Hartford "Uncle Silas" Andrus would grind out cords of Shakespeares, Byrons, Bunyans, and "Alonzo and Melissas," suited for the country trade. In Springfield the Merriams printed Chitty's law books and others, but had not yet begun to work the golden mine of Webster's "Unabridged." Here and there a book would come along with the imprint of Hyde of Portland, Kay of Pittsburg, Howe of New Haven, Metcalf of Cambridge, Gould of Albany, Armstrong of Baltimore; but the three great cities first named, then as now, monopolized the bulk of the bookmaking—Boston rather leading the van.

The young G. P. Putnam who became John Wiley's partner in 1837 had strong convictions and plenty of energy. A year earlier, while he was still a clerk with Wiley and Long, he was chosen secretary of a new society for the establishment of an international copyright law. It was the beginning of a campaign so long that he did not live to see it through. John Wiley also was among the first and most persistent advocates of a copyright law. Putnam no sooner became Wiley's partner than he began to push for expansion. He believed a branch business in England would be a good thing for American books over there as well as for English books in America. In London, too, he would be able to work in the interests of a copyright law. It was

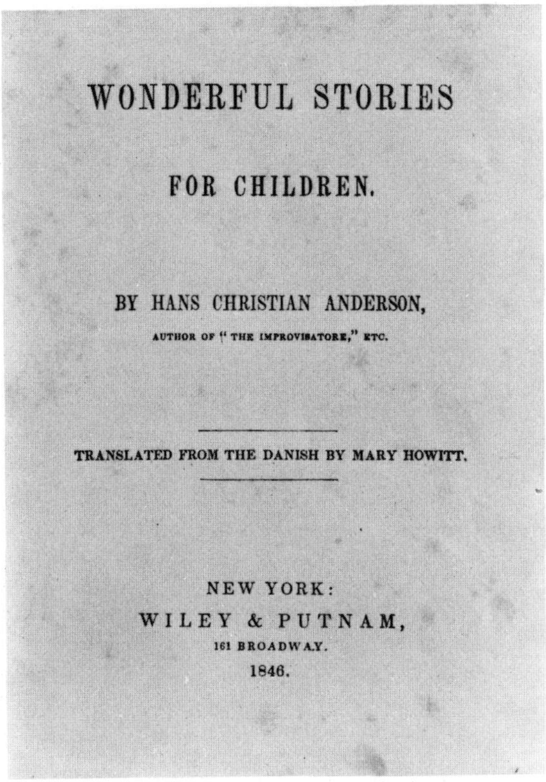

WONDERFUL STORIES

FOR CHILDREN.

BY HANS CHRISTIAN ANDERSON,

AUTHOR OF "THE IMPROVISATORE," ETC.

TRANSLATED FROM THE DANISH BY MARY HOWITT.

NEW YORK:
WILEY & PUTNAM,
161 BROADWAY.
1846.

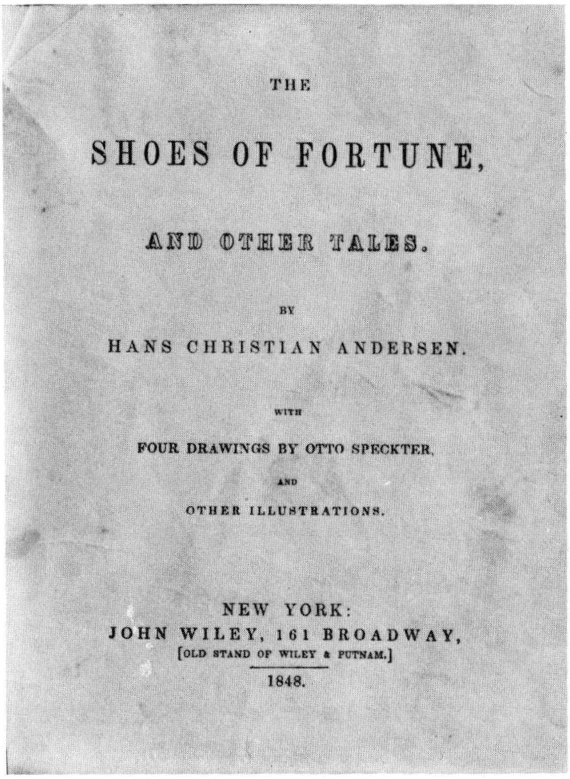

THE

SHOES OF FORTUNE,

AND OTHER TALES.

BY

HANS CHRISTIAN ANDERSEN.

WITH

FOUR DRAWINGS BY OTTO SPECKTER,

AND

OTHER ILLUSTRATIONS.

NEW YORK:
JOHN WILEY, 161 BROADWAY,
[OLD STAND OF WILEY & PUTNAM.]
1848.

Famous juveniles published by Wiley

agreed that he should take charge of a bookshop there and try the theory out. He found a place in the classic street for bookshops, Paternoster Row. According to a description by James Brown of Little and Brown, it was not an impressive centre at that time: "Paternoster Row I was greatly disappointed in. Instead of a street full of splendid booksellers' shops, it is a narrow lane barely admitting a carriage: dirty, dark, gloomy and disgusting. It is for the most part filled with booksellers; but what gives character to the whole lane is a large tallow-chandler's establishment, and the beef market. In this mean street, however, are sold more fine books than in any other in the world. Here, too, booksellers with their families live and here as elsewhere in London you meet the bookseller's wife assisting in the labors of the shop and busy with the pen, or assorting parcels for distant customers, and in discussing the comparative value of the different editions of Boyle and Dumas." Perhaps Putnam, the American, found the street too stuffy; he moved presently to Waterloo Place. His business was mainly exporting English books and periodicals. He tried to sell American books to English readers, but his imported editions had to compete with English reprints. Like Fenimore Cooper and others before and after him, he was continually irritated by the general British ignorance and misunderstanding of American conditions and affairs. In 1845, when he had been in London several years, he published a book of 300 pages called *American Facts: Notes and Statistics Relating to the Government, Resources, Engagements, Manufactures, Commerce, Religion, Education, Literature, Fine Arts, Manners and Customs of the United States of America.*

Sweeping enough! The young bookseller was popular in London and had made many English friends; but their condescension to things American was more than he could easily endure. They professed contempt for American books—and stole them freely. *American Facts* gives a list of 382 American books printed in England from 1841 to 1846, ranging all the way from theology to juveniles. There are sixty-odd books of fiction in the lot, and a dozen books of poetry. "These lists," says Putnam quietly, "might have been used as a convenient answer to the query quoted from Sydney Smith: 'Who reads an American book?' " Putnam's book got more of a hearing than Cooper's "Notions of the Americans" had twenty years earlier, for it ran into several editions, or printings.

During his seven years in London, Putnam had entrée to the best literary society. He hobnobbed with Sergeant Talfourd and Thomas Campbell and Tom Moore. Washington Irving was a guest at his "Knickerbocker Cottage." The plan of a collected edition of Irving, to be issued by Wiley and Putnam, was broached then, though it would not be undertaken for some years. Putnam sent home frequent letters to the New York journals about English people and affairs. He was full of interest in British politics, the corn laws, the tariff, Ireland. He was much concerned about Pennsylvania's repudiation of her bonds, as well as about the raising of the Union Jack in the Sandwich Islands. Meanwhile he gave proof of his honest desire to see fair play in the matter of authors' rights on both sides of the Atlantic. If not its originator (and the point is obscure), he was among the first to recommend and to practice a method of royalty payment. In 1844 he proposed to Elizabeth Barrett to issue her poems in New York "at his own risk and give her ten per cent on the profit." This was not the same thing as the true royalty payment of a percentage on the retail price. But it was a proposal almost incredible to Miss Barrett. "Not that I ever asked for such a thing," she said, reporting the strange affair to Robert Browning: "They were the terms offered. And I always considered the 'percentage' as quite visionary—put in for the sake of effect, to make the agreement look better. But no—you see! One's poetry has a real 'commercial value' if you do but take it far enough away from the civilization of Europe." She had just "miraculously received" a remittance from Wiley and Putnam in New York. Browning was impressed, and praised the American publishers as "fine fellows, who do a really straightforward un-American thing." He saw indeed some glimmerings on the horizon of these benighted States: "I like the progress of these Americans in taste, their amazing leaps like grasshoppers up to the sun—from—what is the from? what depth, do you remember, say ten or twelve years back—to Carlyle, and Tennyson, and—you! So, children, leave off Jack of Cornwall, and go on just to Homer!" Some of the leaping belonged to the poet's fancy rather than to American taste, for the 1830's, at least, had shown a remarkable demand here for the best English books, if the importations and piracies advertised in publishers' lists of the time are evidence.

Putnam must have had a way with him, for even Carlyle the crabbed took to him: "a very intelligent, modest, and reputable-looking fellow." Putnam offered him a true royalty arrangement, one of the first on record—ten per cent "on the selling price of all the copies of 'Cromwell' sent into the market by them"—and also on reprinted editions of his former works, or some of them. Such an offer was a marvel to the sage of Chelsea as well as to the poetess of Wimpole Street. He well-nigh chirps over it in a letter giving his friend Emerson the surprising news. The Boston firm of Little and Brown, with whom Emerson had placed a number of Carlyle's books, had been unable to make a profit out of them in competition with unauthorized editions from Philadelphia and New York. Meanwhile the stay-at-home partner John Wiley was doing an active business in New York. George Haven Putnam says that he was mainly a bookseller; but during those years of George Palmer Putnam's absence, Wiley published much of the best American literary work of the period. The Wiley and Putnam "Library of American Books," unlike most assemblies of the kind, contained original material of high importance, Poe's *Tales* and *The Raven*, Hawthorne's *Mosses from an Old Manse*, Melville's *Typee*.

The London branch of Wiley and Putnam was given up in 1847, and soon afterward the firm was dissolved. There was disparity of temperament between the partners, and there must have been frequent differences of opinion. Putnam's London experiment had not been highly profitable, and perhaps the conservative Wiley preferred freedom to play safe. George Haven Putnam thought it a pity his father and John Wiley had not stayed together, as each was in some fashion the complement of the other. They parted amicably enough, and the property was divided. Putnam kept most of the purely literary material except Ruskin, whom Wiley continued to publish for many years. Ruskin was among the famous writers who have refused to make use of the offices of a professional publisher. Ruskin employed an agent to look out for details, but got out his own editions, and booksellers had to buy of him direct, at a very small discount from the retail price. Moreover Ruskin was a frank hater of America and her ways. Wiley had a very short reply from him to a letter proposing the issuance here of an authorized edition, on terms such as Carlyle had readily accepted. Ruskin seems to have simply washed his hands of the plan. Under the conditions Wiley felt justified in going ahead, and his reprints of Ruskin were excellent specimens of the bookmaking of that period. But after his separation from Putnam in 1848, Wiley undertook little new publication in the field of belles-lettres. Soon he was concentrating upon the scientific and technical works which ever since have been the specialty of the house. In 1875 the firm became John Wiley and Sons, and under that imprint has built up the great business it is known for today.

HENRY WALCOTT BOYNTON

The Riddle of Life

Books in the Biological Sciences

THE RECORDED HISTORY of any nation, institution, or custom reveals that there are few sudden and abrupt changes occurring at distinct and specific dates. On the contrary, most changes take place gradually, and the transition from one stage to another is relatively slow and by successive degrees. Thus in the history of science there is a continuous but slow progression of events extending from the wonder and superstition of primitive man, through curiosity and speculation, to the development of the scientific method involving experimentation, repeated testing, and confirmation or rejection of hypotheses. One of the most interesting and fruitful periods of this history is the nineteenth century, and the scientific books published by Wiley between 1807 and the present day reflect the trend and scope of scientific interest during this period. This was a time of steadily increasing interest, penetrating inquiry, helpful developments, and rich discoveries. During this period biology emerged as a major science in the curricula of the colleges, and it was subdivided into the numerous parts now recognized as important and distinct fields of research and development. As discoveries in the various compartments of biological science were multiplied, the number of biology books increased apace, as the bibliography of Wiley publications clearly indicates.

In the seventeenth century and increasingly during the eighteenth century, exact scientific research in the realm of biological phenomena was effecting a progressive transition from speculative natural philosophy to modern biology. In the curricula of our leading universities, special fields of biology did not appear until near the end of the nineteenth century. As late as 1880, Asa Gray held the title of Fisher Professor of Natural History in Harvard University. Although features of natural history persisted during the nineteenth century, it was during this period that sound scientific investigation, as contrasted with theoretical speculation, produced a wealth of discoveries in the field of biology that has not been equaled in any preceding or subsequent period of history. The contributions of Charles Darwin aroused an intense and widespread interest in the study of biological phenomena, and these studies yielded enormous increases in the knowledge of biology in general.

During the nineteenth century, Wiley published only twenty-one biological books, just one-fourth the number published during the first half of the twentieth century. Prior to the twentieth century, the older educational institutions of Europe were dominant. American students desiring graduate degrees enrolled in German, English, French, and other foreign universities. It should be noted that, beginning with the establishment of Johns Hopkins University in 1867, American students began to find adequate facilities for graduate study in this country, and by the year 1900 it was evident that there was no particular advantage in going abroad except for postdoctorate study. Most of the textbooks in science were written by foreign authors and published in foreign countries. These were the textbooks used by the students in our colleges and universities of that period. All this was changed, however, when the American scholars trained abroad returned to their native land to teach and to carry on their individual programs of specific investigation. As the special subjects to be studied were introduced in the curricula of our universities, making it possible for our native students to complete graduate programs in biological science in our own institutions, these recruits began to produce material for publication. Thus, very soon, there was an increased demand for publication, and books dealing with many different aspects of biology began to appear in greater numbers.

The earliest interest manifested in plants and in animals was taxonomic, and the persistence of this interest is observed in the title of one of the earliest of Wiley's books on biology: *Florula Ludoviciana, or Flora of the State of Louisiana*, by C. S. Rafinesque (1817). It is significant that this series of publications in the field of biology by a pioneer publishing house should begin with the publication of a phase of the work of a taxonomist pioneering in the investigation of American flora. Rafinesque's work has been variously evaluated by different scholars in different periods, but most of them, discounting his eccentricities, think of him as an indefatigable scientific genius, so precocious that his ideas were far in advance of those of his contemporaries. When he was a member of the faculty at Transylvania College in Kentucky (1819–1826), he used the laboratory method in teaching science, and therefore can be credited with introducing laboratory work in American schools. One hundred years after Rafinesque, David Starr Jordan, noted zoologist, called him "the most remarkable man to appear in the annals of American science." More recently, Donald Culross Peattie offered this tribute to him: "Among all the naturalists who have ever worked on the American continent he is the only one who might clearly be called a titan."

Other early Wiley publications of a taxonomic nature are John Torrey and Asa Gray's *Flora of North America* (1838), J. P. Girard's *Birds of Long Island* (1844), John C. Louden's *Encyclopedia of Plants*, and Gray's *General Florae Americae Boreali-Orientales Illustrato* (1848). The surviving interest in natural history is further reflected in such books as *Alphabetical Drawing Book and Pictorial Natural History of Quadrupeds* (1847).

The persistence of natural philosophy is indicated in the bibliography by such titles as *Human Magnetism*, by William Newnham (1845); *Compendium of the Phreno-Philosophy of Human Nature*, by James S. Grimes (1848); *Elements of Somatology*, by George M. Maclean (1859), and also *Physiological Cruelty*, by Francis Heatherley (1883). There are also books that combine natural history with practical aspects, such as Griffin's *An Essay on the Botanical, Chemical, and Medical Properties of the Ficus Edulis of Linnaeus* (1816), Peter Boswell's *Bees, Pigeons, Rabbits, and the Canary Bird* (1842), and J. H. Steel's *Treatise on the Diseases of the Dog* (1888).

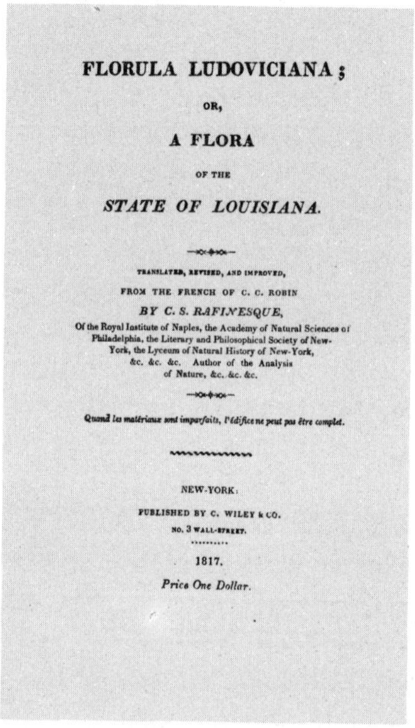

FLORULA LUDOVICIANA;

OR,

A FLORA

OF THE

STATE OF LOUISIANA.

TRANSLATED, REVISED, AND IMPROVED,

FROM THE FRENCH OF C. C. ROBIN

BY C. S. RAFINESQUE,

Of the Royal Institute of Naples, the Academy of Natural Sciences of Philadelphia, the Literary and Philosophical Society of New-York, the Lyceum of Natural History of New-York, &c. &c. &c. Author of the Analysis of Nature, &c. &c. &c.

Quand les matériaux sont imparfaits, l'édifice ne peut pas être complet.

NEW-YORK:

PUBLISHED BY C. WILEY & CO.

NO. 3 WALL-STREET.

1817.

Price One Dollar.

Title pages, then and now

LIFE SCIENCE

A College Textbook of General Biology

THOMAS S. HALL

Dean of the College of Liberal Arts
and Professor of Zoology
Washington University

FLORENCE MOOG

Associate Professor of Zoology
Washington University

JOHN WILEY & SONS, INC.—CHAPMAN & HALL, LTD.
NEW YORK LONDON

During the later years of the nineteenth century, when the subject of biology had achieved widespread popularity, American biological textbooks began to appear. Among the Wiley books there are *The Botanical Textbook*, by Asa Gray (1842), and *Compendium of General Biology*, by Westermaier (1897). There was then a keen interest in heredity and variation and in 1899, on the threshold of the emergence of modern genetics, Charles B. Davenport's *Statistical Methods with Special Reference to Biological Variation* (1899) appeared.

The improvement of the microscope was a very important factor in the development of a greatly increased interest in the study of biology. In 1827 Amici demonstrated his first achromatic lens system, which advanced microscopy incredibly and resulted in an extensive series of discoveries in microscopic biology. The Wiley books that appeared subsequently show clearly the influence of this discovery, as may be observed in such titles as *The Dublin Dissector or System of Practical Anatomy*, by Robert Harrison (1848), *Treatise on Microscopical Diagnosis*, by Von Duben (1874–1876), and especially *Microscopy of Drinking Water*, by George C. Whipple (1899), which remains a classic in its field.

During the latter half of the nineteenth century great advances were made in the physical sciences, particularly in chemistry and in physics. With the development of organic chemistry, colloidal chemistry, and physical chemistry, biologists acquired new tools to aid them in their research, and soon such subjects as biochemics, histochemics, and biophysics appeared in the curricula of our universities. Investigators exploring new fields and using their new tools made enormous progress in the development of biological science. Soon the subject had become so important that it was included in the curricula of almost all high schools, colleges, and universities. Along with this growth in importance came the gradual division of biology into a considerable number of subdivisions, each one representing an area of intensive specialization. Consequently, in addition to the older subjects of taxonomy, morphology, and physiology, we now have cytology, histology, ecology, genetics, endocrinology, virology, vitaminology, embryology, parasitology, bacteriology, mycology, paleontology, and others. In the so-called applied fields of biology there has been a corresponding specialization. The growth, expansion, and subdividing of biological science have brought

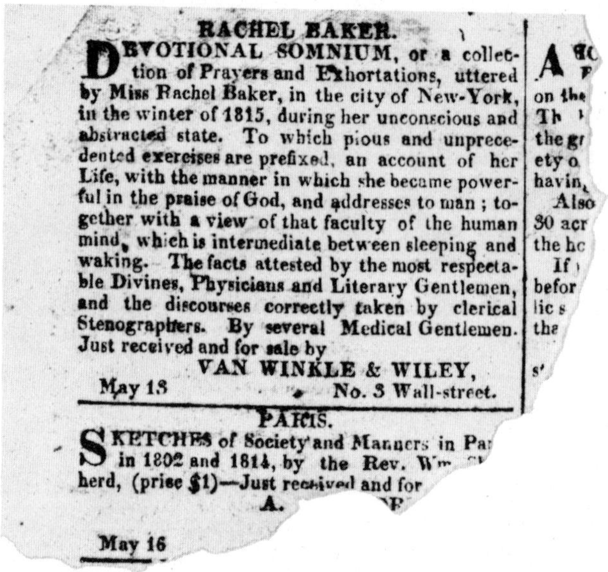

RACHEL BAKER.

DEVOTIONAL SOMNIUM, or a collection of Prayers and Exhortations, uttered by Miss Rachel Baker, in the city of New-York, in the winter of 1815, during her unconscious and abstracted state. To which pious and unprecedented exercises are prefixed, an account of her Life, with the manner in which she became powerful in the praise of God, and addresses to man; together with a view of that faculty of the human mind, which is intermediate between sleeping and waking. The facts attested by the most respectable Divines, Physicians and Literary Gentlemen, and the discourses correctly taken by clerical Stenographers. By several Medical Gentlemen. Just received and for sale by

VAN WINKLE & WILEY,

May 13 No. 3 Wall-street.

PARIS.

SKETCHES of Society and Manners in Pa in 1802 and 1814, by the Rev. W herd, (price $1)—Just received and for

A.

May 16

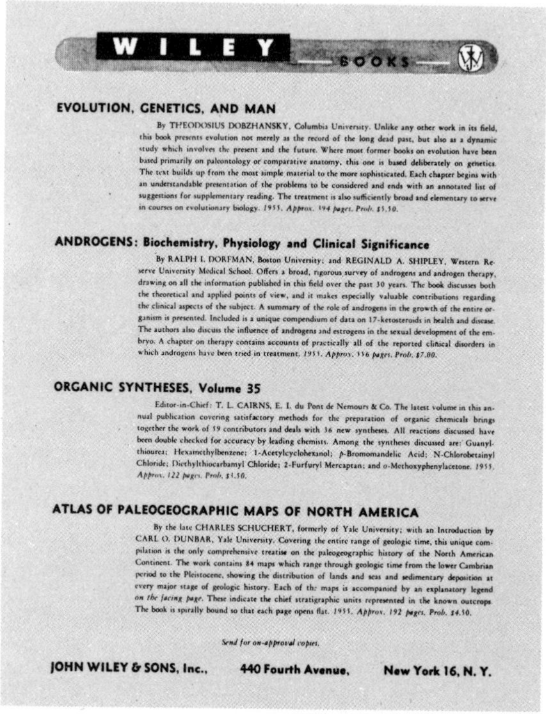

WILEY BOOKS

EVOLUTION, GENETICS, AND MAN

By THEODOSIUS DOBZHANSKY, Columbia University. Unlike any other work in its field, this book presents evolution not merely as the record of the long dead past, but also as a dynamic study which involves the present and the future. Where most former books on evolution have been based primarily on paleontology or comparative anatomy, this one is based deliberately on genetics. The text builds up from the most simple material to the more sophisticated. Each chapter begins with an understandable presentation of the problems to be considered and ends with an annotated list of suggestions for supplementary reading. The treatment is also sufficiently broad and elementary to serve in courses on evolutionary biology. *1955. Approx. 394 pages. Prob. $5.50.*

ANDROGENS: Biochemistry, Physiology and Clinical Significance

By RALPH I. DORFMAN, Boston University; and REGINALD A. SHIPLEY, Western Reserve University Medical School. Offers a broad, rigorous survey of androgens and androgen therapy, drawing on all the information published in this field over the past 30 years. The book discusses both the theoretical and applied points of view, and it makes especially valuable contributions regarding the clinical aspects of the subject. A summary of the role of androgens in the growth of the entire organism is presented. Included is a unique compendium of data on 17-ketosteroids in health and disease. The authors also discuss the influence of androgens and estrogens in the sexual development of the embryo. A chapter on therapy contains accounts of practically all of the reported clinical disorders in which androgens have been tried in treatment. *1955. Approx. 556 pages. Prob. $7.00.*

ORGANIC SYNTHESES, Volume 35

Editor-in-Chief: T. L. CAIRNS, E. I. du Pont de Nemours & Co. The latest volume in this annual publication covering satisfactory methods for the preparation of organic chemicals brings together the work of 59 contributors and deals with 36 new syntheses. All reactions discussed have been double checked for accuracy by leading chemists. Among the syntheses discussed are: Guanylthiourea; Hexamethylbenzene; 1-Acetylcyclohexanol; *p*-Bromomandelic Acid; N-Chlorobetainyl Chloride; Diethylthiocarbamyl Chloride; 2-Furfuryl Mercaptan; and *o*-Methoxyphenylacetone. *1955. Approx. 122 pages. Prob. $3.50.*

ATLAS OF PALEOGEOGRAPHIC MAPS OF NORTH AMERICA

By the late CHARLES SCHUCHERT, formerly of Yale University; with an Introduction by CARL O. DUNBAR, Yale University. Covering the entire range of geologic time, this unique compilation is the only comprehensive treatise on the paleogeographic history of the North American Continent. The work contains 84 maps which range through geologic time from the lower Cambrian period to the Pleistocene, showing the distribution of lands and seas and sedimentary deposition at every major stage of geologic history. Each of the maps is accompanied by an explanatory legend *on the facing page*. These indicate the chief stratigraphic units represented in the known outcrops. The book is spirally bound so that each page opens flat. *1955. Approx. 192 pages. Prob. $4.50.*

Send for on-approval copies.

JOHN WILEY & SONS, Inc., 440 Fourth Avenue, New York 16, N. Y.

Display advertising, then and now. Upper: Advertisement in "New York Herald," July 2, 1815. Lower: Full-page advertisement in "Science," November 11, 1955.

about a tremendous increase in biological literature, and the publication of this literature has become a gigantic enterprise.

During the first twenty-five years of the twentieth century only twelve biological publications were added to the list, but they indicate quite clearly the new emphasis on laboratory work and the increasing development of specialization in biological studies. In 1916 Ward Giltner's *Laboratory Manual in General Microbiology* appeared, and its success is shown by the fact that a second edition was published in 1921. In 1925 two new laboratory guides were published: *A Laboratory Guide for a Course in General Botany*, by Lee Bonar, Richard M. Holman, and Lucile Roush, and *Laboratory Directions in General Zoology*, by Winterton C. Curtis and Mary J. Guthrie. There were also some new books in physiology: *Structural and Physiological Botany*, by O. W. Thome and A. W. Bennett (1900), *Physiology of Alimentation*, by Martin H. Fischer (1907), and *Light and Behavior of Organisms*, by S. O. Mast (1911), which proved to be one of the most significant books in its field. The new interest in histology is reflected in such books as William Mansfield's *Histology of Medicinal Plants* (1916) and Charles W. Ballard's *Elements of Vegetable Histology* (1921). Another classic in its field that appeared during this period is Asa C. Chandler's *Animal Parasites and Human Diseases* (1918), one of the earliest and still one of the best textbooks on parasitology. Other best sellers published at this time were *Entomology*, by E. Dwight Sanderson and Leonard M. Peairs (1917), *Textbook of Botany*, by Richard M. Holman and Wilfred W. Robbins (1924), and *Genetics in Plant and Animal Improvement*, by Donald F. Jones (1924). A. S. Hitchcock's *Descriptive Systematic Botany* (1925) was one of the first textbooks devoted exclusively to the subject of taxonomy.

It was during the second part (1926–1953) of the first half of the twentieth century that the number of Wiley books in the biological sciences increased remarkably. During these twenty-seven years there were sixty-five new publications, twice the number published in the preceding one hundred and twenty-five years. Eighteen of these books proved to be above-average sellers or were given excellent critical attention. Curtis and Guthrie's *Textbook of General Zoology* (1927) and Holman and Robbins' *Elements of Botany* (1928) were very successful. At the beginning of this period there was a general demand for closer integration of the subject matter of animal and plant biology. *General Biology*, by Perry D. Strausbaugh and Bernal R. Weimer

(1938), and *Bio-Ecology*, by Frederic E. Clements and Victor E. Shelford (1939), accomplished this unification in some measure and paved the way for further efforts in this direction. In 1929 *The Plant Rusts*, by Joseph C. Arthur, was published. Other very important publications of this period were Waldo Shumway's *Vertebrate Embryology* (1927), Arthur T. Henrici's *Molds, Yeasts, and Actinomycetes* (1930), Richard Hesse, Warder C. Allee, and Karl P. Schmidt's *Ecological Animal Geography* (1937), Herbert H. Ross's *Textbook of Entomology* (1948), Bradley T. Scheer's *Comparative Physiology* (1948), M. Demerec's *Biology of Drosophila* (1950), Wilfred W. Robbins and T. Elliot Weier's *Botany* (1950), C. J. Alexopoulos' *Introductory Mycology* (1952), Katherine Esau's *Plant Anatomy* (1953), S. E. Luria's *Virology* (1953), Kenneth D. Roeder's *Insect Physiology* (1953), Scheer's *General Physiology* (1953), and Theodosius Dobzhansky's *Evolution, Genetics, and Man* (1955).

The publication of scientific books is not merely a routine business following specific recipes and formulas. It is also an art that requires critical judgment of manuscript and illustrative material. It is an art the objective of which is the production of attractive publications presenting clearly and accurately the facts of science. The success of so many of Wiley's biological publications appearing during the last one hundred and fifty years attests to the high degree of proficiency attained in publishing. These books have contributed richly to the teaching of biological science in the colleges and universities and have also stimulated and encouraged continued investigation. Since further progress in the various fields of biological science depends primarily on the exploratory efforts of capable, resourceful, well-trained workers, the publication of good, sound, reliable scientific books is a necessary and highly significant service.

P. D. STRAUSBAUGH

Atoms, Molecules, and Reactions

Books on Chemistry

PUBLICATION OF BOOKS ON CHEMISTRY has been an important activity of Wiley's for more than a century. Many influential works have borne this imprint since the beginning of the program in 1844. Wiley entered this field at a time when the science of chemistry was in a period of transition. Inorganic chemistry had become well established in the early decades of the nineteenth century, but then it failed to attract the best minds of the profession. Most chemists were struggling to bring order to the confusion of organic compounds, whose numbers were constantly increasing. Neither inorganic nor organic chemists had any firm theoretical basis for carrying on their work, since the fundamental distinction between atoms and molecules had not yet been accepted. Physical chemistry as an organized branch of the science did not exist, and the only biochemistry was carried on by physiologists who did not recognize the chemical implications of much of their work.

The seeds of the modern developments did exist in Europe at that time, and during the next twenty-five years rapid progress was made. Inorganic chemistry was thoroughly systematized in the Periodic Table, structural theory gave organic chemistry its modern form, and tentative developments appeared in the other branches. In America, however, there was little interest in these significant advances, at least in their early stages. America was still a remote province of the scientific world. Such chemists as were active were concerned almost entirely with the analysis of minerals. The geology of the new West, so rapidly being opened to exploration, held public attention. Chemists were as eager as their lay brothers to discover the resources hidden in the new territories. Word of the progress of European chemistry came slowly to the New World and attracted relatively little attention. The advantages of European study were not yet realized.

In such a situation, it might have been expected that the first book on chemistry offered by a publisher newly entering the field would be of a technological nature. Instead, Wiley chose in 1844 to publish *Chemistry as Exemplifying the Wisdom and Beneficence of God*, by the English chemist, George Fownes. This book had won the Acton Prize of one hundred guineas offered for the best essay on this subject. It was an illuminating review of the chemical theories of its time and a detailed survey of the chemistry of animals and plants, with emphasis on their interrelations. Such a book would interest many educated laymen, but, more important, it could stimulate the imagination of chemists and lead them along new paths of study.

At first Wiley approached chemical publication cautiously. Not until 1855 did another major book appear. In that year Wiley published a translation of *Principles of Agricultural Chemistry*, by Justus von Liebig. Here was a book by a leading German chemist, noted for his theoretical studies, but now devoting himself to practical work that had a wide appeal in an agricultural nation such as America then was. The book was evidently a great success, since it continued in print until at least 1876.

As soon as the Civil War ended, Wiley began in earnest to publish chemical books. The first ones were concerned largely with inorganic chemistry, and, as could be expected, included a number of books on qualitative and quantitative analysis. The most important and popular of them were translations of the classic books on analytical chemistry by the great German analyst, Carl Remigius Fresenius. The first Wiley editions of his books appeared in 1864, and there were repeated re-issues until as late as 1903.

Publication of books by important European chemists became a significant part of the Wiley program. The effect of such books in stimulating American chemists to study abroad was very great, and such foreign study in the second half of the nineteenth century was chiefly responsible for developing the United States into a world chemical power.

The results of this foreign study soon became apparent in the list of chemical books published by Wiley. By 1880, books by American authors began to appear with increasing frequency. At first they were largely concerned with analytical chemistry and with technological subjects such as coal gas, lead pipes, water supplies, and metallurgical chemistry. They obviously supplied a need felt in the chemical industries that were beginning to appear in America. At the same time, these books by native authors helped to train the men who would later exert a far wider influence by their own writings. The chief example of such an author was Henry Carrington Bolton, whose books on quantitative analysis were published by Wiley in 1881–1882. They were forerunners of his subsequent writings, which made him almost the first American chemist to view chemistry in its full historical and philosophical perspective.

Wiley's editors who selected the books for the chemical list were not narrow specialists. While supplying the needs of the practical chemists of the time, they continued to offer the best of the European books, such as A. Pinner's *Introduction to Organic Chemistry*, published in 1883, and Hermann Kolbe's *Text-Book of Inorganic Chemistry*, which appeared in 1884.

At the same time, they were alert to the newest and the most promising developments in the science. In 1874 Yale University established the first teaching laboratory in biochemistry in America. It was under the direction of R. H. Chittenden, who was for many years the only professional biochemist in the country. He said near the end of his life that his specialty developed rapidly only after 1890. It is significant that this is just the period in which Wiley began an active publishing program in this field. In 1889 Henry A. Mott's *Composition, Digestibility, and Nutritive Value of Food* was published, and in 1896 John A. Mandel's *Handbook for the Bio-Chemical Laboratory*. In 1893 Mandel translated Olof Hammarsten's *Text-Book of Physiological Chemistry*, which became the leading textbook in its field in America. Later (1927) Wiley again published the ranking textbook when Meyer Bodansky's influential *Introduction to Physiological Chemistry* was issued. A more recent development was the launching in 1949 of *Biochemical Preparations*, a series comparable to *Organic Syntheses*. Four volumes have appeared, edited in order by Herbert E. Carter, Eric G. Ball, Esmond E. Snell, and W. W. Westerfeld. There can be little doubt that the editors at Wiley's early recognized the importance of this new branch of chemistry and by the active encouragement of their publication program did much to bring about the rapid growth of a field in which Chittenden had been working almost alone for twenty years. This is a good example of the stimulating effect of editorial foresight in a field in which the demand has not yet developed.

During the nineties the production of books on practical chemistry continued, with emphasis on analytical chemistry and on problems concerned with water. In 1899 William P. Mason's *Examination of Water* appeared, and it was long the standard reference on the subject. At the same time Wiley produced an increasing number of books on industrial organic chemistry. It is clear that American chemical industries were growing. Americans still relied almost exclusively on Germany for their industrial chemicals, but their knowledge and their interests were broadening. The day of the dominance of mineralogical and geological chemistry was past.

At the beginning of the twentieth century the *Textbook of Organic Chemistry*, by the great Dutch chemist, A. F. Holleman, was published by Wiley. This book ran through many editions and was a powerful molder of thought among American organic chemists. It was particularly effective in university circles, where American research centers had begun to develop. Study in Europe had become almost essential for anyone who planned an academic career. Thus was produced a generation of American chemists who were keenly aware of the latest developments in their science. Such men began to develop research groups among their own students, using the standard textbooks of workers like Holleman. In this way the training of American students began to improve.

These groups of research workers also began to produce original books, and Wiley was active in publishing them. In 1903 and 1904 appeared the books on analytical chemistry by Treadwell and Hall. They set the standards for chemical analysis in the next thirty years. Samuel P. Mulliken in 1904 published the first volume of his *Method for the Identification of Pure Organic*

Compounds. Here for the first time a systematic procedure was presented by which the confused mass of organic chemicals could be classified, separated, and identified as individual compounds. The succeeding three volumes of his book, which appeared in 1910, 1916, and 1922, were at once followed by Oliver Kamm's *Qualitative Organic Analysis.* Kamm's book made possible the application of Mulliken's methods by undergraduate students of chemistry. Many of the leading chemists of today received their first actual appreciation of the systematic nature of organic chemistry by following the procedures of Mulliken and Kamm. Today students in this area of chemistry are likely to study Ralph L. Shriner, Reynold C. Fuson, and David Y. Curtin's *Systematic Identification of Organic Compounds*, which was published in a fourth edition in 1956. The first edition appeared in 1935, the work of the two senior authors.

In 1905 Wiley began to publish *Conversations on Chemistry*, by Wilhelm Ostwald, the father of physical chemistry. This association with the great German chemist led to the subsequent publication of his more important *Introduction to Chemistry* in 1911. The modern physical chemist owes a great deal to Wiley for making these books available. The subject of physical chemistry was introduced to undergraduates in chemistry almost as soon as it became a well-established branch of the science through the well-known books of Frederick H. Getman—the *Laboratory Exercises in Physical Chemistry* of 1904 and the *Outlines of Theoretical Chemistry* of 1913.

As would be expected, the years of the first World War saw the publication of a considerable number of practical textbooks. American chemical industries, under the spur of the loss of German industrial chemicals, were forced to develop almost overnight into giant organizations. This development continued actively after the war, and Wiley publications played an important part in it.

The demand for the production of unusual organic chemicals was heavy at this time. In 1921 this demand was met in part by the inauguration of the series *Organic Syntheses*, the first volume of which was edited by Roger Adams. This series, with a new volume each year and a collective volume issued periodically containing revision of material in the ten previously published annual volumes, has made possible the simplified production on a large laboratory scale of hundreds of compounds needed by organic chemists in the furtherance of their laboratory studies. The series has had an important influence also on standards of laboratory practice by the rigid requirements that it has demanded of authors who contribute to it. The same rigid standards have been applied in the series *Organic Reactions*, begun in 1942. This series has extended Wiley's services to the organic chemist by its critical review of the various general methods that can be used in preparing organic compounds. Also of major importance are the four volumes of *Organic Chemistry*, edited by Henry Gilman, Volumes I and II of which appeared in 1938, and Volumes III and IV in 1953.

At the end of the first World War there was a great growth of interest in the study of chemistry. Wiley met the needs of the increasing numbers of students by an outstanding series of textbooks: Frank H. MacDougall's *Thermodynamics and Chemistry* (1921), William H. Chapin's *Second Year College Chemistry* (1922), Harry N. Holmes' *Laboratory Manual of Colloid Chemistry* (1922), Alexander Lowy and Benjamin Harrow's *Introduction to Organic Chemistry* (1924), I. M. Kolthoff and N. H. Furman's *Potentiometric Titrations* (1926), Carl J. Engelder's *Elementary Qualitative Analysis* (1927), and Ross A. Gortner's *Outlines of Biochemistry* (1929). It was in this decade, too, that Wiley issued the first of a long list of excellent books by Horace G. Deming, beginning with *General Chemistry* in 1923, which still has a strong following thirty-four years later, in its sixth edition. It was by the study of books such as these that the chemical student of the twenties received a thorough grounding in the newest developments of his science. Much of the important work of today rests on a foundation of knowledge obtained from Wiley publications such as these.

While Wiley was supplying the needs of working chemists and laying the basis for further progress in chemistry through its textbooks for training the next generation of chemists, it was not neglecting the less immediately practical phases of the science. As early as 1906 it published *A History of Chemical Theories and Laws*, by M. M. Pattison Muir, a book that is still of great importance to the historian of chemistry. E. J. Crane and Austin M. Patterson's *Guide to the Literature of Chemistry*, published in 1927, also supplied much historical information, though its greatest importance lay in breaking new ground in its discussion of the sources of chemical information. The publication in 1943 by Tenney L. Davis of *The Chemistry of Powder and Explosives* provided not only an outstanding work on a technical subject, but also a contribution to the history of chemistry, of which Davis was a master.

Wiley has given to the American chemist an important series of works to open to him the vast and essential foreign literature. In the days when most chemists studied in Germany, the language problem was not serious; but more recently the chemist has had to make a definite effort to master foreign languages while remaining in an English-speaking community. Perhaps among his most-used reference works have been the two books by Austin M. Patterson, *A German-English Dictionary for Chemists*, first published in 1917, and *A French-English Dictionary for Chemists*, which was first issued in 1921. Both have been revised and enlarged in recent years. They went beyond mere dictionaries, for they pointed out to the chemist specific idiomatic pitfalls never discussed in general dictionaries. Wiley's linguistic services

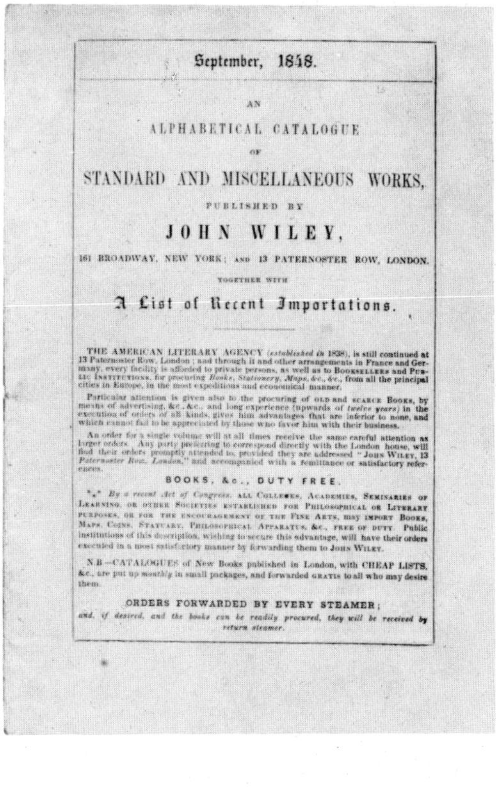

September, 1848.

AN

ALPHABETICAL CATALOGUE

OF

STANDARD AND MISCELLANEOUS WORKS,

PUBLISHED BY

JOHN WILEY,

161 BROADWAY, NEW YORK; AND 13 PATERNOSTER ROW, LONDON.

TOGETHER WITH

A List of Recent Importations.

THE AMERICAN LITERARY AGENCY (*established in 1838*), is still continued at 13 Paternoster Row, London; and through it and other arrangements in France and Germany, every facility is afforded to private persons, as well as to BOOKSELLERS and PUBLIC INSTITUTIONS, for procuring *Books, Stationery, Maps, &c., &c.*, from all the principal cities in Europe, in the most expeditious and economical manner.

Particular attention is given also to the procuring of OLD and SCARCE BOOKS, by means of advertising, &c., &c., and long experience (upwards of *twelve years*) in the execution of orders of all kinds, gives him advantages that are inferior to none, and which cannot fail to be appreciated by those who favor him with their business.

An order for a single volume will at all times receive the same careful attention as larger orders. Any party preferring to correspond directly with the London house, will find their orders promptly attended to, provided they are addressed "JOHN WILEY, 13 *Paternoster Row, London*," and accompanied with a remittance or satisfactory references.

BOOKS, &c., DUTY FREE.

*** *By a recent Act of Congress*, ALL COLLEGES, ACADEMIES, SEMINARIES OF LEARNING, OR OTHER SOCIETIES ESTABLISHED FOR PHILOSOPHICAL OR LITERARY PURPOSES, OR FOR THE ENCOURAGEMENT OF THE FINE ARTS, may IMPORT BOOKS, MAPS, COINS, STATUARY, PHILOSOPHICAL APPARATUS, &c., FREE OF DUTY. Public institutions of this description, wishing to secure this advantage, will have their orders executed in a most satisfactory manner by forwarding them to JOHN WILEY.

N.B.—CATALOGUES of New Books published in London, with CHEAP LISTS, &c., are put up *monthly* in small packages, and forwarded GRATIS to all who may desire them.

ORDERS FORWARDED BY EVERY STEAMER;

and, if desired, and the books can be readily procured, they will be received by return steamer.

Catalogue of 1848

have been expanded more recently by the publications, begun in 1938, of John T. Fotos and R. Norris Shreve and of Fotos and John L. Bray on chemical German readings and grammar.

The pattern set in earlier years continues to be carried on by the present generation of Wiley editors. The diversified fields of modern chemistry are fully covered; and when specialized fields such as chromatography or fluorine chemistry become important, they will be well covered in textbooks and monographs. The current list of Wiley publications in chemistry is a list of the fields of modern chemistry. As in the past, the list also includes such topics as radiochemistry, and such books as Arthur C. Wahl and Norman A. Bonner's *Radioactivity Applied to Chemistry* (1951), Gerhart Friedlander and Joseph W. Kennedy's *Nuclear and Radiochemistry* (1955), to mention only two, which will be the concern of the chemists of tomorrow. In its chemical division, as in the divisions dealing with the other sciences, Wiley has grown as the science has grown. It has supplied the needs of students, technologists, and research workers, and of the dreamers who have built and will build the fundamental structures of chemistry.

HENRY M. LEICESTER

Matter and Energy

Books on Physics

THE PUBLICATIONS OF JOHN WILEY AND SONS have fallen in the era that witnessed the transition from the broad field of natural philosophy to highly specialized fields of physical science. Philosophy among the ancient Greeks originally expressed love of, or striving for, insight into reality, and Plato taught that mathematics was the way to attain this goal. The earlier Greek philosophers first speculated about the principles of Φύσις (Physis), and thereby laid the foundations of natural knowledge. In later antiquity the philosophical poem "De Rerum Natura," by Lucretius, explained the nature of things in terms of associations and disassociations of atoms. In the modern era the various aspects of natural phenomena were included within the scope of natural philosophy, but during the nineteenth century physics as the science of the phenomena of matter and energy acquired an individual status. Within this field there developed the classical subjects of mechanics, electromagnetism, optics, and thermodynamics. Subsequently, theories of molecules and atoms provided bases for constructive microphysical explanations of observable macrophysical phenomena, and during the present century they developed into quantum theories of atom and nucleus. The development of physics to its present high level is exhibited by the Wiley bibliography for one hundred and fifty years.

In colonial America the ideas of the Scientific Revolution were received with enthusiasm from England. Cotton Mather advised candidates for the ministry to study the principles of the "incomparable Sir Isaac Newton"; Benjamin Franklin contributed to the knowledge of electricity; and at Harvard College John Winthrop lectured on natural philosophy to students, among whom was the man now known as Count Rumford, a founder of the mechanical theory of heat. In the early days of the American republic the electrical researches of Joseph Henry were of international significance. The primitive state of natural science during the age of expanding frontiers, however, is reflected in the relatively few titles on physics in the Wiley list during the major part of the nineteenth century. Among American authors was William H. C. Bartlett, professor at the United States Military Academy, who wrote the first Wiley title on physics, *An Elementary Treatise on Optics* (1839), designed for the cadets at West Point. Not until 1855–1857 did the second title appear, a book on the then relatively new art of photography.

The problems set by the Civil War stimulated industrial progress in the United States and scientific activity as well. The Wiley list on physics includes the lectures, *Polar Magnetism* (1868 and 1869), *Acoustics of Public Buildings* (1874–1876), *Textbook of Physics* (1883), *Elements of Wave Motion* (1891), *Thermodynamics of Reversible Cycles in Gases and Saturated Vapors* (the Columbia lectures of Pupin) (1894), and the pioneer work by G. K. Burgess and H. Le Châtelier, *Measurement of High Temperatures* (third edition, 1912). The development of physical laboratories for instruction at the turn of the century is indicated by a succession of manuals. A book with a view to the future was Joseph G. Coffin's *Vector Analysis* (1909). This pioneer textbook may be classified as mathematics, but it was designed to present the beginnings of mathematical physics, including geometry, mechanics, magnetism, electricity, heat, and hydrodynamics. The author expressed the hope that the exposition in terms of vectorial notation of that most beautiful and extensive of all branches of study—mathematical physics—would encourage its study by potential investigators, and thus bring the New World up to the standards of the Old World. How well his prophetic hope has been realized is demonstrated by subsequent Wiley publications.

Classical physics was developed to such a high level in the nineteenth century that the opinion was expressed that all fundamental physical laws had been discovered. But the problem of the ether had been made acute by the Michelson-Morley experiment, an American contribution to Einstein's theory of relativity. A new era began with the discovery of X-rays in 1895. Investigations of electric discharges through gases, the discovery of radioactivity, and demonstration of the existence of the electron launched physics on a new era, the present era of "modern physics." Millikan's precise measurement of electronic charge signalized American participation in the field.

The "new" physics came to fulfillment in the United States subsequent to the first World War. Wiley books on physics continued in the classical field, but as research activities grew atomic physics came to the fore. Ervin S. Ferry's *General Physics* (1921) was notable for its wealth of problems. Architectural acoustics, which had been founded on physical principles by W. C. Sabine, was represented on the Wiley list by Floyd R. Watson's pioneer book, *Acoustics of Buildings* (1923). A subsequent standard treatise in this field was Vern O. Knudsen's *Architectural Acoustics* (1932). Titles for surveys of physical science in the broader sense of the term also began to appear in response to the establishment of courses in general science. A historical survey of physics for the general student was made by Leonard B. Loeb and Arthur S. Adams in *Development of Physical Thought* (1933). The rising standard of instruction in physics for students of science and engineering was indicated by Loeb's *Fundamentals of Electricity and Magnetism* (1931), and by Robert B. Lindsay's *General Physics* (1940), a rigorous exposition of the subject with the aid of the calculus. A superior book for graduate instruction was Paul S. Epstein's *Textbook of Thermodynamics* (1937). A comprehensive presentation of a fundamental field of the "new" physics was Loeb's *Fundamental Processes of Electrical Discharge in Gases* (1939).

The physics of the twentieth century, however, has been characterized especially by the quantum theory. This theory was originated by Planck in 1900 for the statistical theory of thermal radiation, and ascribes an individuality to atomic processes that is symbolized by the quantum of action. The quantum hypothesis was extended by Einstein to radiation, which he inferred to be corpuscular quanta of energy, or photons. A decisive impetus was given to the quantum theory by Niels Bohr in 1913 when he applied the ideas of Planck and Einstein to the hydrogen atom. On the basis of Rutherford's discovery of the nucleus, Bohr assumed that atomic hydrogen consists of an electron revolving in a quantized circular orbit around a positive nucleus, the proton. The extension of the Bohr theory to other elements was correlated with the systematization of spectral lines. Then in the nineteen-twenties the inadequacies of the Bohr theory led to the creation of a new quantum mechanics that has introduced indeterminacy and probability into the foundations of physics.

A Wiley book that set forth the theories of relativity and of quanta within the general system of theoretical physics was Victor F. Lenzen's *Nature of Physical Theory* (1931). This book was followed by Robert B. Lindsay and Henry Margenau's *Foundations of Physics* (1936). Significant textbooks were *The Pittsburgh Outline of Atomic Physics* (1933) and Saul Dushman's *Elements of Quantum Mechanics* (1938). In 1949 Francis O. Rice and Edward Teller's *Structure of Matter*, one of a series in the structure of matter, appeared under the editorship of Maria Goeppert Mayer. A notable Wiley book was an interpretative scholarly book by the Austrian theoretical physicist, Arthur March. His *Quantum Mechanics of Particles and Wave Fields* (1951) gives a uniquely comprehensive treatment of the subject from corpuscular and wave points of view.

The quantum theory of the atom provided foundations for the physics of the solid state, the physics of superfluids, and statistical mechanics.

Upon the discoveries of von Laue and the Braggs in 1912 the structure of crystals became a field of investigation by X-rays. More recent Wiley books in this special phase are William H. Zachariasen's *Theory of X-ray Diffraction in Crystals* (1945), and Harold P. Klug and Leroy E. Alexander's *X-ray Diffraction Procedures* (1954). With the advent of the new quantum mechanics, an approximate treatment provided a theory that linked together the various types of ideal solids, namely, metals, salts, valence crystals, and molecular crystals. Since this primary synthesis was achieved, investigations have centered about properties derived from a study of imperfections. A significant Wiley publication is *Imperfections in Nearly Perfect Crystals*, the record of a symposium, edited by William Shockley, John H. Hollomon, R. Maurer, and

F. Seitz (1952). A recent comprehensive textbook is Charles Kittel's *Introduction to Solid State Physics* (1953).

Quantum mechanics also has been applied to the properties of superfluids, that is, liquid helium and superconducting electrons near the absolute zero of temperature. These phenomena are the subject of a Wiley publication, *Superfluids*, Volume I (1950), and Volume II (1954), by Fritz London, a principal investigator in the field.

The foundations of statistical mechanics have been revised in the light of quantum mechanics. During the nineteenth century a kinetic theory of gases was formulated, a subject represented on the Wiley list by Richard D. Kleeman's *Kinetic Theory of Gases and Liquids* (1920). Statistical mechanics originated in the effort to generalize the derivation of the laws of thermodynamics, a macrophysical theory of heat and energy, from a statistical microphysical theory of the mechanics of molecules. J. W. Gibbs of Yale University contributed especially to the classical phase of the subject. The advances therein during the present century are set forth in Joseph E. Mayer and Maria G. Mayer's *Statistical Mechanics* (1940) and Lindsay's *Physical Statistics* (1941). The last word in the field, however, is the monumental, encyclopedic work by Joseph O. Hirschfelder, Charles F. Curtiss, and Robert B. Bird: *Molecular Theory of Gases and Liquids* (1954).

Although recent Wiley books have indicated increasing interest in quantum mechanics, books on subjects of traditional interest have continued to be published, such as photography, color, acoustics, heat, optics, microscopy, electricity and magnetism, and classical mechanics.

Among Wiley books are some devoted especially to instruments and experimental techniques. Examples of these books are Dushman's *Scientific Foundations of Vacuum Techniques* (1949), Leo L. Beranek's *Acoustic Measurements* (1949), *London Conference on Optical Instruments, 1950* (1952), H. J. J. Braddick's *The Physics of Experimental Method* (an importation, 1954). The application of the rapidly developing field of sound to problems of measurement, control, and processing in industry is set forth in Theodor F. Hueter and Richard H. Bolt's *Sonics* (1955).

A rapid advance in nuclear physics occurred upon the invention of the cyclotron by Lawrence and after Chadwick's discovery of the neutron in 1932. Since then the theory has been developed on the hypothesis that the nucleus is built out of protons and neutrons. The discovery of nuclear fission in 1939, the theory thereof by Bohr and Wheeler, the construction of an atomic reactor in 1942 under the leadership of Fermi, and finally the production of atomic bombs in 1945 under the direction of Oppenheimer, gave enormous impetus to nuclear physics. This increased interest is vividly illustrated by Wiley books of the last fifteen years: Ernest C. Pollard and William L. Davidson's *Applied Nuclear Physics* (1942), Hans A. Bethe's *Elementary Nuclear Theory* (1947), David Halliday's *Introductory Nuclear Physics* (1950). The effects of radiation on living systems is the subject of James J. Nickson's *Symposium on Radiobiology* (1952). The series in nuclear physics has been crowned by two works: John M. Blatt and Victor F. Weisskopf's *Theoretical Nuclear Physics* (1952) and Emilio Segrè's (editor) *Experimental Nuclear Physics*, Volumes I and II (1953). The books edited by Segrè thus far contain the following sections: Staub, "Detection Methods"; Bethe and Ashkin, "Passage of Radiations through Matter"; Ramsey, "Nuclear Moments and Statistics," and "Nuclear Two-Body Problems and Elements of Nuclear Structure"; Bainbridge, "Charged Particle Dynamics and Optics," "Relative Isotopic Abundance of the Elements," "Atomic Masses"; Morrison, "Survey of Nuclear Reactions"; Feld, "The Neutron."

The second World War stimulated research in classical fields of physics. The development of radar, for example, required the expansion of the usable spectrum to frequencies of higher orders of magnitude than usual. Research was conducted in microwaves, which fall between the wavelengths of ordinary radio and light. Among Wiley books are Pollard and Julian M. Sturtevant's *Microwaves and Radar Electronics* (1948), Robert B. Muchmore's *Essentials of Microwaves* (1952), and Walter Gordy, William Smith, and Ralph F. Trambarulo's *Microwave Spectroscopy* (1953).

The war in Korea greatly increased the use of automation, the replacement of men by machines, by servomechanisms and electronic computers. Edmund C. Berkeley's *Giant Brains: or Machines That Think* (1949) was an early Wiley book in the field. A fundamental theoretical book, published by Wiley in co-operation with the Massachusetts Institute of Technology, is *Cybernetics* (1948), by Norbert Wiener. The title of this book is derived from the Greek word for helmsman (κῦβεργήτης), which occurs in the motto of the Phi Beta Kappa Society, "Philosophy, the Helmsman of Life."

As we survey the history of physics during the last century and a half, we appreciate that John Wiley and Sons, by publications beginning with a textbook on optics and currently representing the masterly achievements in theoretical and experimental physics, has encouraged man's striving to gain insight into the physical nature of things, a striving that has been increasing at an accelerated rate in the United States and in the world.

VICTOR F. LENZEN

The Earth's Crust

Books on Geology and Mineralogy

A CENTURY AND A HALF AGO organized study of the geological sciences was about to begin in the United States. The publication of the Scotsman Maclure's geological map of the United States by the American Philosophical Society in 1809 marks the beginning of large-scale geological studies in this country. Earlier publication of geological material in the United States had been limited mostly to brief statements incidental to geographic descriptions and to occasional reports on the finding of fossils. Maclure's work was followed soon by the local and regional studies of several native geologists. The Wiley list contains a single item from this period, Henry R. Schoolcraft's *View of the Lead Mines of Missouri* (1819), one of a long series of studies on a subject that has been of great interest to economic geologists to this day.

The *American Journal of Science*, devoted very largely to the geological sciences, was started by Benjamin Silliman in 1818. The thirties and the forties saw the rise of official geological surveys in many states, some of them rather short-lived. These surveys made a start on the publication of geological materials by government agencies. The entry of the federal government into the field after the middle of the century culminated in 1879 in the establishment of the United States Geological Survey, whose voluminous publications far overshadow those of the states.

During this period Wiley began the publication of geological books and gradually attained an important position in the field, and a dominating one in the mineralogical branch, in which it must be ranked as one of the foremost publishers in the world. A review of this publishing activity is best divided into three parts: consideration of books on geology and some of its recently developed specialties, of books on petrography, and of books on mineralogy.

After the early work of Schoolcraft the next geological item of special interest on the Wiley list is Sir Charles Lyell's *Geological Tour—Travels in North America*, issued in 1845. At that time Lyell was the leading figure in the geological world. His "Principles of Geology," published in England in several volumes, beginning in 1830, went through many editions. It was the first modern textbook of geology and was literally the "standard of the world" for many decades. Publication of the report on his travels in North America must have been a notable event to his contemporaries. The next half century saw the publication by Wiley of several textbooks on geology that are now not so well known, followed in 1894 by Samuel F. Emmons' *Geological Guide-Book for an Excursion to the Rocky Mountains*, bringing to the Wiley list one of the great geological names of that day.

About fifty years ago Wiley's activity in the publication of geological books was greatly expanded. This expansion may be considered to date from the appearance of Heinrich Ries's *Economic Geology* in 1905. This was but the first of numerous successful Wiley books by the well-known Cornell professor and his co-workers. Ries's *Clays: Their Occurrence, Properties and Uses* (1906) was in several editions the standard work in its field, superseded only because of the complete re-orientation of clay studies that followed the introduction of new methods into this area of geology about 1930. C. W. Hayes's *Handbook for Field Geologists*, issued by Wiley in 1909, was one of the earliest books in its class.

The publication of the *Textbook of Geology*, by Louis V. Pirsson and Charles Schuchert, in two volumes (*Physical Geology* and *Historical Geology*), in 1915, marked the beginning of a series of Wiley books in geology that have held an important place in the field. This book and its variants and abridgments, later editions being written by Chester R. Longwell, Adolph Knopf, Richard

F. Flint, and Carl O. Dunbar, successors to the original authors at Yale, have served to introduce countless thousands of American students to geology. The latest in the series, *Introduction to Physical Geology*, by Longwell and Flint, appeared in 1955. The latest edition of *Historical Geology*, by Dunbar, was published in 1949. They also served to spread the influence of Yale in geology over the country, largely displacing the influence gained by the Chicago school of geology, at least in part through its textbooks, in the early years of the century. A later Yale book, Alan M. Bateman's *Economic Mineral Deposits*, first issued in 1942, has also enjoyed success leading to revision and abridgment and has filled a place among American textbooks left vacant by the obsolescence of a famous earlier work by another author and publisher.

Among the more important Wiley books in historical geology, stratigraphy, and paleontology are Charles Schuchert's monographic *Historical Geology of the Antillean-Caribbean Region* (1935), a book such as is rarely found in the lists of commerical publishers, his posthumous *Stratigraphy of the Eastern and Central United States* (1943) and *Atlas of Paleogeographic Maps of North America* (1955), Hervey Shimer and Robert R. Shrock's *Index Fossils of North America* (1944), and Martin F. Glaessner's *Principles of Micropaleontology* (1947).

Recent decades have seen continuing specialization in the geological sciences, and this specialization has gradually had its influence in the appearance of specialized textbooks. Some of the books by Heinrich Ries, mentioned earlier, are in this category, as are Charles M. Nevin's *Principles of Structural Geology* (1931) and Richard Flint's *Glacial Geology and the Pleistocene Epoch* (1947). The last few years have brought an increase in this trend, with the publication of many books intended for specialists whose ranks have swollen to warrant consideration of their needs, while other books aim to make the results of specialization more readily available to the student or general geologist. Many important Wiley books of the second category are to be mentioned here, including P. H. Kuenen's *Marine Geology* (1950), L. Don Leet's *Earth Waves* (1950), Parker D. Trask's *Applied Sedimentation* (1950), Brian H. Mason's *Principles of Geochemistry* (1952), *Nuclear Geology* (1954), edited by Henry Faul, and John R. Schulz and Arthur B. Cleaves's *Geology in Engineering* (1955).

Petrography or petrology, the study of rocks, as distinct from the study of mineralogy, of the components of rocks, or of geology, the history of the earth

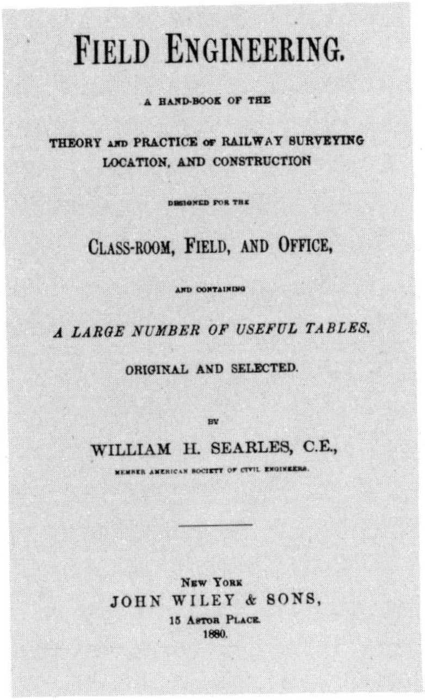

FIELD ENGINEERING.

A HAND-BOOK OF THE

THEORY AND PRACTICE OF RAILWAY SURVEYING
LOCATION, AND CONSTRUCTION

DESIGNED FOR THE

CLASS-ROOM, FIELD, AND OFFICE,

AND CONTAINING

A LARGE NUMBER OF USEFUL TABLES,

ORIGINAL AND SELECTED.

BY

WILLIAM H. SEARLES, C.E.,

MEMBER AMERICAN SOCIETY OF CIVIL ENGINEERS.

NEW YORK
JOHN WILEY & SONS,
15 ASTOR PLACE.
1880.

Earliest Wiley technical book (1880) still in print in a twenty-second edition (1949)

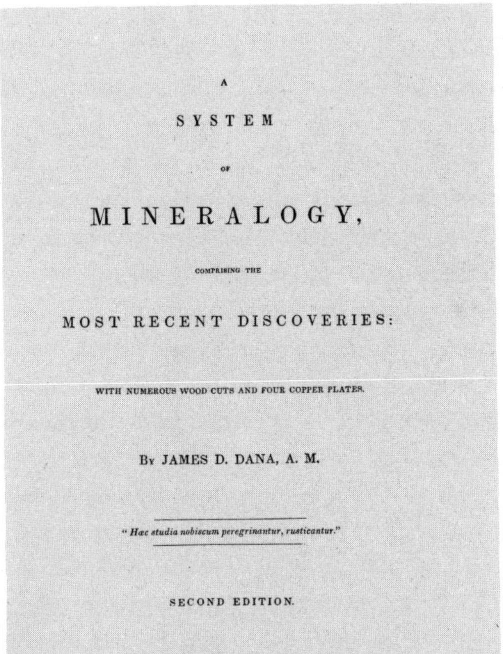

A
SYSTEM
OF
MINERALOGY,

COMPRISING THE

MOST RECENT DISCOVERIES:

WITH NUMEROUS WOOD CUTS AND FOUR COPPER PLATES.

BY JAMES D. DANA, A. M.

"Hæc studia nobiscum peregrinantur, rusticantur."

SECOND EDITION.

NEW YORK AND LONDON:
PUBLISHED BY WILEY & PUTNAM.
1844.

Earliest Wiley book in the sciences (1844), still in print in a seventh edition (Volume I, 1944; Volume II, 1951) as recorded in rocks, began after the appearance in London in 1858 of the classic paper by H. C. Sorby on the applications of the polarizing microscope to the examination of rocks in thin sections. This study was developed into a firm discipline by Ferdinand Zirkel in Leipzig and Harry Rosenbusch in Heidelberg during the last three decades of the nineteenth century. At that time many American students went abroad to study natural sciences, and Rosenbusch attracted most of those interested in the study of rocks. It is no wonder then that the first Wiley book in petrography, issued in 1888, was Joseph P. Iddings' translation of an early edition of H. Rosenbusch's most important book, *Microscopical Physiography of the Rock-Making Minerals*. Within a short time a most active group of native American petrographers was formed. Most prominent among them in the early years of this century was the famous foursome, Cross, Iddings, Pirsson, and Washington, who were the originators of the so-called C.I.P.W. classification of rocks that exercised much influence in its time. Three of these men wrote independent textbooks in various phases of petrography; all of them were published by Wiley. Henry S. Washington's *Manual of the Chemical Analysis of Rocks* appeared in 1904. Used as a guide by generations of chemical analysts or would-be analysts, it has appeared in several revised editions. J. P. Iddings' *Rock Minerals* (1906) and his *Igneous Rocks* (Volume I, 1909, and Volume II, 1913) form a series covering about the same ground as the comprehensive three- and four-volume books of Zirkel and of Rosenbusch. Their appearance marks the end of strong foreign influence on the study of petrography in the United States. Pirsson's *Rocks and Rock Minerals* (1908) proved to be a most successful book for beginners in the study of rocks. Having been revised several times by Adolph Knopf, it is still a standard textbook after nearly half a century.

To these important books, which formed the mainstay of the Wiley group in petrography for several decades, there have recently been added others that are the products of current workers in the field. Ernest E. Wahlstrom's *Optical Crystallography* (first edition, 1943, second edition, 1951), *Igneous Minerals and Rocks* (1947), and *Introduction to Theoretical Igneous Petrology* (1950) form a set rivaling in scope the books of Iddings and designed to make the subject palatable to beginners. The most recent Wiley book in the field, Tom F. W. Barth's *Theoretical Petrology* (1952), highly original and provocative, is sure to be stimulating to the advanced student.

Wiley's entry into the field of mineralogical publication antedated its first publication of an American book in petrography by fully sixty years. This gap is but a reflection of differences in the development of these two branches of geological science, especially in the United States. Whereas petrography developed as a distinct field of inquiry in the last third of the nineteenth century and in its early stages was dominated by a few European personalities, mineralogy had been established as a distinct field of study a century earlier. In the United States several native mineralogists published general textbooks on mineralogy during the first decades of the nineteenth century. Like most books on natural science of their day, all these were influenced by the Linnaean tradition. One of them, however, the *System of Mineralogy*, by James Dwight Dana, the first edition of which appeared in New Haven in 1837, when its author was but twenty-four years of age, was destined to be the forerunner of one of the most important books on minerals. The second edition (1844) and all but one of the later editions have been published by Wiley, and this fact alone would be sufficient to establish the firm as of first importance among mineralogical publishers. The *System of Mineralogy* in a rapid succession of editions was changed and modernized so that the fifth edition (1868) received the world-wide recognition that has also been accorded later editions. Whereas the *System* was originally a textbook, it was gradually modified to become, from the fifth edition onward, a concise and critical compendium of documented data on all mineral species. The sixth edition (1892), by E. S. Dana, son of the original author and, like his father, a professor at Yale, was a completely new book. Until recently it was the best reference book for mineralogical data, a massive book of 1,134 pages, plus 276 pages in three appendices, carrying the work to 1915. In 1944, just one hundred years after the first association of Wiley with the *System of Mineralogy*, the first volume of the seventh edition appeared, no longer a product of the Yale school of mineralogists but that of Professor Charles Palache of Harvard and his co-workers Harry Berman and Clifford Frondel. The second volume, largely the work of Frondel, appeared in 1951, and mineralogists all over the world eagerly await his completion of the third and final volume of the latest and greatest edition of Dana's *System of Mineralogy*.*

* A review and history of the development of Dana's *System of Mineralogy* by A. Pabst appeared in *Rocks and Minerals*, 19: 379–387, 1944.

Besides the *System of Mineralogy*, several other Dana mineralogies have served as textbooks for instruction at various levels over a long period. Most important has been the *Textbook of Mineralogy*, the first and second editions of which, by E. S. Dana, were issued by Wiley in 1877 and 1898. The third edition (1922), prepared by William E. Ford, was soon followed by the important fourth edition (1932), with the descriptive section enlarged to comprehensive scope so that it served as a substitute for the *System* during the latter part of the long interval (from 1915 to 1944) between the appearance of the last supplement of the sixth edition and the first volume of the seventh edition of the *System*. An astonishing popularity has been enjoyed by the somewhat more elementary *Manual of Mineralogy*, which, at the hands of the Danas and of W. E. Ford, went through fourteen editions from 1848 to 1929. This book also has been transferred from Yale to Harvard, the fifteenth and sixteenth editions (1942 and 1952) being by Cornelius S. Hurlbut. The recent increase of amateur interest in mineralogy has also led to the preparation of a third edition by Hurlbut of *Minerals and How to Study Them*. The first edition (1895) was written by E. S. Dana.

Besides these four Dana books in mineralogy, the first editions of which emanated from Yale during the nineteenth century, another outstanding mineralogical product of the same school, the *Manual of Determinative Mineralogy*, by George J. Brush, was first published by Wiley in 1875. The importance of this book is attested to by the fact that it reached its sixteenth and last edition, by Samuel L. Penfield, in 1898. No doubt the lack of later editions is due to the deaths of the authors soon after the appearance of the long-lived sixteenth edition. This book has had a great influence, and the 1898 edition has been repeatedly reprinted over half a century. Its crystal drawings served as the basis for the most widely used set of crystal models. Its tables for the identification of minerals by blowpipe and chemical tests have never been matched for comprehensiveness. A portion of J. Volney Lewis's *Determinative Mineralogy with Tables* (Wiley, 1913), fourth edition by Lewis and Alfred C. Hawkins (1931), is an abridgment of Brush and Penfield's book.

Albert H. Chester's *Catalogue of Minerals with Their Chemical Composition and Synonyms* (1886) and *Dictionary of the Names of Minerals, Including Their History and Etymology* (1896) are still valuable. The worth of such compilations is shown by the fact that modern versions of such catalogues or dictionaries have appeared in both England and Germany in recent years.

Though most Wiley textbooks in general and determinative mineralogy have come directly or indirectly from the Yale school of mineralogists, the Wiley list has also included a few from other sources. Noteworthy among these are G. Montague Butler's *Handbook of Mineralogy* (1918).

Foreign influence in the field is seen in only two Wiley books. They are Hugh Marshall's translation of P. Groth's *Introduction to Chemical Crystallography* (1906) and B. H. Jackson's translation of Groth's *Optical Properties of Crystals* (1910). The latter betokens the rise of optical methods in mineralogy during the first decades of this century. Albert Johannsen's *Determination of Rock-Forming Minerals* (1908) belongs in this same period, but by far the most important of Wiley publications stemming from this era is the *Elements of Optical Mineralogy*, the first edition of which, by Alexander N. Winchell and Newton H. Winchell, appeared in 1909. Split into several parts in separate volumes in later editions, Part II, *Descriptions of Minerals*, is unique in that it is the sole work that aims to treat comprehensively the optical properties of all non-opaque minerals. The latest (the fourth) edition of this part of the *Elements of Optical Mineralogy* (1951) is by N. H. Winchell and Horace Winchell. Together with *Microscopic Characters of Artificial Inorganic Solid Substances*, by A. N. Winchell (1931), it offers the microscopist data on all non-opaque inorganic materials whose optical properties have been recorded. We might only wish that the value of the methods for which these books furnish the reference data were more widely appreciated.

Whereas the Winchell books deal with translucent minerals and these lend themselves especially well to microscopic identification, opaque minerals can also be identified by microscopic means. One of the pioneer books in this field, Joseph Murdoch's *Microscopical Determination of Opaque Minerals*, was published by Wiley in 1916.

In recent decades X-ray diffraction has become one of the most important tools for the student of minerals or crystalline materials of any sort. Wiley's entry into this field is marked by the publication of Martin J. Buerger's *X-Ray Crystallography* in 1942. Buerger's methods, set forth in this book, have become standard practice throughout the world.

ADOLF PABST

The Human Habitat

Books on Geography

INTEREST IN GEOGRAPHY in America goes back to the original settlement by Europeans of a rich land. Government work in geography, in exploration, in surveying and mapping, in land appraisal, and in physical and economic geography began with the establishment of an Office of the Geographer of the United States in 1785. Stimulated by Thomas Jefferson, it flowered in the great land surveys of the late nineteenth century and continues to the present day. Another early center of geographical work was the American Geographical Society, founded in New York in 1852. The Society recently joined with John Wiley and Sons in the publication of *The Geography of the Northlands* (1955).

The pivotal point in the development of geography as a separate academic discipline in America came in 1903. In that year the professional organization, the Association of American Geographers, was founded. In that year also, at the University of Chicago, the first major university department of geography was established.

The rapid expansion of geography into a large number of colleges and universities came only after the first World War. It was at this time, in 1920, that Wiley published its first college textbook in geography—Ellsworth Huntington's *Principles of Human Geography*. Huntington's textbook played a noteworthy role in the spread of geography in American colleges; it was a textbook that delighted generations of both teachers and students with its clear presentation, its grand sweep, and its provocative and stimulating ideas. It has gone through six editions and has sold nearly 140,000 copies, a remarkable record for a comparatively small field such as geography! Ellsworth Huntington happily combined tremendous research drive with the ability to write effectively for the student and the general reader.

W. Elmer Ekblaw, editor of the scholarly journal, *Economic Geography*, wrote in that journal in January, 1927: "Few men of this century have been gifted with such keen vision, such rich imagination, such vibrant joy in research as has Ellsworth Huntington. His active mind has restlessly wandered far and unafraid over the great field of geographic interest, and from its venturous journeys has formulated a number of broad generalizations regarding the relation of man to his environment that have caught the world's imagination."

As geography matured in the United States more specialized courses called for textbooks covering specific regions. Wiley then published George J. Miller and Almon E. Parkins' *Geography of North America* (1928), now in its third edition; Samuel Van Valkenburg and Huntington's *Europe* (1935), now in its second edition; and, much later, L. Dudley Stamp's *Africa* (1953), and Joseph E. Spencer's *Asia, East by South* (1954). In a more detailed treatment of regional subdivisions of the United States, Wiley performed an important scholarly and educational service by providing a unique series. A. E. Parkins' *The South* (1938) and Otis W. Freeman and Howard H. Martin's *The Pacific Northwest* (1942), now in its second edition, launched a regional series that is still being expanded by such books as John H. Garland's *The North American Midwest* (1955).

Concern for man's use and abuse of natural resources grew into the conservation movement under Theodore Roosevelt, vigorously restimulated during the depression of the nineteen-thirties. In 1936 Wiley published *Our Natural Resources and Their Conservation*, written by more than a score of the leading authorities in the field. First edited by Parkins and J. R. Whitaker and later by Guy-Harold Smith, it has gone through several editions and remains today the standard textbook in the field.

Wiley contributed to evolving geographic thought in the topical fields of geography by such books as Huntington's *Economic Geography* (1940) and Arthur N. Strahler's *Physical Geography* (1951). In the field of maps it published Arthur H. Robinson's *Elements of Cartography* (1953).

CHAUNCY D. HARRIS

Numbers

Books on Mathematics

PART I

THE FIRST BOOK ON MATHEMATICS published by Wiley was *An Introduction to Algebra*, by Jeremiah Day. This book was issued in 1815, when Day was professor of mathematics at Yale, of which he became president two years later. In the United States at this time there was a serious shortage of adequate textbooks on mathematics. In the few available, of English origin or written in the English style, mathematics was often presented as little more than a collection of rules. Discussions of principles, when given, were likely to be too highly condensed or insufficiently clear. To provide more adequately for the needs of the rather poorly prepared American college students, Day set himself the task of writing a series of textbooks in which the student was introduced to the subject by easy and gradual steps. For this purpose he took as his model the writings of the French authors, particularly those of Lacroix. The resulting books were widely used and very popular.

The *Algebra*, in particular, ran through many editions, the last appearing in 1852.

The next author on the Wiley mathematical list was Charles Davies, professor of mathematics at West Point, at that time probably the most influential school of mathematics in the United States. After about twenty years of teaching, Professor Davies decided to produce a series of textbooks of his own. In 1835 his *Elements of Algebra*, *Elements of Geometry and Trigonometry*, and *Elements of Descriptive Geometry* appeared. During the next year they were followed by his *Elements of Analytical Geometry* and *Elements of Differential and Integral Calculus*. Overwork in the preparation of these books, all published by Wiley, caused a bronchial affection that forced him to resign his professorship in 1837. He visited Europe and on his return held various positions, the last as professor of higher mathematics at Columbia College in 1857.

For more than fifty years Davies' books were very extensively used in the colleges and advanced preparatory schools of the United States. In fact, some of us even now remember Davies' *Algebra* on the family bookshelf. Like the publications of Jeremiah Day, those of Charles Davies show the French influence. His *Geometry* was a revised form of a translation of Legendre brought out by David Brewster in England, and his *Algebra* was based on the French work of Bourdon. Legendre is regarded as the first writer to present Euclid's geometry in a really teachable form, and Bourdon's "Algebra" was one of the most popular French textbooks on that subject.

Davies was succeeded in the chair of mathematics at West Point by Albert E. Church, whose *Elements of Differential and Integral Calculus* was published by Wiley in 1842. Continuing at West Point until his death in 1878, Church prepared an extensively used series of textbooks.

The Wiley catalogue of 1848 includes Charles Hutton's *Course of Mathematics*. Hutton was professor of mathematics at the Royal Military Academy at Woolwich, England. His *Course of Mathematics* was first published in London (1798–1801). In its day it was probably the best of its kind in the English language. Various editions and revisions of Hutton's *Course* were brought out in this country by Robert Adrian, who was excelled only by Nathaniel Bowditch among American mathematicians of the time.

In the Wiley catalogue of 1848 there also appears a curious little book by Charles Gill entitled *Application of the Angular Analysis to the Solution of*

Indeterminate Problems of the Second Degree. Gill was born in England, became a teacher, and for several years devoted his leisure hours to the study of mathematics. During this time he wrote a number of mathematical articles, and in 1830 when he came to America was already known as an original thinker. In this country he brought out a journal called *Mathematical Miscellany*, and made numerous contributions to other mathematical journals. His principal areas of interest were theory of numbers and actuarial work. Because of his contributions to the latter subject Emory McClintock called him "the first actuary in America."

Another interesting author on the Wiley list of 1848 was William Smyth, who was professor of mathematics at Bowdoin College for more than forty years. He wrote a series of textbooks that were well received, but his principal claim to fame was his introduction of the use of the blackboard at Bowdoin in 1824. At that time Smyth was a tutor specializing in Greek. In teaching algebra to a sophomore section he used a blackboard. This produced such a sensation that many of the juniors requested the privilege of reviewing algebra in order to enjoy the new method of instruction. His success in popularizing algebra led Smyth to abandon Greek and accept a position in mathematics, which he held the rest of his life.

After the Civil War there was a marked increase in mathematical publication, both in number of books issued and the range of subjects covered. Although the Wiley list includes only fifteen books before the war, more than ninety others were added before the end of the century. To this period belong the principal publications of William Woolsey Johnson, professor of mathematics at the United States Naval Academy. Johnson began with a series of books on calculus written in co-operation with J. M. Rice. These were followed by other books on calculus, a *Treatise on Ordinary and Partial Differential Equations* (1889), and his *Theory of Errors and Methods of Least Squares* (1892). He also published a series of papers in the *Analyst*, *Messenger of Mathematics*, and *American Journal of Mathematics*, and was active in the foundation of the American Mathematical Society.

Another distinguished author during this period was Mansfield Merriman. He is better known for his engineering textbooks, but his *Textbook on the Method of Least Squares* (1884) introduced not only engineers but also a generation of mathematicians to this important subject. The Merriman and Robert S.

Woodward *Higher Mathematics* (1896) was also an outstanding handbook of mathematics above the elementary calculus level in an era when few handbooks of that range were available.

H. B. PHILLIPS

PART II

IT IS DIFFICULT TO JUDGE the impact of Wiley's contribution as a publisher of mathematics books in the late nineteenth and early twentieth centuries without some insight into the mathematical atmosphere of America at that time. One of the outstanding mathematical personalities of this period, a Wiley author, was George Bruce Halsted. Halsted not only was an American by birth, being the son of a distinguished American family dating back to pre-Revolutionary days, but he also was trained as a mathematician in the United States. His mathematical reputation in his chosen field, geometry, was international. This was remarkable for this time, since the graduate schools in mathematics were in their infancy in this country and many American mathematicians completed their training in Europe.

Halsted completed the work for his doctorate at Johns Hopkins in 1879 under the direction of J. J. Sylvester, one of the great mathematicians of the midnineteenth century. Almost immediately after receiving this degree, he returned to Princeton, the scene of his undergraduate days, and contributed in far fuller measure than his grandfather, who had donated an astronomical observatory to that institution. Halsted organized a postgraduate school of mathematics, and the reputation of Princeton in mathematics stands today as a monument to this gifted young mathematician. It was at this time that he started writing for Wiley. It is interesting to note that he left another monument, by way of a flourishing graduate school of mathematics, at the University of Texas, where he spent the major portion of his later life.

Halsted's first book for Wiley was *Elements of Geometry*, published in 1885, with a sixth edition appearing in 1903. Halsted presented Euclidean geometry in such a way that an admirable foundation was laid for the later study of non-Euclidean geometry. His best production, from the mathematical point of view, was *Elementary Synthetic Geometry* (1892), which was based on a completely new approach, making no use of congruent triangles, but using instead the circle from the beginning. This work also ran to many editions. Halsted's *Rational Geometry* (1904) was also popular; it was translated into French, German, and Japanese.

Halsted contributed *Synthetic Projective Geometry* as Volume 2 of the twenty-one-volume series of *Wiley Mathematical Monographs*. This distinguished series, edited by Mansfield Merriman and Robert S. Woodward, was begun in 1896, and the most recent volume, the twenty-first, was published in 1921. The American Mathematical Society was founded in 1888, and this date can be thought of as the beginning of the real outpouring of American mathematics, which was only a slight trickle at that time when compared to the flourishing mathematics in Europe. Of this series, G. S. Miller, in reviewing Volume 14, *Algebraic Invariants* (1914), by Leonard E. Dickson, had this to say (*American Mathematical Monthly*, Volume 22, 1915):

> The series of monographs to which the present volume belongs is one of the most praiseworthy undertakings relating to American mathematical publications. . . . Monographs like the one under review are filling a great want in our literature, as they tend to create an interest in some of the rich fields of modern mathematics. Their brevity tends to encourage some who might be overawed by the extent of a comprehensive treatise. . . . To the credit of American publishers . . . there have appeared in America a number of treatises of such high mathematical standing as to make it seem unlikely that these particular works could by themselves be financial successes. . . . Our mathematical development is today impeded more by the lack of such works than by any other one obstacle.

In the textbook area Wiley also made some important contributions. Among these textbooks was Joseph G. Coffin's *Vector Analysis* (1909), a significant and early contribution to the establishment of vector analysis as a part of the common body of information of engineers, scientists, and mathematicians. L. E. Dickson's series of books on the theory of equations, *Elementary Theory of Equations* (1914), *First Course in the Theory of Equations* (1921), *New First Course in the Theory of Equations* (1939), represented distinguished expositions for students by one of the most prominent and productive research mathematicians of topics closely related to his major interests. Henry

B. Phillips' series in analysis, *Analytic Geometry* (1915), *Differential Calculus* (1916), *Integral Calculus* (1917), *Vector Analysis* (1933), contributed much to the development and training of the great numbers of first-rate engineers and scientists on which our society depends in this technological age. Other textbooks contributing in a highly significant way to the training of our scientists and engineers were the following: Harry W. Reddick and Frederic H. Miller's *Advanced Mathematics for Engineers* (1938), Edward S. Smith, Meyer Salkover, and Howard K. Justice's *Calculus* (1938), and their *Analytic Geometry* (1943), Cyrus C. MacDuffee's *Introduction to Abstract Algebra* (1940), Ivan S. Sokolnikoff's *Tensor Analysis* (1951), Charles H. Lehmann's *Analytic Geometry* (1942), Harry W. Reddick's *Differential Equations* (1943), Paul G. Andres, Hugh J. Miser, and Haim Reingold's *Basic Mathematics for Engineers* (1944), Ernest A. Guillemin's *Mathematics of Circuit Analysis* (1949), and John W. Cell's *Analytic Geometry* (1951).

In recent years there has been a widespread movement in the direction of unifying calculus and analytical geometry. An early and successful textbook in the spirit of this movement was Smith, Salkover, and Justice's *Unified Calculus* (1947). Two years later Wiley published Miller's *Analytic Geometry and Calculus* (1949). At a slightly higher level there has been, and is, a continuing movement to introduce the advanced aspects of subjects usually taught at the graduate level in an elementary way to undergraduates. Among the textbooks published by Wiley in support of this movement are Marie J. Weiss's *Higher Algebra for the Undergraduate* (1949), Raymond L. Wilder's *Introduction to the Foundations of Mathematics* (1952), and Dick Wick Hall and Guilford L. Spencer's *Elementary Topology* (1955). At the same time Wiley has continued to support advanced mathematics by publishing significant treatises and textbooks for graduate students and research workers.

GUILFORD L. SPENCER

DICK WICK HALL

Collecting and Using Data

Books on Statistics

THE WORD "STATISTICS" is used in two senses. On the one hand, it refers to numerical data collected by government agencies, business houses and industrial firms, trade associations and economic research groups. In this widely used sense statistics appear in published form as tables, graphs, and charts in reports, yearbooks, and other such documents. As an organized activity it has been developing and expanding as an indispensable basic tool of modern government, business, and industry for more than a century.

In the second sense, statistics is a science concerned with the collection of observations on a population of objects and drawing inferences from the observations about the population. In many situations the observations can be made only on a sample of objects from the population, in which case the problems of inference become especially important. These situations occur not only in connection with economic problems of government, business, and industry but also with equal importance in medical research, agricultural research, industrial research and development, and in all fields of the natural sciences.

The science of statistics had its beginning hardly more than fifty years ago under the leadership of Karl Pearson at University College, London. The early statistical methods developed by Karl Pearson and his school were methods of correlational analysis and curve fitting, motivated largely by problems in the biological sciences.

In the early nineteen-twenties a new direction was given to the science of statistics by R. A. Fisher at the world-famous Rothamsted Agricultural Experiment Station in England. Fisher's main contribution was the development of statistical methods involved in the design of experiments and in drawing inferences from the data supplied by scientifically designed experiments. Fisherian methods are becoming increasingly more widely used, not only in agricultural experimentation but also in many other fields of science and more recently in industrial research.

It was not until the late nineteen-twenties—after the beginning of Fisher's work in England—that modern statistical science began to take hold in the United States. The early leaders in this new field included B. H. Camp, H. C. Carver, E. L. Dodd, H. Hotelling, P. R. Rider, H. L. Rietz, and W. A. Shewhart. The pioneering efforts of these men culminated in the formation of the Institute of Mathematical Statistics in 1935, a society devoted to the development of the mathematical theory of statistics and its applications in many different fields.

John Wiley and Sons has been publishing books on statistics since the beginning of organized interest in statistical science in this country. Actually, its first venture in this field was the publication in 1899 of Charles B. Davenport's *Statistical Methods*, which dealt mainly with some of the simpler problems of biological variation. The first Wiley book in modern statistics was Mordecai Ezekiel's *Methods of Correlation Analysis*, published in 1930. Ezekiel was a government agricultural economist, and his book was devoted to correlation and regression methods that he had found useful in his economic research.

In 1938 Wiley published its first elementary textbook on mathematical statistics, William D. Baten's *Elementary Mathematical Statistics*, and in the next year a similar book by Paul R. Rider, entitled *An Introduction to Modern Statistical Methods*, was published. In these books, particularly in the second,

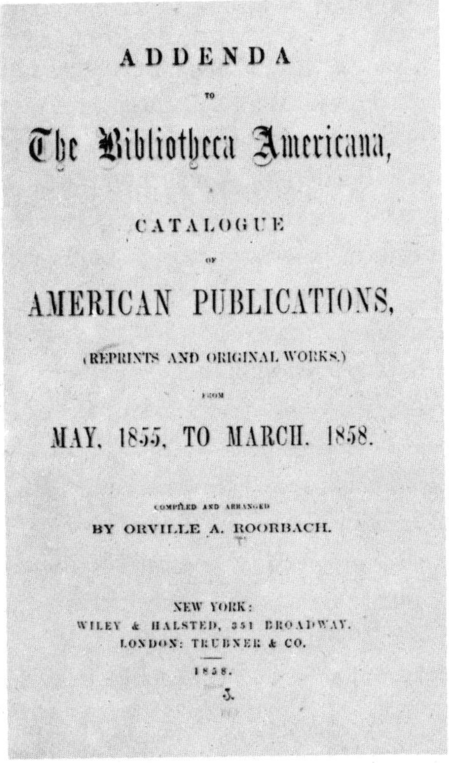

ADDENDA

TO

The Bibliotheca Americana,

CATALOGUE

OF

AMERICAN PUBLICATIONS,

(REPRINTS AND ORIGINAL WORKS,)

FROM

MAY, 1855, TO MARCH, 1858.

COMPILED AND ARRANGED

BY ORVILLE A. ROORBACH.

NEW YORK:
WILEY & HALSTED, 351 BROADWAY.
LONDON: TRUBNER & CO.

1858.

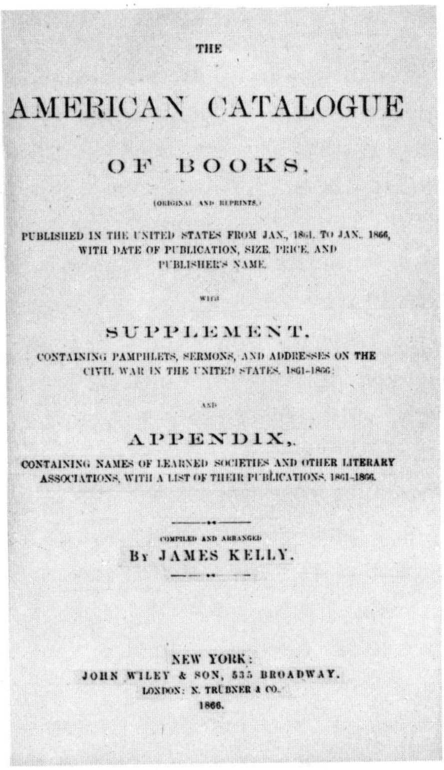

THE

AMERICAN CATALOGUE

OF BOOKS,

(ORIGINAL AND REPRINTS,)

PUBLISHED IN THE UNITED STATES FROM JAN., 1861, TO JAN., 1866,
WITH DATE OF PUBLICATION, SIZE, PRICE, AND
PUBLISHER'S NAME.

WITH

SUPPLEMENT,

CONTAINING PAMPHLETS, SERMONS, AND ADDRESSES ON THE
CIVIL WAR IN THE UNITED STATES, 1861-1866;

AND

APPENDIX,

CONTAINING NAMES OF LEARNED SOCIETIES AND OTHER LITERARY
ASSOCIATIONS, WITH A LIST OF THEIR PUBLICATIONS, 1861-1866.

COMPILED AND ARRANGED

BY JAMES KELLY.

NEW YORK:
JOHN WILEY & SON, 535 BROADWAY.
LONDON: N. TRÜBNER & CO.
1866.

Ventures into bibliography

the authors introduced the elementary mathematical aspects of Fisherian statistical methods.

Early in the second World War, and under the pressure of the war materiel production, statistical methods of industrial quality control, which had been introduced in the mid-twenties by Walter A. Shewhart, Harold F. Dodge, and Harry G. Romig of the Bell Telephone Laboratories, began to attract the attention of engineers responsible for inspection and mass-production operations. Three books in the general area of engineering and industrial statistics appeared in the Wiley Statistics Series in 1941, 1942, and 1944. The first of them was a book entitled *An Engineer's Manual of Statistical Methods*, by Leslie E. Simon, who was then director of the Aberdeen Proving

Ground in Maryland, and who has long been an ardent advocate of the use of modern statistical methods in military research and development work. The second book was Harold A. Freeman's *Industrial Statistics*, which was devoted to the application of Fisher's principles of the design of experiments to industrial experimentation. The third was *Sampling Inspection Tables*, by Dodge and Romig of the Bell Telephone Laboratories, which presented for general distribution what are now widely known in quality-control engineering as "the Dodge-Romig tables" for acceptance sampling plans used in deciding whether to accept or to reject lots of mass-produced articles.

It was at this time—early in the second World War—that Wiley, largely on the advice of W. A. Shewhart of the Bell Telephone Laboratories, began to realize that the science of statistics was a field with a promising future. The applications of statistical methods to industrial quality control and to the design of experiments in various fields not only were showing considerable growth by now, but new lines of development of statistical theory and applications also were in evidence. Accordingly, a decision was made to intensify its publication efforts in statistics, and arrangements were made to retain Shewhart's services as its statistical adviser.

Beginning with Shewhart's appointment, plans were laid for a comprehensive publication program not only in theoretical and applied statistics but also in the foundation subjects of probability theory. The first book to appear in the probability program was Norbert Wiener's *Extrapolation, Interpolation, and Smoothing of Stationary Time Series*, published in 1949 in co-operation with the Technology Press. It is a treatment of time series based on modern theory of stochastic processes. In the same year Wiley published the American edition of Niels Arley's book, *On the Theory of Stochastic Processes and Their Application to the Theory of Cosmic Radiation*. The American edition of Arley and K. Rander Buch's *Introduction to the Theory of Probability and Statistics* appeared in 1950. In the same year William Feller's *Introduction to Probability Theory and Its Applications*, Volume I, was published. This has been an extremely popular probability textbook dealing with the theory of discrete random variables and its application to a wide variety of probability problems. The book has given a strong impetus to the study of the theory and applications of probability in this country. Feller's Volume II, which will deal with continuous random variables, is expected to appear in the late nineteen-fifties. Another important book on advanced probability theory is Joseph L. Doob's *Stochastic Processes*, published in 1953, which will be an authoritative treatment on this subject for some years to come. The American edition of Harold Cramér's elementary textbook, entitled *Elements of Probability Theory and Some of Its Applications*, appeared in 1955.

The new effort toward a more comprehensive program of statistics publications began to bear fruit in 1947 with the appearance of Abraham Wald's *Sequential Analysis*. This book contains a body of statistical theory, with applications developed during the second World War for the design and analysis of certain kinds of experiments in which provision is made for experimenting and analyzing results sequentially.

An area in mathematical statistics that was becoming increasingly important in the early nineteen-forties was survey sampling. Survey sampling plays an important role in government census work, market research, and other fields where, because of cost factors, sampling methods must be employed in place of full-scale surveys or censuses. The leading theoretical and applied work in this area was being done in the Bureau of the Census in Washington, and arrangements were made by Wiley to publish some results of the work. The first book on the subject was W. Edwards Deming's *Some Theory of Sampling* (1950). Three years later a comprehensive two-volume treatise, *Sample Survey Methods and Theory*, by Morris H. Hansen, William M. Hurwitz, and William G. Madow, was published by Wiley. Volume I was devoted to applications, and Volume II to theory. This book is expected to be the standard one for some time. Also in 1953 a textbook by William G. Cochran, entitled *Sampling Techniques*, was published in the Wiley Statistics Series.

As pointed out earlier, one of the directions in which probability and statistical theory and their applications have had a great deal of influence in other fields of science is in the design of experiments. Wiley has published several books devoted to this subject. A book that contains many of the original papers in this field is Ronald A. Fisher's *Contributions to Mathematical Statistics* (1950), a photo-offset collection of forty-three of the most important of Fisher's original papers. The second book was *Experimental Designs* (1950), by Cochran and Gertrude M. Cox. The primary emphasis in this widely known book is on applications of experiment designs of many different kinds. The third book is Oscar Kempthorne's *The Design and Analysis of Experiments*, published in 1952. This book stresses both the theory and the applications of principles of experiment design. A fourth book in this field is Carl A. Bennett and Norman L. Franklin's *Statistical Analysis in Chemistry and the Chemical Industry* (1954), which is aimed, as its title indicates, at problems in statistical analysis and experiment design of special interest to chemists and chemical engineers. The Bennett-Franklin book was preceded, in 1951, by W. J. Youden's popular primer on the design of experiments, entitled *Statistical Methods for Chemists*.

Other Wiley books on statistics that are of interest in engineering and technology have appeared from time to time. Particular reference is made to the American editions of Leonard H. C. Tippett's *Technological Applications of Statistics* and *The Methods of Statistics*, included among Wiley's statistics books in 1950 and 1952, respectively. A comprehensive reference book for engineers is A. Hald's *Statistical Theory with Engineering Applications* (and Tables), the American edition of which was published in 1952.

One of the more recent fields in mathematical statistics to be investigated is statistical decision theory, initiated by Abraham Wald. This theory was motivated in some respects by the theory of games as developed by John Von Neumann and Oskar Morgenstern. Wald's work in statistical decision theory was published in 1950, shortly before his tragic death in an airplane crash in India. It appeared in book form under the title *Statistical Decision Functions*. Wald's work in this field and the Von Neumann-Morgenstern ideas in game theory have stimulated a considerable amount of work among American mathematical statisticians. Two other books on decision theory, published in 1954 by Wiley, are David Blackwell and Meyer A. Girshick's mathematical treatment, entitled *The Theory of Games and Statistical Decisions*, and *Decision Processes*, by Robert M. Thrall, Clyde H. Coombs, and Robert L. Davis. The second book is devoted to decision processes with particular reference to the social sciences. Another Wiley book published in 1954 and strongly influenced by statistical decision theory is Leonard J. Savage's *The Foundations of Statistics*.

Wiley has published several statistics books of special interest to economists in recent years. One of them is Bruce D. Mudgett's *Index Numbers* (1951).

Another is Gerhard Tintner's *Econometrics* (1952). A third is Herman Wold and Lars Jureen's *Demand Analysis: A Study of Econometrics* (1953). Books containing material of substantive interest to economists are Philip M. Hauser and William R. Leonard's *Government Statistics for Business Use* (1946) and R. G. D. Allen and J. Edward Ely's *International Trade Statistics* (1953).

Similarly, statistics books of particular interest to psychologists include Quinn McNemar's textbook entitled *Psychological Statistics*, which appeared in 1949, and Harold Gulliksen's *Theory of Mental Tests*, published the following year. Gulliksen's book deals with the statistical methods of psychometrics—the methodology of construction tests for personnel selection that are becoming widely used in colleges, business, industry, government, and the military services. A theoretical book of interest to psychologists is Robert R. Bush and Frederick Mosteller's *Stochastic Models for Learning* (1955). This book is devoted to some newer concepts concerning learning theory based on the application of probability theory. Another Wiley statistics book of interest to psychologists and other scientists who make extensive use of correlation and regression methods is Paul S. Dwyer's *Linear Computations* (1951).

Recent Wiley books of value to researchers and students in the biological sciences include the second edition of Cyril H. Goulden's *Methods of Statistical Analysis* (1952) and D. J. Finney's *Introduction to Statistical Science in Agriculture* (1953). Both these books are concerned with the applications of statistical methods in agricultural research. A book of particular interest to biometricians is C. R. Rao's *Advanced Statistical Methods in Biometric Research* (1952). This is one of the first books to give extensive consideration to ways of applying some of the modern multivariate statistical methods that have been developed since the advent of correlation and regression methods.

Statistics is a young and expanding science with possibilities of application in many fields. Wiley early showed an awareness of the importance of a publication program in this field. In 1953 arrangements were made for S. S. Wilks of Princeton University to become co-editor with Shewhart for the Wiley Statistics Series. Some areas have only recently matured to the point where books can be written on them. In the last ten years many such books have appeared in the Wiley Statistics Series. Other forthcoming theoretical books to appear in the Series include one by T. W. Anderson on multivariate analysis, one by D. A. S. Fraser on non-parametric statistical theory, one by E. L. Lehmann on the theory of testing statistical hypotheses, one by H. Scheffé on analysis of variance, and an advanced treatise on mathematical statistics by S. S. Wilks. Books dealing with applications of statistical methods to various new fields will also appear within the next few years.

SAMUEL S. WILKS

Graphic Communication

Books on Drawing and Descriptive Geometry

WILEY, IN PROVIDING BOOKS useful to engineers and architects, has kept in mind the dictum of the earliest author of technical books, Vitruvius, who, more than nineteen hundred years ago, thought that an architect-engineer should be a man of letters and a skillful draftsman, understanding geometry, handy with ruler and compass, and capable of executing colored drawings in perspective—an ambitious goal, even for modern times.

No one in our day would think of outlining the historical development of orthographic projection without going back nearly two centuries to Gaspard Monge, to whom modern engineers and architects owe their foundation science of descriptive geometry. For many years Monge taught this beautiful subject to French cadets training to be officers, and required them to vow to keep it a military secret.

Although he never wrote a book on the subject, a number of his pupils or followers did. One of them, Potier, wrote in French "Application of Descriptive Geometry to the Art of Design"; it was published at St. Petersburg in 1817. At least one copy of this book found its way many years ago into an American college library. On the first page the following appears:

> Permitted to print, on condition that the Censorship Committee be furnished, after the work is printed and before it is offered for sale, one copy for the said Committee, one for the Department of the Minister of Public Instruction, two for the Imperial Public Library and one for the Imperial Academy of Sciences.
>
> (Signed) SOHN, Counseller of the Court and Censor

The first American teacher of descriptive geometry was the French-born Claude Crozet, professor at West Point. For some years he taught from a French textbook, then in 1821 he wrote Part 1 of his "Treatise on Descriptive Geometry" in English. He planned to issue Part 2, with "applications to perspective, shades and shadows, and dialling," but he never got around to it. A decade later Charles Davies, the West Point mathematician who wrote the English textbook that succeeded Crozet's, remarked in his preface that the subject "has not found its way into other seminaries with a rapidity at all proportionate to its usefulness."

In 1852 Professor Dennis Hart Mahan of the Academy, whose pioneer *Civil Engineering* Wiley had published fifteen years earlier, wrote his *Industrial Drawing* for the use of "academies and common schools." This may well have been the earliest attempt in the United States to teach the subject to young men who lacked a suitable educational background. The book was based on a series of lectures the author had given to apprentices in New York City's famous West Point foundry. In this book the author advises his young readers that the drawing instruments he describes may be bought from John Wiley, 167 Broadway. A third edition appeared as late as 1877.

The Davies descriptive geometry textbook was used for some years at Rensselaer, until S. Edward Warren of that pioneer institution wrote his comprehensive *General Problems from the Orthographic Projections of Descriptive Geometry* in 1860. This book of more than 400 pages and 166 drawings seems to have made other books almost unnecessary for more than a generation. The author comments on the paucity of books on the subject in English. His book, he suggests, will be useful "to Architects, Engineers, Masons and Machinists, as well as to mere draftsmen."

Although the book found wide acceptance, Professor Warren soon realized that few of the rapidly increasing number of engineering and science students would be able to read so formidable a treatise. He therefore wrote in 1861 his *Elementary Projection Drawing*, which reached its fifth edition in 1880 and exercised a considerable influence on the teaching of drawing for several decades. Professor Warren may rightly be called the most prolific of Wiley authors down through the eighteen-seventies, his twelve titles exceeding Mahan's nine.

In 1875 Warren produced one of the last books ever to be called *Stereotomy*. To him, stereotomy "embraced, either by etymology or established usage," shades and shadows, perspective, dialing, cinematics, structural articulations, carpentry, and stone cutting. His book covered only stone cutting. Evidently there was, even at this period, a great need for standardized nomenclature.

Warren's textbooks covered a period of some twenty years; after he left Rensselaer he served for a time at the then quite new Massachusetts Institute of Technology. After his era of activity, there was a time during which not many important textbooks appeared. Instead there were slight unpretentious books prepared for local use in secondary schools and some colleges, and printed privately. Some of the authors seem to have expected students simply to reproduce drawings from the textbook, a practice that did harm to the subject in certain academic circles for years. Late in the nineteenth century a new group of teachers took over the writing of textbooks on the theory and practice of engineering drawing. Professor Charles W. MacCord of Stevens Institute, with his *Practical Hints for Draftsmen* (1888), was the earliest of these Wiley authors; his *Mechanical Drawing* (1892) and *Elements of Descriptive Geometry* (1895) soon followed.

During the first three decades of the twentieth century increasing numbers of such books were written. The American Society for Engineering Education, originally called the Society for the Promotion of Engineering Education, which dates from 1893, has had a stimulating effect on engineering textbook writers. Not a few of the Wiley authors of this period were associated with large and fast-growing Midwestern engineering schools. Widely used were Alpha P. Jamison's *Elements of Mechanical Drawing* (1904), and the same author's *Advanced Mechanical Drawing* (1905), considered by many authorities as the direct forerunners of today's best-selling books on

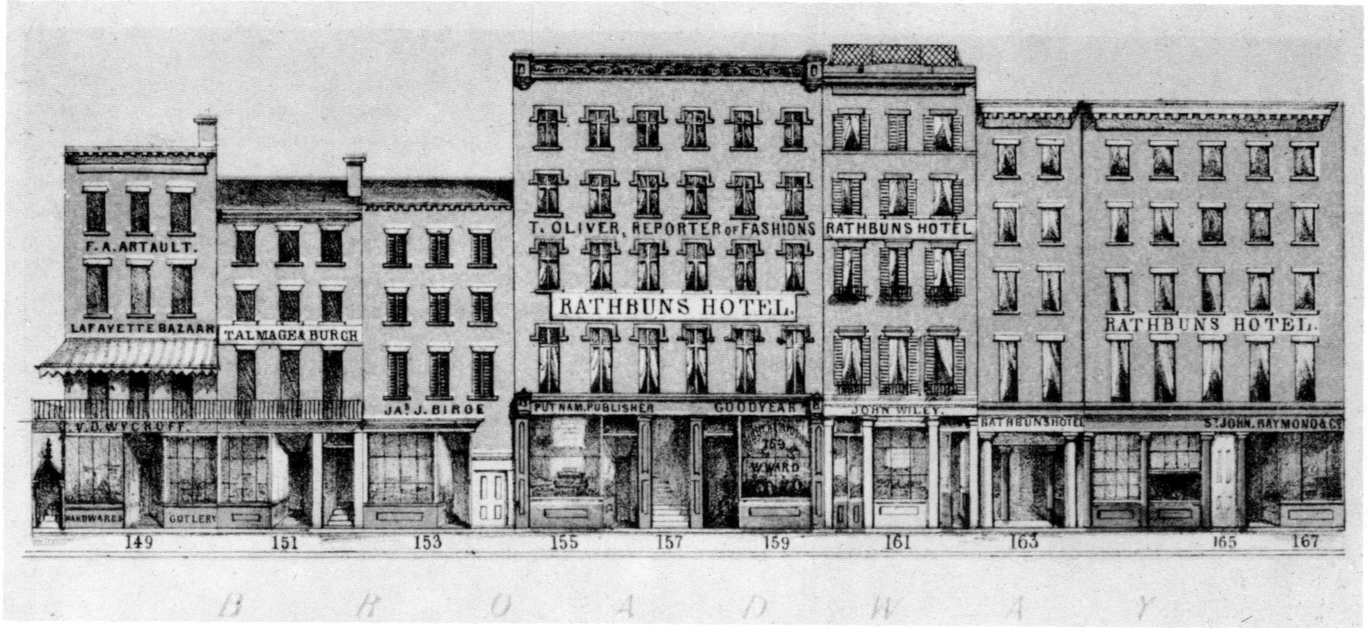

John Wiley's office, 1835–1850, at 161 Broadway

engineering drawing, George F. Blessing and Lewis A. Darling's *Elements of Drawing* (1912), John S. Reid's *Mechanical Drawing* (1919), Harvey H. Jordan and Randolph P. Hoelscher's *Engineering Drawing* (1923), the last, now superseded by Hoelscher and Clifford H. Springer's *Engineering Drawing and Geometry* (1956), Frederic G. Higbee's *Drawing Board Geometry* (1938), and Alexander S. Levens' *Graphics in Engineering and Science* (1954). The more recent books, in keeping with modern teaching methods, aim not to develop skills but to inculcate in the student the ability to express his ideas graphically as a form of communication.

Structural drafting techniques advanced after 1810—three years after Charles Wiley went into business. In that year Judge James Finley of Fayette County, Pennsylvania, explained how he made his drawings for the world's first suspension bridge with level floor as follows:

> To find the proportions of the several parts of a bridge of one hundred and fifty feet span, set off on a board fence or partition one hundred and fifty inches for the length of the bridge, draw a horizontal line between these two points . . . on this line mark off the spaces. . . .

This is a far cry from the meticulous procedure outlined in Carlton T. Bishop's *Structural Drafting* one hundred and thirty-one years later.

Early West Point authors turned instinctively to the Wileys. It was natural, therefore, for artistic Seth Eastman to arrange with Wiley and Putnam to publish his unique *Treatise on Topographical Drawing* in 1837, and for Lieutenant Richard Somers Smith to follow it with his *Manual of Topographical Drawing* in 1854. The latter book had a long life; a posthumous edition appeared as late as 1885. Certain government publications eventually made such books less necessary.

The standards of technique of engineering drawing have been raised considerably in the last century or more. Even as late as 1900 a draftsman might be expected to provide fancy lettering for his titles; sometimes this took more time than the drawing itself.

A milestone in the development of technique was the publication in 1895 of Reinhardt's thin book, "Lettering for Draftsmen, Engineers and Students." The author, who for years had been chief draftsman for *Engineering News*, literally took each letter of the single-stroke alphabet to pieces, stroke by stroke, and put it together in the simple style that has been named for him. A few years later (1902) a Wiley book, Victor T. Wilson's *Free-hand Lettering*, appeared. It was a rather complete textbook on the subject, based in part upon Reinhardt, but the work of a teacher who had already written *Free-hand Perspective.* The engineering type of lettering dates from this period. It shortly found its way into such diverse Wiley textbooks as John C. Tracy's *Plane Surveying* (1907) and Charles B. Howe's *Mechanical Drafting* (1916).

A publishing house that has flourished as long as Wiley may issue two or more books in succession on the same subject reflecting different points of view and meeting specific professional demands. This was true of the last of Professor Warren's books, *Elements of Machine Construction and Drawing* (1870) and John S. Reid's *A Textbook on Mechanical Drawing and Elementary Machine Design* (1900). Both authors in their day canvassed many representative machine shops in order to give their readers samples of current design practice; this, for Warren, was a new idea. A comparison of the two books shows progress during the generation in which reciprocating steam engines were increasing in power, and internal combustion engines and electric motors were on the eve of being invented. These two Wiley books led up to more recent works on machine drawing and design, such as Calvin D. Albert's *Machine Design Drawing Room Problems* of 1923.

Early in the twentieth century, especially after the first World War, as new types of mathematical engineering problems not involving shape description increased in complexity, engineering graphics began to expand into an entirely new field, that of graphical computation or nomography. This word, "nomography," was so new at the time that the fifth edition of "Webster's Collegiate Dictionary" defined it as a "treatise on drafting laws." The idea that mathematical relations could be represented on some sort of system of co-ordinates dates from René Descartes, seventeenth century French philosopher. Monge built on Descartes' idea. Nomograms seem to have been in large part brought into this country from France, where they were developed by the engineer-scientist, Maurice d'Ocagne, and others. An early Wiley book in this field was Joseph Lipka's *Graphical and Mechanical Computation* (1918). This whole subject is expanding and gradually finding a place for itself in engineering, science, and business curricula. The latest Wiley books in this field are Levens' *Nomography* (1948), and Lee H. Johnson's *Nomography and Empirical Equations* (1952).

Wiley broke into a new and theretofore almost undeveloped field with its publication in 1953 of William L. Healy and Arthur H. Rau's *Simplified Drafting Practice*. This book, described as a "modern approach to industrial drafting," and put out with the blessing of the General Electric Company, aims to demonstrate that simplified drafting practices will save time and money for manufacturing concerns. The book may well have some influence on the practice of drafting during the next few years as the subject becomes less pictorial and more pictographic.

RICHARD S. KIRBY

Stresses and Strains

Books on Engineering Mechanics and Strength of Materials

THE STUDY OF THE FORCES acting on a body at rest or in motion is older than engineering itself, and the strength of materials has been the concern of every builder and fabricator who ever conceived a plan for a lasting structure or a useful device.

The historical development of mechanics as a systematic body of scientific knowledge started with the perception, by astute thinkers and observers, of general principles that appear now to be simple. Many of these principles were derived by observation of commonplace phenomena. The earliest recorded writings in mechanics, for instance, are those of Archimedes (287–212 B.C.) concerning the principles of the lever and of the buoyancy of bodies in a liquid. Similar processes of deduction led to the development of the laws of vectors by Stevinus in the early seventeenth century and the work of Galileo on dynamic problems during the same period. By the time Newton formulated his laws of motion, later in the same century, mechanics had been established as a fundamental area of physics.

The application of the laws of physical mechanics to the solution of engineering problems was in a sense a reversal of the procedure by which these laws had been developed. As various areas of engineering evolved from the category of "arts" to professional scientific disciplines, the principles of physics and mathematics received increasing attention in an effort to interpret their engineering usefulness. During the nineteenth century these applications were confined largely to the specific needs of individual engineering fields. Strength of materials, for instance, was taught by departments of civil engineering, with specific reference to structural problems; and dynamics and kinematics were in the particular realms of interest of mechanical and electrical engineers. It was not until the early part of the twentieth century that a broader viewpoint began to prevail. Mechanical engineers became concerned with aspects of the strength of materials that received only scant interest among civil engineers of the time, and increasing attention was given to problems of dynamic loading, resilience, and stress concentration. This broadening of interest led to the establishment of separate departments of engineering mechanics, serving the interests of various departments, and bridging the gap between certain important aspects of the professional fields of engineering and science.

Wiley entered the field of engineering mechanics with *Lessons in Elementary Mechanics*, by Sir Phillip Magnus. This little book was published in England in 1875 and was imported shortly thereafter. It covers statics and a little dynamics without the use of calculus, and was designed for the use of schools and candidates for the London Matriculation and other examinations. Almost simultaneously with this import DeVolson Wood's *Elements of Analytical Mechanics* was published by Wiley. Wood was on the staff of the Stevens Institute of Technology in 1876, when his *Elements* was published. *Elements of Analytical Mechanics* is a remarkable beginning textbook in that it is quite advanced for its day, makes extensive use of calculus, and contains a large number of problems of direct interest to engineers. Certainly this is a fitting book with which to start Wiley's long list of books in mechanics, written by Americans. Wood makes no excuses for his extensive use of analytical geometry and calculus in what he considers a beginning treatment. In fact, he refers those who desire a more elementary text to Magnus's *Lessons in Elementary Mechanics*, which, as he says, avoids the use of calculus and is full of practical examples. As was quite common before the turn of the century, the book treats some topics that today we would call mechanics of materials, such as internal stresses in a body, principal stresses, and certain problems concerning the bending of beams and the design of trusses. It is interesting to note that many of his examples are to be found in textbooks on mechanics that have been written since 1950, attesting to their excellence as vehicles for teaching the subject.

In 1875 Wiley published *Elements of Graphic Statics and Their Applications to Frame Structures*, with a supplemental volume containing thirty-two plates, by A. J. DuBois, who was the Higgin Professor of Dynamic Engineering in the Sheffield Scientific School of Yale College. DuBois's book covered the fundamentals of graphic statics, with applications to cranes, bridges, roof and suspension trusses, braced and stone arches, pivot and draw spans, and continuous girders. It is a monumental book rich in detail, containing lucid explanations, and is in the spirit of Culmann's "Die Graphische Statik," published in Switzerland in 1866. It is one of the first books on this subject published in America that made extensive use of the graphical techniques developed in Europe.

A few years later, in 1881, Wiley published *Textbook of Elementary Mechanics*, by Edward S. Dana of Yale College. The author's objective was to present the fundamental principles of the subject in logical order and in as clear, simple, and concise a form as possible. Dana states that the study of elementary mechanics is one of very great value in a course of liberal education and an excellent kind of mathematical training. The material contained in the book is much the same as that in Magnus's early book, and it is written in the same style. Extensive use is made of geometry and trigonometry but calculus is avoided.

As the engineering schools in the United States began to grow rapidly in the last two decades of the nineteenth century, additional books on mechanics were published. Some outstanding examples are Gaetano Lanza's *Applied Mechanics* (1885), Irving P. Church's *Mechanics of Engineering* (1887), and DuBois's *Elementary Principles of Mechanics*, in three volumes (1894). These textbooks were followed by William Woolsey Johnson's *Theoretical Mechanics* (1900), Frank B. Sanborn's *Mechanics and Problems for Engineering Students* (1902), and Professor Edward R. Maurer's well-known book, *Technical Mechanics* (1903).

At this time a general pattern for engineering textbooks in mechanics was beginning to take shape. There was a noticeable desire for a greater emphasis on the physical nature of situations faced in engineering practice, and the trend in books moved toward more detail and less utilization of calculus and allied mathematics. This trend was represented by several textbooks in the early years of the twentieth century. By 1913, when *Applied Mechanics* by Charles E. Fuller and William A. Johnston was published, the pattern had become fixed, and textbooks in the field were to follow this pattern for the next forty years. The famous textbook by Fred B. Seely and Newton E. Ensign, *Analytical Mechanics for Engineers*, was published in 1921, and began its long career as the most popular textbook in the field ever written in the United States. A whole generation of engineers received their mechanics training from this book, and revised editions have kept it in the front ranks to the present day.

In 1952, thirty-one years after the original "Seely and Ensign," another fine treatment of engineering mechanics appeared with the publication of J. L. Meriam's *Mechanics* in two parts, *Statics* and *Dynamics*. These textbooks are particularly well written and have proved in a short time to have unusual appeal for both teachers and students.

In 1938 Wiley published the *Proceedings of the Fifth International Congress for Applied Mechanics*. This was the first and last time to date that the International Congress has met in the United States, and these proceedings, written partly in French and German as well as in English, are a part of the basic literature in theoretical mechanics. The practitioners in applied mechanics have benefited tremendously from Wiley's decision to undertake the responsibility of publishing this book.

The long list of Wiley books in the general area of strength of materials starts with the *Treatise on the Resistance of Materials with an Appendix on the Preservation of Timber* by DeVolson Wood. This book was published in 1871, while Wood was on the civil engineering staff of the University of Michigan. The *Resistance of Materials*, by Wood, is an amazing book. One could today teach an excellent course from this book that would meet most of the requirements and objectives of our present-day courses on the same subject. Indeed, the material is somewhat more sophisticated than the treatment of today. It is a well-blended treatment of mechanics of materials and material properties, including some of the elements of metallurgy and the preservation of timber. The author states that the book was intended for the senior year in the civil engineering curriculum. In subsequent editions the material contained in the earlier book was expanded and a second appendix concerned with the integration of differential equations was added. Wood apparently had difficulties not uncommon to modern authors when it came to selecting the topics that were to be treated. In fact, he starts the preface of his third edition with this sentence: "The subject which forms the title of this book is inexhaustible."

Wood's treatise in 1871 was followed by a series of books by Robert H. Thurston, *Materials of Engineering* (1883), *Textbook on Materials of Construction* (1885), and *Materials of Engineering Construction* (1900). They were concerned primarily with material properties and represent the state of the art in the eighteen-eighties. In 1883 William H. Burr wrote his *Elasticity and Resistance of the Materials of Engineering*, and in 1885 Wiley published Mansfield Merriman's (of Lehigh University) famous book, *Mechanics of Materials*. These books were followed by textbooks by Lanza, Church, Henry T. Bovey, and Charles E. Greene on mechanics of materials, and the book by John B. Johnson, *Materials of Construction*, in the late eighteen-nineties. Shortly after 1900 Rolla C. Carpenter's *Testing Machines and Methods of Testing Materials*, Albert W. Smith's *Materials of Machines*, and H. E. Smith's *Strength of Materials* were published. Of special note is a little book by Irving P. Church entitled *Mechanics of Internal Work*, published in 1910. Church in 1879 was first in the United States to publish a textbook on elastic energy methods based upon the work of the Italian, Castigliano, although William Kane and George F. Swain had previously written papers on the subject for the American journals. The book, written in lucid fashion, contains numerous applications to structures and machines.

The second decade of the twentieth century saw the beginning of several trends in the teaching of strength of materials. As in engineering mechanics, there was in beginning textbooks a general emphasis on practical design calculations and problem-solving techniques; graphic and arithmetic methods began to be emphasized, and advanced mathematical methods curtailed. Teachable textbooks and lucid explanations appeared, and among the most noteworthy of them were two Wiley titles: Fred B. Seely's *Resistance of Mate-*

rials (1925), and *Mechanics of Materials*, by Philip G. Laurson and William J. Cox (1938). An interesting experiment in teaching was provided by Roland H. Trathen in his *Statics and Strength of Materials* (1954). Seely's *Advanced Mechanics of Materials* (1932) is an important book and constitutes a major reference in the field to the present day.

A second trend in strength of materials research after 1920 was the increasing attention to the applications in engineering of the mathematical theories of elasticity and plasticity. Based on the work of Love and others around the turn of the century, research in applied elasticity theory received its major impetus through the many publications of Stephen P. Timoshenko in this country, beginning in 1925. A few years later there were important developments in the application of classical theories of plasticity to problems of engineering design beyond the elastic range.

A third development in strength of materials research, in part from studies in applied elasticity and plasticity, has been the study of the behavior of materials based on their molecular constitution; the work of the solid-state physicist has been extremely influential in this phase of the development.

These advances in research during the second quarter of this century have had an inevitable influence over a wide range of activity, from advanced structural research to undergraduate teaching in strength of materials. Although the pioneering books of Timoshenko in applied elasticity and of Nadai in applied plasticity are not on the Wiley list, several books appeared among its publications that represent significant developments in these fields. Among them are Francis R. Shanley's *Basic Structures* (1944), John A. Van Den Broek's *Theory of Limit Design* (1948), and *The Theory of Perfectly Plastic Solids*, by William Prager and Philip G. Hodge (1951). The subject of photoelasticity was treated comprehensively in a two-volume book, *Photoelasticity*, by Max M. Frocht (1941 and 1948); and the *Handbook of Experimental Stress Analysis*, edited by M. Hetenyi (1950), provided an exhaustive reference in this area that was treated in textbook form in George H. Lee's *An Introduction to Experimental Stress Analysis* (1950). The publication in 1950 of Alfred M. Freudenthal's *The Inelastic Behavior of Engineering Materials and Structures* was a major step in the formulation of a new and independent theory of strength of materials arising from the experimental study of the behavior of materials under increasing loads. In the posthumously published book, *Theory of Elasticity and Plasticity* (1952, Number Three in the Harvard Monographs on Applied Science), the late Harold M. Westergaard considered the fusion of these developments into a new body of theory. "In its advanced phases," he stated, "mechanics of materials may emerge as a more advanced subject than the theories of elasticity and plasticity."

The nineteen-fifties are witnessing the beginnings of the emergence of these new ideas into the undergraduate engineering curriculum. The fourth edition of *Resistance of Materials*, by Seely and James O. Smith (1956), has made a considerable departure from its predecessors in introducing concepts of inelastic behavior as an integral part of the basic course contents. And in the year 1957 Wiley will publish *The Science of Engineering Materials*, edited by Jacob E. Goldman, a symposium prepared under the sponsorship of the American Science Foundation, the American Society for Engineering Education, and two leading universities, to encourage and to accelerate the introduction of the concepts of basic science into a more fundamental approach to the study of engineering materials.

PAUL F. CHENEA

Ores, Metals, and Alloys

Books on Metallurgy

IN THE EARLY NINETEENTH CENTURY, metallurgy showed many signs of change. Metallurgists, no longer content to restrict themselves to Agricola's "De Re Metallica," began to seek out, study, and devise other books to contain and explain a new knowledge gained through new curiosity and new methods.

The middle of that century saw the beginnings of larger-scale and more economic refining of metals from their ores. Great strides were taken in the improvement of the blast furnace, and both the Bessemer and Siemens open-hearth processes for making steel came on the scene. At this time, when the ancient art of metallurgy was passing into a period of ferment and rapid development, Wiley began its publications in the field. The arts of metal refining and working were being altered by the new chemistry and mechanical engineering. Chemistry itself was attempting to understand the mysteries of the refining of minerals and the transmutations of metals, while new mechanical devices were finding their way into the working of iron and steel.

The Civil War brought about the transition from cast iron to cast steel for cannon, and new ways of steel making were transplanted to this country for a permanent place in the technology of the United States. It is not surprising that the first several books in the Wiley series were devoted to the metallurgy of iron and to the fabrication and manufacture of structural members of steel for pillars.

About the same time a great exploitation of the mineral resources of the western United States began. The discovery of fabulous quantities of gold, copper, silver, and lead ores led to the historic Gold Rush, which in turn provided a stimulus to the rapid growth of the United States in the following decades. The Wiley books of that time were devoted largely to extraction or process metallurgy on copper, lead, and the precious metals.

Typical of the books published in the period following the Civil War, prior to 1900, were *Metallurgy of Copper* (1874) and *Metallurgy of Silver and Lead* (1874), by Robert H. Lamborn, and John A. Allen's *Tables for Iron Analysis* (1896), which gave the basic information necessary to the refining of metals from their ores and determination of the values of ore deposits. In that early day of metallurgical mining in the United States this basic information was all that was necessary. The new sources of electricity made possible not only the practical electrolytic refining of copper, such as that described in Titus Ulke's book, *Modern Electrolytic Copper Refining* (1903), but also made possible other electrolytic methods, such as those for aluminum and lead. Anson G. Betts described lead refining in his book, *Lead Refining by Electrolysis* (1908), and the new aluminum industry was anticipated in Adolphe Minet's *Production of Aluminum and Its Industrial Use* (1905).

At the turn of the century the application of the microscope to the study of metal surfaces by Sorby, Austin, Sauveur, and others signified a new era in metallurgy. Soon it was possible to recognize internal structure, revealed by the microscope, as a determining factor of many of the properties of metals and alloys. No longer was the control of composition man's dominant means of mastering the material; control of structure had given him a new mastery by means of heating, cooling, and working of metals.

The dean of American metallurgy teachers of this period (and almost to the present) was C. H. Mathewson of Yale. His first book (in collaboration with Ruer and Rudolf), *The Elements of Metallography* (1909), is a landmark in American publication in this field.

A number of significant books were published immediately after the first World War. During that war metallurgists learned even more clearly how heat treatment affected the properties of alloy steels through minor changes in microstructure. Ernest E. Thum's *Elementary Metallurgy*, published in 1917, was the first of many books dealing with the rapidly growing subject of physical metallurgy in contrast to earlier textbooks that were devoted exclusively to process metallurgy and refining. Shortly books were published that were written by men who are renowned in the history of metallurgy, such as John H. G. Monypenny, author of *Stainless Iron and Steel* (1926), who was largely responsible for the development of special stainless alloys. These alloys were possible only because of a new understanding of the factors controlling microstructure, particularly the equilibrium relations determined by thermodynamic principles. Here the confluence of the application of thermodynamics to metal systems and the application of the metallographic microscope was most evident. Colin J. Smithells' *Impurities in Metals* (1928) and Monypenny's book indicate that methods of development using thermodynamic principles could make possible new materials with tremendous industrial importance. These two books first appeared in England under the imprint of Chapman and Hall.

During the 1930–1940 period the number and coverage of Wiley publications decreased. It was a time not only of fewer books, but also of fewer children and fewer jobs. Great men of metallurgy, such as Grossman, Bain, and Campbell, did indeed write books for Wiley during this period, but authors were rare. The Marcus A. Grossman and Edgar C. Bain book, *High Speed Steel* (1931), described in detail the characteristics of newly developed high-speed steels in terms of phase equilibria and the related effects of heat treatment and composition on the microstructure. Harry L. Campbell's book, *The Working, Heat Treating and Welding of Steel* (1935), used the same sort of approach to these processing problems.

A major event in technical publishing occurred during this depression decade (1930–1940) when Wiley brought out, in 1938, the two-volume revision (the fourth edition) of Dennison K. Bullens' *Steel and Its Heat Treatment*, prepared by the metallurgical staff of the Battelle Memorial Institute. Bullens' book, which for twenty years had been a major link between the theory and the engineering uses of heat-treated steels, and which emphasized the

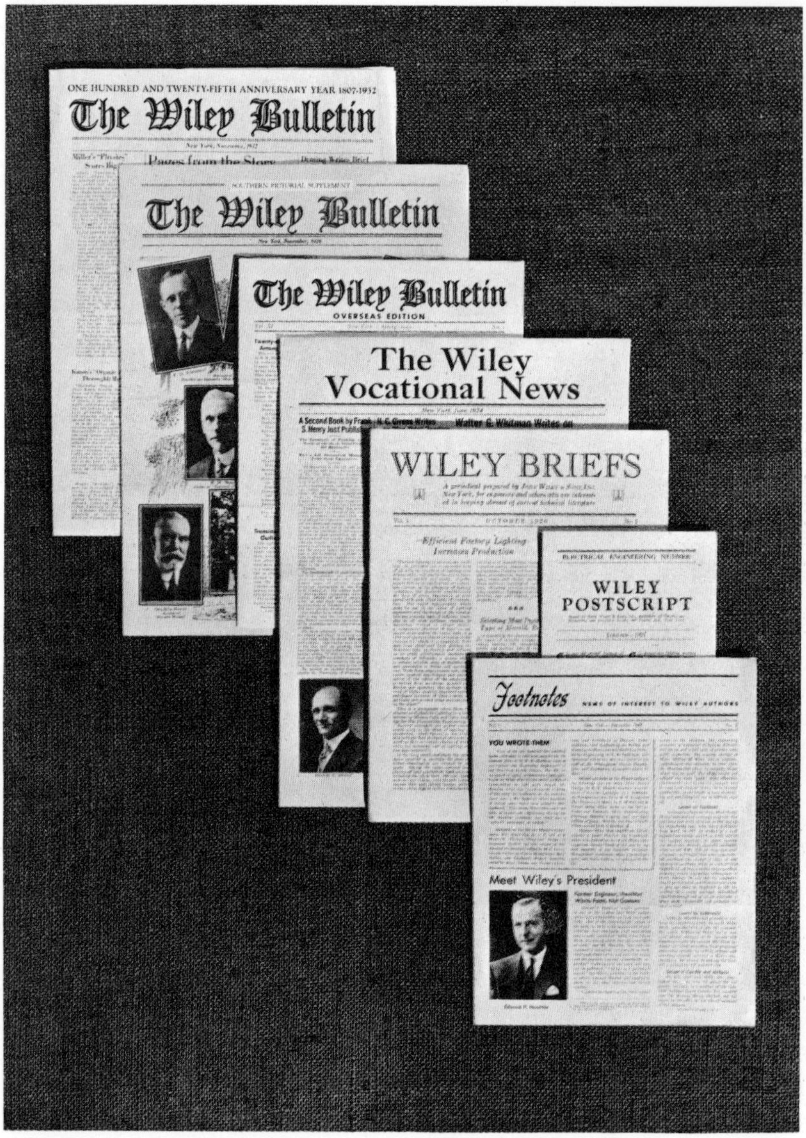

Wiley house organs

importance of the human element, had been out of date for more than ten years, and this new enlarged edition was badly needed by metallurgist and engineer alike. A three-volume edition was published in 1949.

With the increasing application of new and special materials and the use of metals toward the limit of their properties, failures were to be expected. One of the most useful books on metallurgy ever written, *Prevention of the Failure of Metals under Repeated Stress* (1941), describes the procedures used by the intelligent metallurgical engineer in his analysis and relates them to inappropriate or inadequate design and to the inadequacy of the microstructure and properties of the metals. It discusses the behavior of metals from the classic viewpoint, based on microscopic examination and the principles of applied mechanics. The book was written by the staff of the Battelle Memorial Institute and was edited by the great metallurgical engineer, H. W. Gillett, who had much to do with the growth of Battelle.

This book, as well as those by Campbell, Grossman, and Bain, and the book by Ralph L. Dowdell and collaborators, *General Metallography* (1943), and Joseph Newton and Curtis L. Wilson's book, *Metallurgy of Copper* (1942), would seem to indicate that the future growth of metallurgy would come only through more applications of the sciences of metallography and thermodynamics to metallurgical systems. Little further progress, except to extend the principles to other alloys and to the various types of metal processes, seemed possible. But advances in physics had begun that were to have great effect on metallurgical science and engineering.

X-ray and electron diffraction had been applied to a few metal systems by this time. This use of X-ray diffraction in revealing the structure of metals was described in an introductory way in some of the earlier Wiley books. Newton's *An Introduction to Metallurgy* (1938) mentions crystal structure and the arrangements of atoms in metals, but the idea did not appear to be related to the materials presented in the remainder of the book. An English import by Wiley, *An Introduction to X-Ray Metallography* (1946), by A. Taylor, was published only a few years after the application of X-rays to such systems had begun in earnest. Thus the importance of the crystal structure of metals to the development of metallurgy was recognized.

With only a few exceptions, new alloy development had been carried on in a more or less empirical way, with little consideration of the quantitative laws of heat flow or of reaction kinetics. A Wiley book by John H. Hollomon and Leonard D. Jaffe, *Ferrous Metallurgical Design* (1947), attempted to present new logical and quantitative development procedures and proposed that future metallurgical engineering could be based on quantitative principle and calculation rather than simply upon empiricism.

For centuries the problem of the corrosion of metals and alloys has limited their use and made their practical application, for some purposes, exceedingly expensive. The understanding of surface chemistry and some of the principles of electron-ion interactions in metals based on quantum mechanics made possible a further understanding of the corrosion process and led to the knowledge that could prevent or ameliorate corrosion losses. A full and clear summary of this step in the understanding of the problem of corrosion is given in the *Corrosion Handbook*, edited by Herbert H. Uhlig and published by Wiley in 1948.

P. L. Teed's book, *Properties of Metallic Materials at Low Temperatures* (1950), not only reflects an increasing interest in the study of materials and matter at low temperatures (made possible by the ready production of liquid hydrogen and helium) but also emphasizes the lack of understanding surrounding the brittleness and strength properties of metals when deformed at temperatures below room temperature.

During the last several years Wiley has published a number of books that summarize the advances made in the engineering behavior of metals during and since the second World War. Noteworthy among these is the new "Alloys of Iron Monograph Series," which summarize for the busy metallurgist and engineer the world's literature on the effect of certain important alloying elements on the structure and properties of steel and cast iron. The first of these books, *Aluminum in Iron and Steel*, was published in 1953; the second, *Nickel in Iron and Steel*, in 1954; and the third, *Titanium in Iron and Steel*, in 1955. Additional books are in preparation.

Other important books concern fatigue and fracture related to welding and express the broad interest in welded structures during the second World War. The books also indicate the increased interest of mechanical engineers in materials, as evidenced by the book by John Wulff, Howard F. Taylor, and Amos J. Shaler, *Metallurgy for Engineers* (1952).

Two new trends in metallurgy are apparent in books published recently by

Wiley. One of these is present in Bruce Chalmers' book, *The Structure and Mechanical Properties of Metals* (1951), wherein he states that defects in crystals, such as vacancies and dislocations, are very important to the behavior and properties of metals. As a part of solid-state physics, dislocation theory has been advancing rapidly and after the second World War came to be used quantitatively to predict the properties of crystalline solids. Its importance to practical metallurgy is difficult to foretell exactly, but it will be very great.

Another trend in the practical use of metals is also clear. Mechanical, electrical, and aerodynamic engineers are all recognizing that further advances in new apparatus and new devices and new systems for aircraft electrical or mechanical machinery are limited by materials. Thus the properties of materials and their structural reliability determine whether or not new steam turbines, new aircraft power plants, new nuclear reactors are possible or can be manufactured economically. The importance of metallurgy and metallurgical engineering to the future engineering of such devices is now becoming recognized. The demand for books by engineers and scientists who understand the properties of materials and of structural defects as well as those who understand the application of the knowledge of quantum mechanics to these problems will influence the Wiley publications of the future.

Wiley has begun a new series in the science and technology of materials where these principles and these needs will be reflected, not only in books on metallurgy but also in books on semi-conductors, on polymers, and on ceramics.

JOHN H. HOLLOMON

Shafts in the Earth

Books on Mining

ONE OF THE GREATEST ENGINEERING BOOKS ever published is Agricola's "De Re Metallica," an engineering best seller of 1556—four centuries ago.

Agricola did not, of course, originate all the many techniques he describes in his great book. He brought together and, although many of his statements are far from clear, described with greater than earlier clarity technical procedures that date back to the dawn of the metal arts, to the earliest days of mining and of civilized life. Much of this had to do with assaying and metallurgy and much, like the "Pirotechnica" of Biringuccio published some fifteen years earlier, would be characterized today as recipe or cookbook in nature. Yet we marvel that Renaissance man, lacking the aid of modern science, evolved such effectively workable yet often complex procedures for refining metals from their ores.

But the outstanding feature of Agricola's masterpiece is his treatment of mining *per se*. He was the first to describe methods of mining, problems of mine surveying, of shaft sinking, of tunnels and drifts, stopes and timbering, fire-setting, ventilation and pumping—all the techniques of finding and bringing hidden ores to the surface. It was close to three centuries before the purely manual, pick-and-shovel hand methods of mining described by Agricola felt the impact of new advances, of power tools, of machinery, and of modern explosives.

The evolution of other branches of engineering has been especially characterized by the replacement of older, empirical, qualitative techniques by more fully rationalized, quantitative procedures. Mining, however, has baffled such analysis. Experience has been the teacher, and other, nonrationalized, factors have exercised the preponderant influence. Prospecting and discovery have, of course, been reborn, with the rise of geological knowledge and understanding. Similarly, assaying and metallurgical operations have been clarified and reinforced through the growth of chemical science. But in the evolution of "hard rock" mining methods, it has been primarily the development of steam and, later, other power machinery, of explosives and power drills, the challenge of deep mining, the mounting pressures of increased demand, and the need to handle low-grade ores economically that have conditioned development. Science has unquestionably played a part in this advance, but mining has long remained an art evolving from practical operations.

Such evolutionary influences have been particularly characteristic of progress in American mining. After a relatively slow start, there was tremendous expansion in the United States after the Civil War. By the close of the century, American mining engineers were widely recognized as foremost in these new practices and were called upon to apply their new techniques in mining work throughout the world. The mining publications of Wiley, the growth of which was concurrent with this American development, have kept pace with these technical changes.

As early as 1819 Wiley published Henry R. Schoolcraft's pioneer book, *A View of the Lead Mines of Missouri*. This book reflected the wave of interest in the natural resources of a new continent—and notably mineral resources—that followed the explorations of Lewis and Clark, beginning in 1804, and continued by such later explorers as Frémont. Easterners took pride in collections of minerals, and it was Egleston's mineral collection that, in large measure, was the basis for the establishment of the first successful mining school in the United States at Columbia College in 1864. There was, to be sure, a lead "rush" in the early eighteen-twenties to which Schoolcraft's work undoubtedly contributed; but, outside the small iron mines of the North Atlantic states and the opening of the anthracite coal mines of northern Pennsylvania (which, it should be noted, led to the construction of one of our greatest pioneer undertakings, the Delaware and Hudson Canal of 1827–1830), mining in the States was slow in getting under way.

Wiley's next related publication did not appear until 1865, almost a half century later; it was a treatise on the assaying of lead, copper, silver, gold, and mercury. In short, mining in the States was still limited, and, as it had been for centuries, was a completely practical art of specific skills obtained through experience.

There had been an early mining school at Freiburg in Germany, and the École des Mines in France had been established in 1785 and revived after the Revolution in 1816, but the instruction centered largely in the auxiliary areas of geology, assaying, and metallurgy. A handful of American engineers had—like Egleston—studied abroad, but their notebooks recorded only hand tools, picks and shovels, hammers and drills. Although Watt's first invention had been an economical mine pump, the steam-driven rock drill did not appear until 1849, and the Burleigh was not in use before 1865. Similarly, it was not until 1829 that electric ignition came into use, thus increasing the safety of blasting with gunpowder; and, while the blasting machine was provided in 1857, it was not until 1867 that Alfred Nobel invented dynamite, a safe and effective means of using nitroglycerine.

By the sixties these advances had entered mining practice. A start had been made as early as 1844 in developing the great deposits of copper in the Lake Superior region, and it was here in 1864 that the first air compression and air rock drills were employed. It was here, also, that the first use of dynamite occurred, and hoists with large diameter drums were first used.

In 1877 Wiley published a modern classic in H. S. Drinker's *Tunneling, Explosive Compounds and Rock Drills.* Herein all the new techniques and tools that were in use in underground excavation were described. The application, to be sure, was to tunneling, but Drinker's book has long been regarded as a general mining book, for it summarized the earlier advances of the new era in underground operations.

Perhaps the new vistas and their accompanying changes opened by these advances are best exemplified in the story of a famous and historic mining center. The discovery of the Comstock lode in 1859 had come about as a consequence of the search for the mother lode after the rapid exhaustion of the placer gold deposits in the West. But the great days of Comstock succeeded the discovery of silver in 1873. They ended when operations ceased in 1886, but here for the first time American mining engineers had problems of deep mining, of water and ventilation, of high temperatures running up to 130 or 150 degrees, and of hoisting from shafts that went down 3,500 feet. Here also the problem of silver smelting was met for the first time in the United States. A later visitor might wonder at Comstock's abandoned but enormous shaft houses, huge engines of antiquated design from which, nevertheless, modern winding engines had clearly evolved. When we recall that modern shafts in the Rand area are almost two miles deep and that oil drills have reached almost four miles, these efforts at Comstock seem puny indeed. Comstock was an important American mining school, however, and its teachings were clearly reflected in Wiley publications of the day, such as M. C. Ihlseng's *Manual of Mining* and such later books as Walter R. Crane's *Ore Mining Methods.* It was here, in fact, that the change from individual initiative, from the lone prospector of placer days to the modern mining company with adequate resources and employing special engineering personnel, was most clearly marked.

But, paralleling these changes, another modern tool was brought into mining service to become one of the most widely used machines of modern mining. Copper was its sponsor.

As the demand for the red metal increased, Butte, Montana, emerged from its earlier gold and silver days as a great copper center. Here a new chapter in the history of mining geology was written, and it was here also that American copper smelting reached new levels for, even up to 1892, copper matte had been shipped for reduction not only to Baltimore but also to Swansea in Wales. The flotation process, now standard in the concentration of all but ferrous ores, also was further developed at Butte. But Butte could not "corner" copper. The ever-increasing demands of an electrical age stimulated another vital change in the mechanization of mining operations.

Steam shovels had been used to excavate and load the huge shipments of iron ore from the Mesabi Range in the Superior region that found their way to the eastern mills through the Soo Canal opened in 1855. This railroad construction device was now employed in meeting the problem of mining profitably low-grade copper ores, ores carrying only 2 per cent or less of metal. Great volumes had to be handled, and at Bingham Canyon, near Salt Lake City, huge electrically operated shovels and 100-ton cars have taken out more rock than was excavated in building the Panama Canal. Similarly, at Bisbee, in the Southwest, a hill of barren rock was removed with shovels to reach ore averaging only 1.7 per cent copper. This so-called stripping method has also found particular application in coal mining along with other tools such as mucking and loading machines and belt conveyors. In fact, the largest shovels in the world are used in the modern mining of coal. It should be noted that this development is also especially well covered by Wiley books. In 1874 Wiley published Warrington W. Smyth's *Coal and Coal Mining*, and related books on mine accidents and mine gases and explosives have followed, including Elwood S. Moore's *Coal* of 1922.

Probably, however, the wide scope of interests and understanding that the modern mining engineer was being called upon to possess and apply is better grasped by a review of the contents of a famous handbook that Wiley first published in 1918 than through any story of the ever-widening horizons of American mining. Robert Peele's *Mining Engineer's Handbook* has been carried by mining engineers to the four corners of the earth. From mathematics and chemistry to assaying and metallurgy, from geology and prospecting to mechanics and mine structures and plant, from physics to electrical and mechanical power tools and equipment, from operating costs to the marketing of mineral products, from mining law to mineral economics—all these are covered in Peele's vast compendium, exemplifying the wide scope and the variety of information that the modern sons of Agricola are required to have at their command. One of the major problems of today is devising methods of underground working that will permit the economical mining, as the more easily available deposits are worked out, of more deeply hidden ores. That man's ingenuity is not yet exhausted is shown by the invention of the "block caving" method of undermining huge blocks of ore that break up in settling—a plan hailed in 1929 as the greatest forward step in underground mining of modern times. Such developments are fully reflected in modern Wiley textbooks.

The modern trend, however, is toward specialization. The advent of the petroleum industry, born of the daring venture that sent "Colonel" Drake to Titusville in 1859 to drill the first oil well, has created an entirely new mining activity with techniques that have emphasized new problems of mining geology and of petroleum refining. Just before the first World War gasoline replaced kerosene as the major product, and just after the war (1920) Wiley published Louis S. Panyity's *Prospecting for Oil and Gas.* Joseph E. Pogue's *Economics of Petroleum* followed the next year, and, in 1922, David T. Day's *Handbook of the Petroleum Industry* made its appearance in this new field. In fact, in the early twenties Wiley's offerings included also R. H. Johnson, L. G. Huntley, and R. E. Somer's *Business of Oil Production*, V. R. Garfias's *Petroleum Resources of the World*, and Victor Ziegler's *Oil Well Drilling Methods.* More recently (1942) there has been Paul Paine's *Oil Property Valuation.*

Similarly, with increasing costs of transportation, the more effective concentration of ores close to the mine has been an important factor in turning ever greater attention to ore dressing methods and techniques. Intermediate between the work of the mining engineer and the metallurgist, mineral dressing promises to become a mining specialty, involving as it does special understanding of the newer teachings of physical chemistry and new areas of highly specialized research. Wiley issued Arthur F. Taggert's *Handbook of Ore Dressing* in 1927, which to a major degree launched this reborn art and science on a new and far more scientific career. The search for, and the mining of, the newer ores, not only those of aluminum and nickel but also of tungsten and other vital alloying metals—and now uranium—also emphasize the specialized modern interests of a profession and an industry not only basic to our national well-being but also vitally affecting international policies and relationships.

JAMES KIP FINCH

The World of Construction

Books on Civil Engineering

American civil engineering was in its infancy when the first Wiley books appeared. A few timber bridges, notable precursors of record-breaking works to come, had, it is true, been built or were in process. Several short canals supplemented the rivers. Although Fulton had demonstrated on the Hudson the practicability of steam navigation, mechanical engineering was not even dreamed of. The American civil engineer still faced the tremendous challenge of providing for the transportation and the urban needs of a seaboard nation that was about to spread across and conquer a continent. There were only the earliest stirrings of a movement destined to carry a new civilization, reinforced by and increasingly dependent on engineering, to the farthest confines of a rapidly expanding nation. The original coastal states were about to take the first steps in the development that has made the United States today the leading engineering and industrial nation of the world.

In 1807 American engineers could be counted on one's fingers. They were the able, gifted, resourceful, and vigorous products of pioneer American life.

West Point had been founded as a military academy a few years earlier, but none of the American engineering schools, which now number some one hundred and twenty, had come into being. In short, the engineers essential to this continent-wide expansion and new way of life had to be prepared for service. For this preparation, engineering books were a basic and essential need. To this challenge was added another and almost revolutionary problem: the technique of the ancient art of civil engineering was shortly to undergo a fundamental evolutionary change.

Some steps had been taken in France in the eighteenth century toward the development of a science of engineering, but engineering in 1807 was, as it had been for centuries, largely an empirical art. Design was based on knowledge and judgment derived from practice, from first-hand contact with construction, from the accumulations of past experience, the records of earlier practice and of the successes and failures of earlier workers. These hard-won understandings were passed on from master builder to apprentice. A revolutionary and fundamental change in technique was essential to the more effective and widespread extension of engineering practice and to meeting the ever more challenging scale and scope of engineering needs that America's growth demanded.

Some of the most interesting and beautiful engineering books ever printed were published in the late eighteenth century in France and England, but, reflecting earlier needs and practices, they were naturally largely descriptive. They were records of earlier constructions. It was in Great Britain in the early years of the nineteenth century that pioneer efforts were made to bridge the gap between natural science and engineering and, thus, to transform what had so long been a qualitative, empirical art into what has since become in large measure a far more certain, exact, and quantitative science. Wiley's history as a publisher of engineering books thus not only spans and reflects the rise of engineering and industry in the United States—the making of a nation—but this house has also led the way with one forward-looking textbook after another in furthering this basic change in the technique of the engineering profession. It was, in fact, this change in technique that led to the replacement of apprenticeship by the more effective methods of the classroom—that is, to the birth of the modern engineering school. Wiley's story and that of American engineering education have developed simultaneously.

We would naturally expect to find in the earlier books of this house, therefore, some overlapping of content, some mixture of descriptive data with more highly theoretical and scientific material. We thus find Wiley importing such early descriptive textbooks as David Stevenson's *A Sketch of the Civil Engineering of North America*, printed in 1838 by the famous British engineering publisher, John Weale, in London. Similarly, Wiley also co-operated with other American publishers in bringing out Duggan's *Specimens of Stone, Iron and Wood Bridges . . . of the U.S. Rail-roads*, in 1850. These books reflected the strong European interest in even early American practice. Yet the change in technique we have noted did not take place overnight, and it is far from complete even today. The art element in civil engineering can never be fully replaced by engineering science. In fact, the descriptive book still has its role to play in civil engineering education. Later Wiley books of this type have included George S. Morison's *Memphis Bridge* of 1894, and Edward Wegmann's *Water Supply of the City of New York, 1658–1895* (1896), as well as very many editions of the latter's famous historical and descriptive treatise on dams.

Probably no book better reflects the nature of earlier Wiley engineering books than Mahan's *Civil Engineering* (1837), a publication of the Wiley and Putnam era. Here we find, for example, not only much sage advice drawn from practice and experience but also a correct, but brief statement of the modern formula for the design of rectangular beams in bending; data on the "coefficient of rupture" from early tests of materials; and, in a supplement, outlines of the earlier search for the more exact design of arches and retaining walls based, as the author states, "on the researches of the French savant, Coulomb." In short, here are the beginnings of the modern engineering science of mechanics of materials and structures. But the general situation is still clear. No data, Mahan states, "can be relied upon with more security than those which are obtained by examination of structures which have already withstood the test of time."

But, even in Mahan's day, new and impelling forces were influencing the evolution of the civil engineering profession. "The first American engineers," a group of remarkably able and gifted itinerant native master craftsmen, were active around the turn of the century when Wiley's was born. Lacking the aid of modern structural mechanics, dependent solely on an intuitive structural judgment and the practical skills and resourcefulness essential to a pioneer age, they, nevertheless, built a number of local timber highway bridges which set precedents still valid in modern construction. Their work marked the advent of a new era of framed construction, and from it the truss as a bridge form—long known but sparingly used—emerged to set the pattern for the great majority of American nineteenth century bridges.

The truss, in contrast to the older stone arch, was an architectural structure, depending not only on the proper functioning of its parts for safety and a proper apportionment of material for economy but also on a framework, the parts of which carried stresses not easily evaluated by judgment alone. Furthermore, a new and more costly material, iron, was coming into use. Simultaneously, the needs of the new railroads with their constantly increasing locomotive loadings were challenging the skill of the bridge engineer, as they continued to do throughout the nineteenth century.

This new era forced two basic developments in the techniques of the bridge builder. On the one hand, it was essential that means be found to determine the actual stress in the parts of a truss under assumed loads. A special branch of structural mechanics, the analysis of framed structures, was born. Second, materials had to be tested to determine the stresses that they could carry with safety in the unit forms used—columns, ties, etc.—and the testing and mechanics of materials became a complementary part of this development.

The contributions of Wiley to the general field of engineering mechanics and the strength and mechanics of materials have been discussed in another chapter. Suffice it to say that their publications played a vital role in introducing these new techniques to both student and practitioner. In the more specialized area of structural mechanics, one can likewise follow the entire history of advances in understanding and application in Wiley publications. Here the emphasis was on the railroad bridge, a framed structure first of wood, then of cast and wrought iron, then, when several failures proved that cast iron was an unreliable bridge material, the all wrought-iron truss (1863). The all-steel bridge was not to come until later (1879), and the arch received rather scant attention until the advent of concrete and reinforced concrete after 1900.

When thinking of the earlier days, the name of DeVolson Wood comes to mind. Bridge engineering was becoming a specialty in the civil engineering field. In the period 1870–1900, distinguished authors were drawn from the field of consulting practice and from the classroom to publish pioneer works. Among these contributions may be cited such significant books as Clemens Herschel's *A Handbook for Bridge Engineers* (1874); Alfred P. Boller's *Practical Treatise on the Construction of Iron Highway Bridges* (1876); William H. Burr's *A Course on the Stresses in Bridge and Roof Trusses, Arched Ribs, and Suspension Bridges* (1880); John A. L. Waddell's *Designing of Ordinary Iron Highway Bridges* (1885); Mansfield Merriman and Henry S. Jacoby's *Textbook on Roofs and Bridges* (1888); Charles H. Wright's *The Designing of Draw Spans* (1897); Waddell's *De Pontibus—Pocket Book for Bridge Engineers* (1898), and his *Specifications for Steel Bridges* (1900). Some of these early books became classics in engineering education and in professional practice and, with successive revisions, continued to instruct and inspire students for half a century.

One of the earliest, and perhaps the authentic forerunner of many modern, textbooks was the widely used John B. Johnson, C. W. Bryan, and F. E. Turneaure's *Theory and Practice in the Designing of Modern Framed Structures*, which is still on the Wiley list sixty-seven years after publication, having gone through numerous editions, although other books in this area by Hale Sutherland and Harry L. Bowman (1930), Thomas C. Shedd and Jamison Vawter (1931), and others, have taken the place held so long by this pioneering textbook. But, with the turn of a new century, new factors began to affect this ever-widening evolution in planning and design. In the last years of the nineteenth century, bridge engineers were building railroad bridges in steel for ever-heavier loads. The advent of concrete and reinforced concrete gave the engineer a new material. Earlier American textbooks also had emphasized simpler structures avoiding such problems as the use of continuity in design, statically indeterminate structures and secondary stresses, by what would be considered today to be uneconomical over-design. The need for an extension of earlier methods became apparent, and the economical use of reinforced concrete demanded that advantage be taken of continuity. The bridge engineer, ever seeking in design to balance the costs of labor and materials, began to recognize the economy of the more involved structural forms. The great increase in bridge spans, following the demands of the Highway Era, made it essential to seek more effective means of handling secondary stresses.

Although it is true that a few examples of "continuous construction" had appeared before 1900, this change was not fully evident before the first World

War. In the interval a few books, such as two textbooks of 1905 by William H. Burr and Myron S. Falk, *Design and Construction of Metallic Bridges* and *Graphic Methods by Influence Lines for Bridge and Roof Computation*, also Malverd A. Howe's *Symmetrical Masonry Arches* (1906), C. R. Grimm's *Secondary Stresses in Bridge Trusses* (1908), W. H. Burr's *Suspension Bridges, Arch Ribs, and Cantilevers* (1913), and J. Melan's *Plain and Reinforced Concrete Arches* (1915), opened the door to the newer techniques. They have been followed by even more highly specialized studies, such as Hardy Cross and Newlin D. Morgan's *Continuous Frames of Reinforced Concrete* (1932), considered by many competent critics to be one of the greatest modern contributions to structural analysis, and John I. Parcel and Robert B. Moorman's *Statically Indeterminate Structures* (1955), which stems from Parcel and Maney's earlier work.

Various types of structures have also been subject to similar, more exact analysis, as is exemplified by more recent books on bridge engineering and the numerous textbooks on concrete structures, such as David B. Steinman's *Suspension Bridges, Their Design, Construction, and Erection* (1922), Otis E. Hovey's *Movable Bridges* (in two volumes, 1926 and 1927), Conde B. McCullough and Edward S. Thayer's *Elastic Arch Bridges* (1931), and Frederick W. Taylor, Sanford E. Thompson, and Edward Smulski's *Reinforced Concrete Bridges* (1939).

Thus, although differences in the conditions influencing American and European practice resulted in a special emphasis abroad on the advancement of engineering science, America also had its pioneers, men who were constantly seeking to bridge the gap between the more mathematical theories and actual practice and to extend the applications of mechanics. In no field of engineering endeavor has there been closer co-operation between author and publisher than is found in Wiley's contributions to the ancient art of the bridge engineer.

Turning from framed to masonry works, we note immediately the challenge the engineering publisher has faced in maintaining leadership in modern days, even in this limited area. For many years there was relatively little change in the nature of text material in this subject. There is much in common between Mahan's pioneer *Civil Engineering* of 1837, for example, and Ira O. Baker's widely used *Masonry Construction* of 1889. Indeed, some of the practical observations and shrewd advice contained in both these Wiley works are reminiscent of the famous treatise of Vitruvius just prior to the Christian

Era. Masonry construction had been confined for centuries to stone and brick, to lime, and to a very limited use of hydraulic cement. Masonry arches had been built for at least twenty centuries, retaining walls were no novelty, and stone dams were at least four centuries old; but when he came to publish a new edition of his book in 1899, Baker remarked that an almost complete revision was necessary. An age of concrete was suddenly and rapidly replacing this long era of stone and brick.

Brought about by the development of the manufacture of a relatively low-cost hydraulic, "portland," cement, this mass-produced, machine-made product rapidly replaced the older, terribly laborious, and increasingly costly hand-built stone and brick work. In fact, Baker did not go far enough. Very few engineering students of today have ever heard of such terms as "ashlar" or "quoins" of cut stone days. Indeed, this grand old man of engineering education may have written not only the best but also the last important book on masonry construction. Stone work today is used merely as a thin veneer or facing over concrete and largely for appearance' sake alone. Frederick E. Turneaure and Edward R. Maurer's *Principles of Reinforced Concrete Construction*, published by Wiley in 1907, prefigured this change and was the first of a group of textbooks that have continued to follow this remarkable development.

Probably the most detailed treatise published in this area is the two-volume book, *Concrete, Plain and Reinforced*, by Taylor, Thompson, and Smulski (1925 and 1928). The senior author of these books is known today chiefly as the father of industrial management. Over the years there were other excellent textbooks on concrete, principally those by Sutherland and Reese, and by Peabody. The new field of prestressed concrete is represented by Tung-Yen Lin's *Design of Prestressed Concrete Structures* (1955).

In the field of liquid mechanics, notably hydraulics and hydraulic design, we also find some important Wiley books of earlier as well as recent days. For example, the pioneer book of Hamilton Smith, Jr., on orifice flow, was published in 1886; the first translation of E. Ganguillet and W. R. Kutter's *Flow in Open Channels*, which introduced American engineers to the famous Kutter formula, was made in 1889. One of Merriman's books, which was later revised and remained a standard engineering school textbook well into the twentieth century, *Treatise on Hydraulics*, also first appeared in 1889.

The nineteenth century may be characterized as primarily an era of "coefficient" hydraulics, distinguished for its search of modifying factors that, applied to the few basic equations of pure hydromechanics, would allow for the many unresolved factors that entered practical hydraulic design. Some fifty years ago, stimulated by the advent of modern aerodynamics and the petroleum and chemical industries in new eras, this older hydraulics began to change. Gardner S. Williams and Allen Hazen's *Hydraulic Tables* of 1905 was one of the last of these earlier studies, but today the more inclusive "fluid mechanics" has taken over, and followers of the late Professor Bakhmeteff of Columbia, in such books as John K. Vennard's *Elementary Fluid Mechanics* (1940), Hunter Rouse's *Elementary Mechanics of Fluids* (1946), and Rouse and J. Warner Howe's *Basic Mechanics of Fluids* (1953), are carrying on this new advance in an ancient technique. That the new approach has extensive civil engineering application was emphasized by the publication in 1950 of *Engineering Hydraulics*, a symposium volume edited by Rouse.

In the related area characterized as hydraulic engineering, which includes public water supplies, water power, irrigation, drainage and canalization and river control, Wiley has published titles well known to the civil engineering profession. America was somewhat backward in meeting many of her urban problems, and ideas of sanitary engineering were rather sketchy until the discovery of the typhoid bacillus in the eighties turned attention to the problem of sanitation. A pioneering book was William R. Nichols's *Water Supply from a Chemical and Sanitary Standpoint* (1883). Several publications followed in the nineties. Allen Hazen's *Filtration of Public Water Supplies* of 1895 emphasized the bacterial efficiency of a method hitherto largely used for the physical improvement of public supplies. Mason, Fuertes, and others made important contributions in this relatively new science. Turneaure and Harry L. Russell's *Public Water-Supplies* summed up earlier and current practice in the water supply field. Published in 1901, it was and still is a standard college textbook. Gordon M. Fair and John C. Geyer's *Water Supply and Waste Water Disposal* (1954) has reunified these two areas of interest to sanitary engineers. Among early specialized books that have continued to this day are George C. Whipple's *Microscopy of Drinking Water* (1899), revised by Gordon Fair and Melville C. Whipple in 1927, and Samuel C. Prescott and Charles-Edward Winslow's *Water Bacteriology* (1904). Also worthy of inclusion in this group are Horace W. King, Chester O. Wisler, and James G. Woodburn's *Hydraulics*, now in its fifth edition (1948), and Wisler and Ernest F. Brater's *Hydrology* (1949). Herbert M. Wilson's *Irrigation Engineering* of 1893 was another well-known work in the field of hydraulics, as was James D. Schuyler's *Reservoirs for Irrigation, Water-Power and Domestic Water-Supply* (1901). Older engineers will also recall B. F. Thomas and D. A. Watt's *Improvement of Rivers*, first issued in 1903; various other books appeared later, including Harold E. Babbitt's *Sewerage and Sewage Treatment* (1922) and Karl Imhoff and Gordon M. Fair's *Sewage Treatment* (1940). Earle B. Phelps's *Stream Sanitation* (1944) directed attention to the increase of pollutional load on streams and other bodies of water, and Phelps and Clarence J. Velz' *Public Health Engineering* (1948) expanded the horizon of sanitary engineers into the whole field of environmental health. The power field has likewise

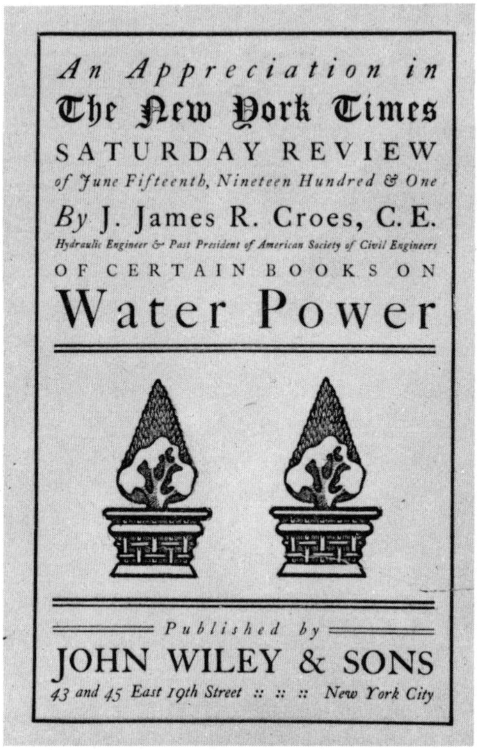

Promotional piece of 1901

received attention with books ranging from Joseph P. Frizell's *Water Power* (1900) to William P. Creager and Joel D. Justin's *Hydroelectric Handbook* (1927).

Probably no other engineering publisher has followed so closely as Wiley the remarkable development of the design of a basic form of hydraulic construction, namely, masonry and other types of dams. Wegmann's book has been noted, as has Schuyler's of 1901. The literature of this entire era of engineering was brought up to date in 1945 by the appearance of Creager, Justin, and Julian Hinds' three-volume book, *Engineering for Dams*.

Returning again to the change in engineering techniques, we must note the important area of foundations and soil mechanics. The basic and fundamental art of providing adequate foundations and of predicting the behavior of soils and earth structures has been the most recent of age-old empirical civil engineering practice to give way to more exact and scientific analysis. The obstacles to such rationalization, the many variables and uncertainties encountered in practice, have for years discouraged attempts to bridge the gap between laboratory tests and analysis and the conditions encountered in actual construction. It was largely as the result of the work of Karl Terzaghi, who came to this country in 1925, that the practical possibilities of such studies became apparent. Wiley published Karl Terzaghi's *Theoretical Soil Mechanics* in 1943, and Terzaghi and Ralph B. Peck's *Soil Mechanics in Engineering Practice* in 1948. More recent books are *Foundation Engineering*, by Peck, Walter E. Hanson, and Thomas H. Thornburn (1953), and Elwyn E. Seelye's *Foundations* (1956), which make available to the civil engineer the results of later advances.

We must also take note of the Wiley list in the vital domain of transportation. The first American textbook on road making, by a famous pioneer teacher of civil engineering at Union College, William H. Gillespie, was published in 1847. Then, for fully half a century, nothing was published on this subject. With railroads taking over transportation, road work was long regarded as a purely local problem of manual labor. When Wiley published Ira O. Baker's pioneer and widely used "modern" textbook, *Roads and Pavements*, in 1903, the author stated in the preface:

> It is frequently claimed that the public would be benefited by placing the care of the roads in the hands of engineers, but there is no evidence that any

> considerable number of engineers comprehend either the principles of road making . . . or the economic limitations and political difficulties of the problem.

The advent of the automobile has since focused even greater attention on one of the greatest present-day engineering problems, as is fully reflected in recent Wiley publications.

Highway engineering attained major professional stature after the first World War on the publication of Arthur H. Blanchard's *American Highway Engineers' Handbook* (1919). This book brought together in one volume the many diverse phases of the subject. Blanchard's *Handbook* was never revised; its place in the field was taken by Laurence I. Hewes' *American Highway Practice*, in two volumes (1942). From this treatise the current standard textbook in the field has developed—Hewes and Oglesby's *Highway Engineering* (1954).

On the other hand, this earlier period of highway neglect was paralleled, as has been suggested, by a plethora of railroad textbooks. Wiley issued such classics in this field as Arthur M. Wellington's monumental treatise, *The Economic Theory of the Location of Railways* (1887) and Walter L. Webb's *Railroad Construction* (1900), the latter going through nine editions before going out of print in 1955. A few years earlier (1880), William H. Searles' textbook on railroad surveying had appeared under the somewhat misleading title, *Field Engineering*. His *Railroad Spiral* was published in 1882. But this picture began to change in the earlier years of the twentieth century. The major American railroads had been built. Operation, maintenance, and management had become the dominating problems. As early as 1897 Henry S. Haines's *American Railway Management* was issued. Early in the present century an era of "trolley transportation" was ushered in, reflected in H. B. Andrews' *Handbook for Street-Railway* of 1902. Today, although we find few new and valuable civil engineering textbooks in this once dominant field of civil engineering activity, there is to be noted William A. Hay's *Railroad Engineering*, Volume I, published in 1953, superseding William G. Raymond's *Elements of Railroad Engineering* (1908), a standard textbook for several generations.

Wiley was a pioneer in the field of engineering surveying. One of the first engineering publications was *Elements of Surveying* (1835), by Charles Davies of the United States Military Academy at West Point. Throughout the period of development of the West and the advance of a railroad network across the continent, Wiley books were responsible for the training of many engineers. Many of these books became "pocket companions" for the field engineer. In later years the tables by such men as Crandall, Merriman, and Searles and Ives became standard works. The basic textbook on surveying by Breed and Hosmer has been the textbook of literally tens of thousands of civil engineers. Revisions of these books have added new information as it was developed.

The engineering handbook, or pocketbook as it was called before it became too big to permit such transportation, is also of ancient lineage. Carpenter's, bridge, and some other handbooks appeared in the earlier Wiley days; then, between 1872 and 1894, some seventeen editions of John C. Trautwine's famous *Civil Engineer's Pocketbook* were issued. This book, however, was a product of the old school. The preface had stated:

> The writer does not include Rankine, Moseley, and Weisbach because their books . . . exhibit a profundity of knowledge beyond the reach of ordinary man. . . . They are but little more than striking instances of how completely the more simple facts may be buried out of sight under heaps of mathematical rubbish.

Actually, Rankine, Moseley, and Weisbach were prophets of the new era of engineering science to which, as we have noted, Wiley has made many contributions. Wiley brought out in 1911 the first of a continuing series of editions of *The American Civil Engineer's Pocket-Book*, with Mansfield Merriman of textbook fame as editor-in-chief, which was superseded in 1956–1957 by Robert W. Abbett's *American Civil Engineering Practice*, in three volumes. Another publication in this special field is the *Handbook of Engineering Fundamentals*, edited by Dean Ovid W. Eshbach of Northwestern University, and published in 1936. This more specialized work may well mark the beginning of a new era in such publications, for it seems clear that with the increased proliferation and specialization of technical understanding and knowledge, it will be increasingly difficult to put even the bare essentials between two covers. Further evidence of this trend can be seen in the publication in 1955 of Douglas F. Miner and John B. Seastone's *Handbook of Engineering Materials*, which provides a single source of data on the materials of manufacturing and construction in all branches of engineering. Although not a handbook in the accepted sense, Elwyn E. Seelye's *Data Book for Civil Engineers* (1945–1946–1947) covers essentially the same field, but with all data presented graphically or in other easily read forms. These practical volumes are very highly regarded today by the men who actually build structures.

It has frequently been remarked that engineering is one of the most dynamic professions, ever changing and ever progressing in scope and power. The challenge that thus faces a publishing house that has aimed not only to serve but to pioneer and lead in this never-ceasing progress and advance is obvious. Furthermore, in no period have this growth and this change been more rapid than in the United States during the century and a half of Wiley history. To have met this challenge, to have led in this advance, and to carry forward in the even more rapid changes of the present day constitute a record of which Wiley may indeed be proud as it marks its one hundred and fiftieth anniversary. The truly progressive and pioneering technical publisher has, in fact, come to have a vitally important—in some respects almost controlling—role in the development of the engineering profession. New ideas (one of Wiley's most recent textbooks, for example, deals with the new problem of airport design), improved practices and methods, must be made available to the profession through early, far-sighted, and adequate publication. We cannot afford in these days of technological nationalism, when so much depends upon rapid and effective advance in engineering and science, to await publication until a full market for a new book has been developed. Furthermore, instruction in established current practice does not suffice for the engineering student of today. He must be ready to play his part in the future some four or five years distant, when he is graduated and when the standard textbook of yesterday is almost certain to be obsolete. To pioneer has thus become not only more risky and more costly, but the element of choice, of judgment in selecting works for publication, has become more complex while, at the same time, such decisions would appear to have increasing influence on the evolution and growth of the engineering profession.

JAMES KIP FINCH

Machines and Power

Books on Mechanical Engineering

NO SINGLE FACTOR in man's age-long upward climb from the jungle to the life of today has exercised a more vital, a more widespread and compelling influence on his life than his evolution from tool builder, through machine maker, to the mastery of the miracle of modern mechanical and electrical power. This remarkable advance in man's ability to shape, control, and use nature's forces and resources better to meet his needs, wants, and conveniences not only has been basic to the birth and progress of Western civilization but has also vitally changed the methods and practices of all sister professions of mechanical engineering. Both modern life and modern engineering would be impossible were it not for machines and power. In this continued and continuing evolution the technical publisher has played, and plays today, a basic and essential role.

Many of the tools and machines of modern life are of very early origin. Ancient Egypt has been called "The Mother of the Mechanical Arts." Archimedes and Hero of Alexandria were inventive geniuses of the first order. But it was in the Renaissance that the possibilities of machinery seem to have suddenly been brought to light. Leonardo, it is said, lacked but the gift of mechanical power to have anticipated by three centuries the Industrial Revolution. But Leonardo held his ideas in secret as part of his "stock in trade," whereas the publication of the notebooks of his successors not only marked a new era in the exchange of professional knowledge but also the advent of the technical publisher in the mechanical field. It is only in comparatively recent years that Leonardo's wonderful drawings and notes have been seen, but in 1579 one of the first of these machinery notebooks, that by Jacques Besson, "Theaters of Machinery," was published in France. Remelli's famous "Diverse and Artificial Machines" followed in 1588, with a Paris imprint. It is a wonderful and beautiful book, illustrating and describing water wheels and pumps—all the machines of an age when man and animal power were supplemented only by the uncertain gifts of wind and water. Zonca's Italian work of 1607 was another of these pioneer machine publications of the pioneer technical publisher.

Thus, while it was the highly skilled planner and builder of these earlier machines, the resourceful and inventive millwright, who became the immediate ancestor of the modern mechanical engineer, it was unquestionably Watt who not only added a new technique to this ancient art that ultimately resulted in the birth of a new branch of the engineering profession but also initiated a new era in human history, a new epoch in man's life, a new economy and way of living. For some years after James Watt and Matthew Boulton were manufacturing steam pumps and steam engines this development remained part of the practice of such versatile British civil engineers as Telford and Rennie. But the emergence of a new branch of the profession, while delayed, could not be denied. George Stephenson, the "Father of the Locomotive," became the first president of the British Institution of Mechanical Engineers, founded in 1847.

Watt did not, of course, invent the steam engine, but he did produce the low-pressure, low-speed, condensing, reciprocating steam engine that was to dominate the nineteenth century. But it had been only a few years before Wiley entered the publishing field that this engine had been applied to turning the wheels of industry. As has been noted in earlier chapters, in the same year that Charles Wiley went into business, 1807, the successful application of steam power to navigation was demonstrated by Fulton's *Clermont.* John

Wiley was just beginning his long career some twenty years later when, in 1829, the railroad locomotive revolutionized land transportation. The first century of the Wiley firm witnessed the continued evolution of Watt's epoch-making invention and its application in industry and transportation and to the other needs of an unfolding "Power Age."

This pioneer American technical publishing house not only published a fine list of American books covering all phases of this growth and evolution but imported a number of epoch-making textbooks. One of these early importations was the famous book of the Scottish engineer-teacher, William John Macquorn Rankine, his *Manual of the Steam Engine*, of 1859. Watt, it was said, had been the practical inventor and builder; Rankine was his mathematical complement, developing the theory of that art of which Watt represented the practical side. The strength of Rankine's contribution is well illustrated by the fact that his *Manual* survived to reach a tenth edition in 1882 and also by the fact that the cycle that Watt invented has to this day borne the name of Rankine, who first described it. But, as was later observed, Rankine still left great gaps between theory and practice. These gaps one of Wiley's nineteenth century authors led in bridging.

Robert Henry Thurston (1839–1903) taught first at Stevens Institute and later at Cornell. He was not only a great teacher and a prolific writer but also a beloved personality, a man of character, a leader of his profession. His interests ranged from educational methods and programs of study to materials and boilers, from the steam engine as a heat engine to friction and lost work in machinery and millwork. Wiley published eight books for Professor Robert H. Thurston, but the book that he regarded as his masterpiece was his *Manual of the Steam Engine*, which appeared in 1891–1892 in two volumes. Here he sought "to reduce or eliminate the wastes of the steam engine," the difference, as he put it, between "the steam engine of Rankine and Clausius and the actual engines of industry and transportation."

It is impossible in brief space to note all the other authors and books on mechanical subjects that Wiley brought out during the period just before and following the advent of the American Society of Mechanical Engineers, organized in 1880 with Professor Thurston as its first president, and Major William H. Wiley as one of its charter members. The entire range of mechanical interests from fuels and boilers to locomotive, marine, and stationary engines, from gears to propellers and from belts and pulleys (the power transmission of a mechanical era) to the founding, casting, and making of machine parts—all these areas were covered with ever-increasing emphasis on reconciling theory and practice, on the rationalization and more effective quantitative analysis of earlier and current practices, on the reduction or elimination of the wastes and lost work that had so irked Professor Thurston. Perhaps in view of present-day activities, one of the most surprising of these early interests is in the field of heating and ventilation. As early as 1858 Wiley published David B. Reid's *Ventilation in American Dwellings*, and this was followed in succeeding years by several books dealing with mechanical applications to this supposedly modern problem.

But in spite of this century of notable advances—of locomotives spanning and opening up a new continent, of great steamships, of steam power replacing the earlier water power about which New England had been developed, of steam drills, of steam shovels, hoists, and dredges—the nineteenth century seems backward indeed when compared to the twentieth. Three major developments, started in the last years of the nineteenth century, were primarily responsible for the rise of our modern mechanical era; they were the electrical distribution and utilization of power, the replacement of the reciprocating engine by the steam turbine, and the evolution of the gas engine.

It seems difficult in these days of "electric life" and the Motor Age to realize that but fifty years ago our parents lived in a power era, to be sure, but one that lacked the now casually accepted conveniences "we could not do without." The American Industrial Revolution had developed around the many small water powers of New England. A "giant," an incredible Corliss engine of 1,400 horsepower, had furnished the power needs of the Philadelphia Centennial of 1876. By the nineties the ocean steamers *Campania* and *Oceanic* had both been equipped with tandem engines of 15,000 horsepower each. These were truly remarkable advances, although they seem today but the making ready for a new era to come.

The status of mechanical engineering in the United States about the turn of the century is clearly reflected in one of Wiley's famous family of pocketbooks or handbooks. In 1895 Wiley published *The Mechanical Engineer's Pocket-Book* by William Kent, one of Thurston's younger assistants and associates, which has since evolved into a two-volume work. Here, of course, we do find a hint of things to come, but Kent was clearly writing for the era of the reciprocating, the Watt engine, although, as it was to turn out, the *Campania* and *Oceanic* engines marked the culmination of this development; they were the largest reciprocating engines ever built.

The changes and advances of the new power era of the twentieth century are also revealed by some statistical comparisons. In 1900 available power equipment in the United States was estimated as equivalent to about two manpower per capita. Today it is a hundred or more. Man's physical resources have been multiplied fiftyfold, and use of electricity and the gas engine account for much of this increase. In 1900, although the incandescent light was in use, the application of electric motors in American factories was estimated to total less than 500,000 horsepower, or an application to about 4 per cent of the tools and machines then in use. In slightly more than a quarter of a century this use had grown to over 30,000,000 horsepower, and over 75 per cent of the tools and machines were electrically driven. The jump from Edison's pioneer Pearl Street Station of 1882 with a capacity of about 750 kilowatts to a modern power plant of a million kilowatts supplying electricity for all sorts of service in factories, in the home, and on the farm, emphasizes also the vital stimulus to power development that has come from the mechanical engineer's sister profession of electrical engineering. Wiley's publications in this allied field are noted in another chapter. They clearly reflect these remarkable trends and developments.

Likewise, although De Laval's steam turbine had been invented in 1883, it was not until 1894 that Parsons built his famous turbine-driven steamship, the *Turbinia*. Even ten years later, in 1904, when the power house for the first New York subway was built, a battery of reciprocating engines of 7,500 horsepower each—the largest of this type ever built for land use—was installed, although turbines of approximately the same capacity had been put in service by the Commonwealth Edison Company in Chicago in 1903. The rapid rise of the steam turbine to its dominating position in the central power plants of today—single units of 400,000 horsepower—has posed many new thermodynamic and mechanical problems. Wiley published Carl C. Thomas' *Steam Turbines* in 1906 and Cecil H. Peabody's *Thermodynamics of the Steam Turbine* in 1911, both marking this change; but progress was continuous and

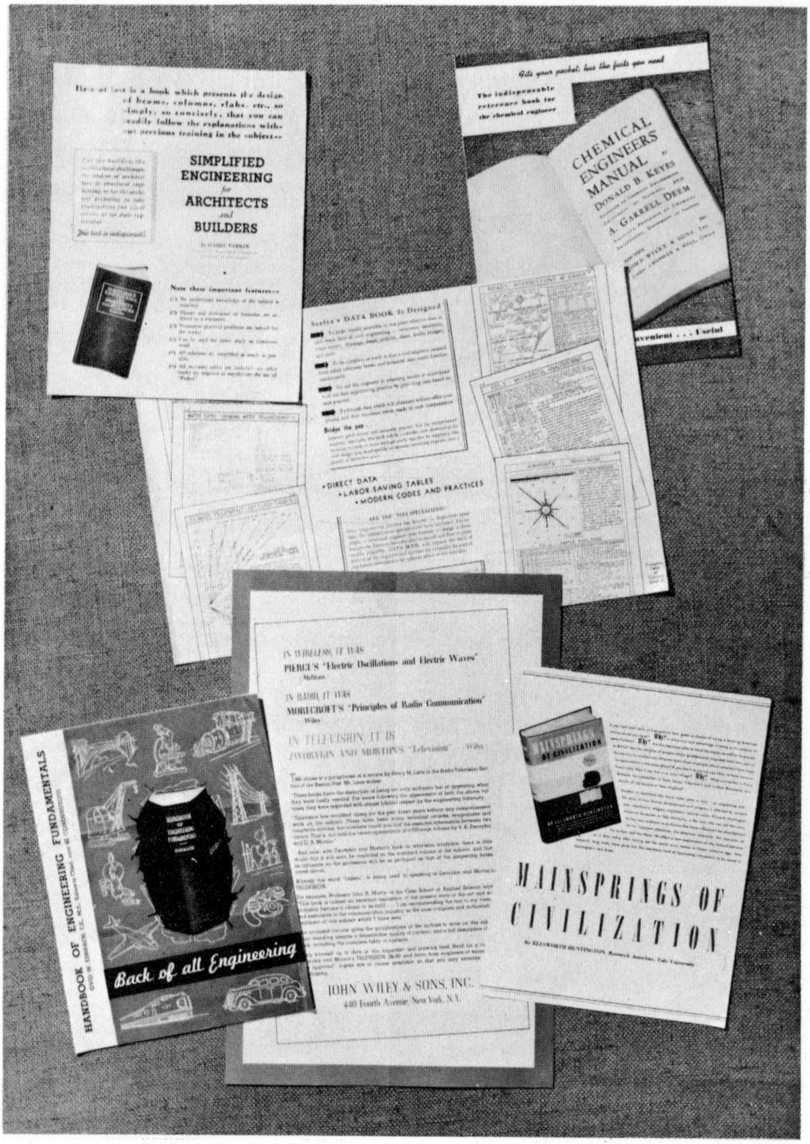

Recent promotional pieces

rapid, and these early books have been followed by new textbooks at frequent intervals.

The steam turbine has won out over the reciprocating engine because of lower weight and cost and thus has made it possible in the best modern power plants to produce a kilowatt hour—the equivalent of about nine or ten man-power hours—from less than a pound of coal, as against an average requirement of over seven pounds in 1900 and, perhaps, twenty to thirty in Edison's pioneer plant of 1882. The evolution of the steam boiler and of condensers has been equally revolutionary. And here again Wiley's books have marked these changes, step by step. Thurston had written on boilers in 1888, and Kent had followed in 1901, but one must turn to later Wiley imprints for the story of the great modern boilers, several stories high, burning powdered coal and evaporating enough water to supply a city of 25,000 population. Hand firing was on the way out in 1900, and today the entire problem of handling fuel has been mechanized while condensers, using as much as 35,000 gallons of water per minute, make the cooling water supply problem of a modern power plant one of the first magnitude. All these changes and the host of detailed operations, devices, and equipment that has accompanied this truly remarkable development have been reflected in specialized Wiley books.

It seems difficult in this motor age to realize also that, in 1900, the internal combustion engine was still more or less an experimental curiosity. Wiley had published Dugald Clerk's famous book, *The Gas Engine*, in 1886. But Professor Frederick R. Hutton in the preface to his *The Gas Engine*, which Wiley published in 1903, still emphasized the gas engine as a means of conserving "the fuel value of what are called the waste gases from the blast furnace." He noted the advantages of direct fuel consumption in "getting rid of the boiler and its plant," and he foresaw that "the recognition of carburetion as a process in the handling of liquid fuels had enormously widened the scope and field of the internal combustion motor." But while Hutton, an early motor car enthusiast, lived to see the motor era well launched, it is doubtful if he could have foreseen how important the gas engine or the internal combustion engine, as we now term it, was to become not only in the field of omtor transport but also on the farm and in construction, wherever a portable power unit could be used to advantage. The internal combustion engine has created the highway era, posing, as the locomotive had done a century earlier, new problems for the civil engineer, but it has also given man wings, command of the air, and a new means of transport, for it has made the aeroplane possible. Today gas turbines and jet engines give promise of even more powerful power units.

Wiley's contribution to this great epic of human achievement has been, of course, primarily educational—not only the education of students, but also the continued education of practicing engineers, for new advances have forced the engineer to become a perpetual student. When one turns back to the books of Wiley's centenary, fifty years ago, the largely descriptive character of those textbooks is apparent. On the other hand, ever-increasing emphasis on the basic science, notably thermodynamics, and with special application to heat engines and the dynamics of machinery, has been fundamental to the tremendous strides in mechanical engineering of the twentieth century. Education has turned from overemphasis on what has been called the "case system" to ever greater attention to "fundamentals."

In the thermodynamics field, for example, the Wiley books that contributed most to the understanding were Thurston's translation of N. L. S. Carnot's *Temperature Entropy Diagram* (1905), and the first edition of Paul J. Kiefer and Milton C. Stuart's *Principles of Thermodynamics* (1930), the first simple engineering treatment of the steady flow process, and a book that greatly influenced subsequent literature on the subject through clarification of troublesome earlier approaches and the introduction of methods better adapting the study to current types of heat power and related equipment. The later edition (1954), with G. F. Kinney collaborating, further introduced notably useful techniques for the analysis of processes and equipment developed during and since the second World War, and, of course, Joseph H. Keenan's *Thermodynamics* (1941) was the first engineering textbook that based its elementary exposition on the "operational" methods of Poincaré and Max Planck and used Gibbs's treatment of equilibrium as an objective.

The development of steam tables is an interesting subject in itself. Peabody seems to have been the originator of the modern steam table. His *Tables of the Properties of Saturated Steam and Other Vapors* of 1888 was probably the first publication of steam tables as a separate entity. He later added properties of the superheated vapor with tabulations along lines of constant entropy as well as constant pressure and constant temperature. The next set of tables, George A. Goodenough's *Tables of the Properties of Steam and Ammonia* (1915), constituted the first tables in which the available data were critically surveyed to check conformity with basic mathematico-physical requirements. Frederick G. Keyes's *Thermodynamic Properties of Ammonia* (1916) was another major engineering aid, and then came the Joseph H. Keenan and Keyes *Thermodynamic Properties of Steam* of 1936, and *Gas Tables* of Keenan and Joseph Kaye in 1948. The last was a new kind of compilation of numerical data for calculations in gas dynamics. The Keenan and Keyes book represents the results of the first international co-operation in extending the range and in critical appraisal of data on the properties of water. The Hottel, Williams, and Satterfield book of 1949 was an ingenious presentation of thermodynamic data for engineering calculations relating to combustion processes occurring at chemical equilibrium. Thus it would seem that Wiley published all of the tables in this area, beginning with *Peabody* (1888), up to the current period with the lone exception of the Marks-Davis "Tables" published in 1909 by Longmans, Green. In a related field, Max Jakob's *Heat Transfer* (1949) was a milestone. It was a compendium of analytical, as well as experimental, data of its field. A more recent dramatic development of thermodynamics is nuclear power, where the need for authoritative literature for engineers is of the greatest urgency. In the articles on chemistry and physics, mention has been made of the Wiley books in these areas. Here we should mention a 1956 book, *Thermal Power from Nuclear Reactors*, by A. Stanley Thompson and Oliver E. Rodgers, which provides an introduction to the mechanical engineering aspects of nuclear power plant design, including an analysis of nuclear reactors.

Earlier books in the field of industrial practice, such as George M. Price's *The Modern Factory* (1914), for example, played a part in the rise of industrial engineering as a separate branch of the engineering profession. Orlan W. Boston's *Engineering Shop Practice*, Volume I (1933) and Volume II (1935), circulated as mimeographed notes as early as 1923, and *Metal Processing* (1941, second edition 1951), were some of the first books to introduce processing to co-ordinate design, materials, and manufacturing, involving machine tools and accessories, cutting tools and cutting fluids, machinability of metals with speeds and feeds. This book accompanied the development of a complete curriculum dealing with production or manufacturing engineering, one of the first in this country. Myron L. Begeman's *Manufacturing Processes* (1942) and James F. Young's *Materials and Processes* (1944) have also constituted important contributions in this field.

One of the few criticisms that can be made of mechanical engineering is that so dominating and important has the power field been that mechanical engineering education was too long confined almost entirely to power problems. The vitally important area of machine tools and processes was too often neglected. Recent years have witnessed marked advances in this direction. As a matter of fact, Wiley has sponsored over the years a number of books dealing with the application and use of power and with machines and machine tools.

One of the early textbooks in the machine design area was S. Edward Warren's two-volume one, *Elements of Machine Construction* of 1870, which he followed in 1883 with the translations of two Philip J. Weisbach books, *Manual of the Mechanics of Engineering* and *Kinematics and the Power of Transmission.* The increased use of the electric motor, steam turbine, and gasoline engine about 1900, as mentioned previously, increased the rotative speed of many units some tenfold. It also necessitated the development of power gears able to reduce the speeds of these prime movers to a reasonable value for the driven machines. This situation was reflected in the books of the design field; for instance, in Schwamb and A. L. Merrill's *Elements of Mechanism* (1904), which had originally been presented by Peter Schwamb in printed notes in 1885 and is the basis for Venton L. Doughtie and Walter H. James' book of the same title published in 1954, and Dexter S. Kimball and John H. Barr's *Elements of Machine Design* of 1909. Both of these books were for many years deservedly popular in most engineering colleges. Also to be mentioned in this connection are Louis J. Bradford and Paul B. Eaton's *Machine Design* (1926), George L. Guillet's *Kinematics of Machines* (1928), and Calvin D. Albert and Fred S. Rogers' *Kinematics of Machinery* (1931). The solution of problems attendant on the design of modern machinery is aided by such books as John A. Hrones and George L. Nelson's *Analysis of the Four-Bar Linkage* of 1951 (a Wiley–Technology Press publication), and Alfred R. Holowenko's *Dynamics of Machinery* of 1955.

The fluid machinery field has not been neglected. From Du Bois' translation of Philip J. Weisbach's *Hydraulics and Hydraulic Motors* of 1877 through Arthur M. Greene's *Pumping Machinery* of 1911 to Alexey J. Stepanoff's *Centrifugal and Axial Flow Pumps* of 1948 and *Turboblowers* of 1955, this area has been adequately covered by a multitude of books.

During the nineteen-thirties vibration problems became more prevalent, and books dealing with this subject were written. One of the earliest of them was Arthur L. Kimball's *Vibration Prevention in Engineering* of 1932. This has been followed by a number of books, including W. Ker Wilson's *Practical Solution of Torsional Vibration Problems* of 1935 and Charles E. Crede's *Vibration and Shock Isolation* of 1951.

We may well ask not only where do we go from here, but where can we go. There are times when it would seem that the possibilities of further power applications in the life of man and in our modern industrial economy must have been exhausted. But it is only "seems," for the demand for more power and for further mechanization seems to have no end. The use of power is still increasing enormously and the power miracle of today that transforms less than a pound—a handful—of black rock, costing less than a cent, into the equivalent of a long day's physical toil by a strong man, now promises to be supplemented by a still more miraculous age of nuclear power. Whereas the gas engine brought power to the service of men and women on the remote farm and in areas devoid of any other power sources, nuclear power may, in the end, be applied not only in larger plants but also to further extending power services and, thus, reducing the geographical irregularities that have retarded the spread of modern standards of life and living.

It has been said that it is the aim of the modern mechanical engineer to make it unnecessary for man to do any work that can be done by machine. Yet it has been argued that even this relief from physical toil has led to man's becoming the slave of the machine, to his being tied to the monotony of repetitive machine production. New controls, "automation," the gift of electrical engineers and stemming from recent advances in the electronic field, now give promise of relieving many even of these responsibilities.

JAMES KIP FINCH

Men and Machines

Books on Industrial Engineering and Management

WITH THE INCREASING COMPLEXITY of society brought about by the Industrial Revolution, the role of the manager began to be recognized and studied as an important function in business and industry. In 1776 Adam Smith wrote in his "Wealth of Nations" about the division of labor necessitated by the rapid expansion of industry in the eighteenth century, and in the same year the appearance of Watt's steam engine foreshadowed the vast power resources that were to be applied to industrial production in the years following. Specialization of labor and harnessing of power created tremendous gains in production output, but they did so at the cost of managerial control. Methods had to be developed to cope with new and intricate problems of production and inventory control, equipment selection and replacement, plant layout, maintenance, inspection, materials handling, and personnel relations.

Several explorations were made during the nineteenth century into the application of scientific methods to the solution of these managerial problems. Charles Babbage, the versatile English mathematician and inventor, had been concerned as early as 1832 with the scientific determination of the proper uses of machines and the most effective organization for production. Records of research by contemporaries and predecessors of Babbage indicate that a considerable and widespread study of scientific management was under way in the decades prior to the significant work of Frederick W. Taylor, around the turn of the twentieth century. The framework for Taylor's work was provided in an address by the industrialist Henry R. Towne before the American Society of Mechanical Engineers in 1886. "*The management of works*," he said, "has become a matter of such great and far-reaching importance as perhaps to justify its classification also as one of the modern arts."

It is no accident that this "modern art" of scientific management was developed into a systematic discipline at this particular time by a man with a lifetime of work in the steel industry. The perfection of new applications for steel and other basic materials of construction was opening the new world of industrial production. Taylor's contribution to the field of materials had been well established by his "The Art of Cutting Metals" (presented to the American Society of Mechanical Engineers in 1906); and his *Concrete, Plain and Reinforced* (with Sanford E. Thompson), published by Wiley in 1905, was the forerunner of a group of books on concrete structures that were to be authoritative for many years after Taylor's death. But his restless mind was most concerned with the development of a scientific methodology for analyzing industrial production and human capabilities in industry. By observing workers in the steel industry, Taylor developed techniques for producing startling increases in production, with a corresponding increase in the value of the individual worker's efforts. By the time his "Principles of Scientific Management" was published (Harper's, 1911), Taylor had retired, and he was able to write of his system: "At least 50,000 workmen in the United States are now employed under this system of scientific management, and they are receiving 30 to 100 per cent higher wages daily than are paid to men of similar caliber with whom they are surrounded."

Taylor's concepts met with considerable resistance from management and labor leaders of his day, and it was only when his successors made it clear that scientific management was compatible with respect for human values that the movement was able to achieve widespread recognition. The industrial pressures of the first World War helped to speed this acceptance, and by

1924, when the International Committee on Scientific Management was formed, the field of industrial engineering had become a recognized branch of study in engineering colleges.

As early as 1914, the Massachusetts Institute of Technology had established a distinct curriculum in "Engineering and Management," but the responsibility for developing academic programs elsewhere became largely that of the mechanical engineering departments, since the early courses were concerned with the management of manufacturing processes employing machines and machine operators. Thus the first important textbook was the "Principles of Industrial Management" (McGraw-Hill, 1913), by Dexter Kimball of the Sibley School of Mechanical Engineering at Cornell. The fallibility of even the most experienced of technical publishers is attested to by the fact that the firm of Wiley declined the offer to publish this new book by its distinguished author and friend.

Wiley had not been idle in this new field, however. By 1916 the firm had published three books that have considerable historical value in the early literature of scientific management: H. W. Jacobs' *Betterment Briefs* (1909), a collection of papers on organized industrial efficiency; and two books by Frederic A. Parkhurst, *Applied Methods of Scientific Management* (1912) and *The Predetermination of True Costs and Relatively True Selling Prices* (1916). But it was the publication in 1923 of *Industrial Management*, by Richard H. Lansburgh, of the University of Pennsylvania, that marked the first significant entry of the company into the area of management. This basic textbook has achieved a formidable record of longevity through a series of revisions by Lansburgh and William R. Spriegel.

By the time Lansburgh's book was published, the field of industrial engineering had begun to undergo the diversification that inevitably accompanies an expanding area of study. Although in the academic world it continued to be a part of the mechanical engineering program, a number of intermediate courses were being offered in specialized phases of the area, and the introduction of industrial engineering "options" foreshadowed the identity of the field as a distinct branch of engineering. Concurrently with this activity in the engineering colleges, schools of business administration were devoting an increasing amount of time to the study of management principles and techniques, and the groundwork was being laid for the significant economic and sociological ideas that underlie present-day thinking in this field.

One of the early areas of specialization was a natural outgrowth of the main stream of Taylor's studies on the physical performance of men at work. Motion and time study, or methods engineering, became an important field of research through the work of Frank and Lillian Gilbreth and others. With the publication of *Motion and Time Study*, by Ralph Barnes, in 1937, and the subsequent *Work Methods Manual* (1944) and *Motion and Time Study Applications* (1942), Wiley achieved a long-term leadership in this area. As these books went through revisions, new concepts from mathematics and statistics were included, to meet the problems caused by the rapid development of industrial techniques. The advent of automation demanded the use of a variety of new tools for work measurement, and some of these tools have been dealt with in Helmut C. Geppinger's *Dimensional Motion Times* (1955) and Barnes's *Work Sampling* (1957). The latter is based on the work of another Wiley author, Leonard H. C. Tippett, in "ratio delay analysis."

The subject of the human being in his business and industrial environment was also a matter of serious study in the years following Taylor's studies. Personnel and labor relations officers faced problems of a magnitude and complexity unheard of prior to the great depression of the thirties, and the resources of economists, psychologists, and sociologists have been called on by management to augment the work of the industrial engineer. Wiley's publications have reflected these developments in many areas since Paul F. Gemmill's *Present Day Labor Relations* was published in 1929. Most of these books, such as J. Keith Louden's *Wage Incentives* (1944), Robert W. Gilmour's *Industrial Wage and Salary Control* (1956), and *Job Evaluation*, by Forrest H. Johnson, Robert W. Boise, and Dudley Pratt (1946), were written by industrial men with experience in dealing with personnel matters on the job. With the publication in 1956 of *Work and Authority in Industry*, by Reinhard Bendix, Wiley launched a series of volumes written by staff members of the Institute of Industrial Relations at the University of California.

Another branch of research, stemming from Taylor's work, that has had a profound effect on concepts of management is the study of the planning and control of production activities. The step from the "progress chart" of Taylor's disciple, Henry Gantt, to *Introduction to Linear Programming*, by

Abraham Charnes, William W. Cooper, and Alexander Henderson (1953), is a long one, but the problems attacked are essentially the same, the allocation of limited resources to the production of a desired output. The forty-year intervening period was one of considerable valuable and practical work by men with an intimate knowledge of actual production practice. Wiley books of this period include Charles A. Koepke's *Plant Production Control* (1941), *Science of Production Organization* by Edward H. Anderson and Gustav T. Schwenning (1938), and E. H. MacNiece's *Production Forecasting, Planning, and Control* (1951), revised in 1957 with many interesting additions resulting from the author's postwar experiences with European industry. Much of the important work arising from the second World War research in applying mathematical techniques to production problems was collected in the Cowles Commission Volume, *Activity Analysis of Production and Allocation*, edited by T. C. Koopmans (1951). The impact of the papers in this book on many phases of management research clearly indicated the profound influence of basic mathematics and science on the solution of management problems.

This influence, which had been perceived by Taylor, was felt in many ways and from many directions. The "Second Industrial Revolution" after the second World War was brought about through the combined efforts of scientists and engineers in a variety of fields, and the managerial complexities created by this revolution have demanded the resources of an equally diverse group of research specialists. Serious explorations are being conducted into the implications for management of concepts of mathematics, statistics, electrical engineering, economics, and psychology.

Theoretical developments in mathematics have formed the basis for a number of powerful managerial tools. Linear programming, queueing theory, Monte Carlo methods, game theory, analysis of variance—all these would be strange terms indeed to Taylor and to industrial managers of his time. Yet present-day management has begun to recognize the power of these tools, and is exploring their applications to inventory and production control, transportation, accounting, and many other areas. The role of a technical publisher is particularly important in presenting these mathematical concepts to an audience eager for enlightenment, and the firm of Wiley is in the forefront of this activity. The pioneering work, *An Introduction to Linear Programming*, is to be followed by a comprehensive treatise entitled *Management Plan-*

ning and Mathematical Programming, by Charnes and Cooper. Andrew Vazsonyi's *Scientific Programming in Business and Industry* (1957) is a guide to management, explaining in non-mathematical terms many of these new techniques. *Theory of Games and Statistical Decisions*, by David Blackwell and Meyer A. Girshick (1954), though not directed primarily at the management reader, contains a lucid exposition of the important work of Von Neumann, Morgenstern, and Wald that has powerful implications for management. *Decision Processes*, edited by Robert M. Thrall, Clyde H. Coombs, and Robert L. Davis (1954), is a symposium on decision making under uncertainty by a group of scholars from a variety of disciplines. *Symposium on Monte Carlo Methods* (1956), edited by Herbert A. Meyer, contains the results of recent research in this useful application of probability theory.

The branch of mathematics that is the special concern of the statistician has produced many significant contributions for management. Many books in the Wiley Publications in Statistics (more fully described in another chapter) reflect the pioneering work in quality control of the editor of this series, Walter Shewhart, whose own book, "Economic Control of Quality of Manufactured Product" (Van Nostrand, 1931), was the literary guidepost to the field. *Sampling Inspection Tables*, by Harold F. Dodge and Harry G. Romig (1944), provided a guide to the organization of an effective inspection system. Several other general books on statistical applications in engineering contain useful material for managerial activities: Harold A. Freeman's *Industrial Statistics* (1942), Leonard H. C. Tippett's *Technological Applications of Statistics* (1950), and A. Hald's *Statistical Theory with Engineering Applications* (1952). *Government Statistics for Business Use*, by Philip M. Hauser and William R. Leonard (1946), provides an invaluable guide to the identity and sources of most collections of government data.

The united efforts of mathematicians, statisticians, physicists, and engineers during the second World War produced some profound advances in the theory and application of automatic control and information transfer. The provocative ideas on these subjects in Norbert Wiener's *Cybernetics* (Technology Press–Wiley, 1948), and in the publications of Shannon and others, have been reflected and amplified in literally dozens of books intended for various audiences and purposes. Many of these recent researches have some bearing, direct or indirect, on the solution of managerial problems, but none has

Some recent Wiley books in the social sciences

exceeded the rapid emergence of the high-speed electronic computer as a powerful tool for industrial research and business data processing. When Edmund C. Berkeley's *Giant Brains* was published in 1949 the electronic computer industry was in its infancy. Eight years later it has become a multimillion dollar business, although it is still in its burgeoning adolescence. If Charles Babbage thought of the possible applications of his ingenious calculating machine of the eighteen-thirties to the production problems that interested him, he would be no less astounded today at the tremendous burden of work being lifted from the shoulders and minds of today's workers by the complex descendants of his device. Computers and automatic controls have been the subject of many Wiley books. They have been interpreted for managerial readers in Richard G. Canning's *Electronic Data Processing in Business and Industry* and Howard S. Levin's *Office Work and Automation*, both published in 1956.

The economist has provided among other things new insights into inter-industry relationships that have an important bearing on the perspective of the business manager. Using the electronic computer and various mathematical techniques, he has been able to study the complex network of industrial activity in a national framework and to explore the possibilities of exerting control on the activities within this network. Several of the Cowles Commission Monographs have dealt with these studies, and the symposium on *Economic Activity Analysis*, edited by Oskar Morgenstern (1954), contains an important summary of research in the "Mathematical Structure of American Type Economies."

From the psychologist has come significant research in several areas of vital concern to management. Automation has brought with it many new problems of displacement, high speeds, and human integration into the man-machine system. An important early publication in the field of "human engineering" was *Applied Experimental Psychology* (1949), by Alphonse Chapanis, Wendell R. Garner, and Clifford T. Morgan, a study of the application of psychological techniques to the solution of engineering design problems. Norman R. F. Maier's *Principles of Human Relations: Applications to Management* (1952) is a guide to the effective development of leadership on all levels of industry.

The high degree of specialization involved in these diverse fields contributing to managerial activities made it clear that complex problems could best be attacked by a group of experts acting in an advisory capacity to management. The concept of "system engineering" advanced during the wartime programs of aircraft development came to have considerable significance in its application to peacetime industrial management. The term "operations research" was also formulated during the second World War to describe the exhaustive application of the methods of scientific research to problems of military strategy and tactics. A summary of this wartime activity was published in *Methods of Operations Research*, by Philip M. Morse and George E. Kimball (Technology Press–Wiley, 1951), a book that served as a guide to the intensive applications in general business and industrial activities after the war. Several centers of research were organized, and a considerable body of industrial case studies was made available for instruction. From one of the first of these centers, the Operations Research Group at Case Institute of Technology, a comprehensive book was developed under the editorship of C. West Churchman, Russell L. Ackoff, and E. Leonard Arnoff. Published in 1957, *The Principles of Operations Research* is a presentation, in textbook form, of the various mathematical techniques available to management, and an exposition of the philosophical foundation underlying the most effective use of these techniques.

The rapidity with which scientific management has developed in the half century since Taylor is no more breathtaking than the general advance of technology during that period. Indeed, through the necessity of keeping pace with this general advance, the field has been in danger of losing its identity, and the explosive developments of the postwar years have only added to this ferment. It seems most likely that considerable thought will be devoted in the next few years to the formulation of definitions of the roles of industrial engineers and management scientists in the modern industrial age. The task of a publisher in this process is an important and difficult one, necessitating the employment of all the resources gathered from experience in publishing books in a dozen related fields. The contributions of the firm of Wiley to the literature of industrial engineering and management have been considerable in the past, and it is indicative of the future direction of its activities that in its anniversary year it publishes *Automation in Business and Industry*, edited by Eugene M. Grabbe, a collection of lectures by a group of the pioneers of tomorrow's technology. In this same year the final work is being done on a multi-volume *Handbook of Automation, Computation and Control*, a comprehensive reference work being edited by Simon Ramo, D. E. Wooldridge, and E. M. Grabbe.

CHARLES B. STOLL

Volts in Action

Books on Electrical Engineering

THE ELECTRIC TELEGRAPH spread its first loose net over the United States about the time of the Civil War. Philadelphia's famous display of electric arc lights at the Centennial Exposition was made in 1876. The American Institute of Electrical Engineers was founded in 1884, and the French and British societies were founded about the same time. Early electrical industries were started and were received with great enthusiasm toward the end of the nineteenth century. There were, however, very few electrical engineering books published.

Harris J. Ryan and his co-authors, Henry H. Norris and George L. Hoxie, published their *Textbook of Electrical Machinery* with Wiley in 1902. Looking back into the nineteenth century, we see that Robert Sabine's *Electric Telegraph*, McGregor's *Practical Telegraphy*, and Bond's *Handbook of the Telegraph* appeared in the early years, around 1870. An *Elementary Treatise on Electric Batteries* was written by A. Niaudet and L. M. Fishback in 1880, and, just as the century closed, William A. Anthony wrote *Lecture Notes on the Theory of Electrical Measurements*. Looking forward into the twentieth century, we find that the book by Ryan, Norris, and Hoxie, published earlier, was being read with great interest.

Ryan had spent ten years at Cornell studying the transformer. "I was put in the department of physics," he once told the author of this chapter, "because at that time there wasn't any electrical engineering department." But three years later, when Ryan left Cornell for Stanford University, the ripple of interest started by Ryan, Norris, and Hoxie had grown into a wave. The titles of Wiley books reflected the excitement. There were such books being published as *Alternating Currents*, by George T. Hanchett (1904), *Circuits and Machines*, by Henry H. Norris and Boyd C. Dennison (1909), and *Lead Accumulators*, by Friedrich Dolezalek and Carl L. von Ende (1904). There was even a *Manual of Wireless Telegraphy and Telephony*, by A. Frederick Collins, in 1906, which seems remarkably ahead of its time.

In this same decade Vladimir Karapetoff's first two books on experimental electrical engineering appeared. And just at the end of the decade, in 1910, the first of the famous Timbie books was published. *Elements of Electricity* was its name, and the fourth edition is still a best seller.

Excitement over applied electricity lasted into the second decade, augmented by two more books by Karapetoff, two by William H. Timbie, two others by Timbie and Henry H. Higbie, a three-volume book, *Design*, by W. T. Ryan, and Harold Pender's *American Handbook for Electrical Engineers*. Books by Chester L. Dawes and Ralph G. Hudson, Herbert B. Dwight's *Constant Voltage Transmission*, and Timbie and Higbie's *Essentials of Alternating Currents* were of this decade. Sixty-three electrical engineering books had been published by Wiley by the end of 1925.

The electrical knowledge of the era was reflected in some excellent textbooks. *Principles of Electrical Engineering*, by Timbie and Vannevar Bush, appeared in 1922, and Arthur L. Cook's *Elements* in 1924; Timbie brought out *Industrial Electricity* in the same year, and in the following year L. Frank Woodruff's *Electric Power Transmission* was published.

The number of new books on electrical engineering, for a time, was less. Interest in the subject broadened, however, and some titles of the twenties reflected such special fields as *Storage Batteries*, by George W. Vinal, and *Illuminating Engineering*, by Francis E. Cady and Henry B. Dates.

In the meantime, John H. Morecroft had written *Principles of Radio Com-*

munication. This important book, published by Wiley in 1921, was one of the first written on this subject. Morecroft's book stood almost alone in its field throughout the twenties. It is hard to know why, but despite the glamour of radio, the tremendous amateur interest, and the professional achievements, major radio books did not appear. It was not until 1929 that Rudolph L. Duncan and Charles E. Drew wrote for amateurs *Radio Telegraphy and Telephony* and *How to Pass United States Government Radio License Examinations.*

Then Keith Henney's *Principles of Radio* was published just at the end of the nineteen-twenties, a successful book that enjoyed a phenomenal sale during the war years and is now in its fifth edition, with Glen A. Richardson as co-author. Publications now were many, with Knox McIlwain and J. G. Brainerd's *High Frequency Alternating Currents* appearing in 1931, *Electronics*, by Ralph G. Hudson, the next year, and Morecroft again, with *Electron Tubes* (1933), followed by Arthur L. Albert's *Electrical Communications* (1934), Elmer D. McArthur's *Electronics and Electron Tubes* (1936), and William G. Dow's *Engineering Electronics* (1937). Again a book foreshadowed the future: *First Principles of Television*, by A. Dinsdale, was brought from England in 1932. It was not until 1940, 1945, and 1949 that Vladimir K. Zworykin, with George A. Morton, Edward G. Ramberg, and other co-authors, wrote *Television*, *Electron Optics*, and *Photoelectricity*.

In the decade of the thirties, powerful means of analysis were brought to bear on electrical engineering subjects. The formal thinking called mathematics was applied to circuit theory with great effect, giving us some books of greater erudition when Vannevar Bush's delightful *Operational Circuit Analysis* appeared in 1929. *Communication Networks*, by Ernest A. Guillemin, followed: Volume I in 1931 and Volume II in 1935. Gabriel Kron's books, *Tensor Analysis of Networks* (1939) and the others, are a part of this group, and so is P. LeCorbeiller's *Matrix Analysis of Electrical Networks* of 1950. The recent books by Guillemin, the *Mathematics of Circuit Analysis* in 1949 and his startling *Introductory Circuit Theory* of 1953, surely belong in this classification also.

With this same emphasis on mathematical thought, yet different enough to demand special mention, was the book by Murray F. Gardner and John L. Barnes that brought Laplace transformation into circuit analysis. It appeared in 1942, camouflaged under the title *Transients in Linear Systems.* This name for the book is without doubt accurate, but it quite fails to suggest that a new concept had arrived, and that ten years later electrical engineers would be thinking in different terms because this book was written.

The well-known textbook by Russell M. Kerchner and George F. Corcoran, *Alternating-Current Circuits*, was published in 1938. Even today it dominates its field, and "K and C" is enough to mean "Kerchner and Corcoran" to teachers and bookmen.

In the early forties the staff of the Massachusetts Institute of Technology, by a more or less co-operative effort, produced a trilogy, *Electric Circuits*, *Magnetic Circuits*, and *Applied Electronics* (Technology Press–Wiley). These three are a valuable set of reference books, and the last-named reappeared in 1954, still under the title *Applied Electronics* but this time with the sole and disclosed authorship of Truman S. Gray.

Then in the years of the second World War there was new interest in electromagnetic theory and centimeter waves. Perhaps H. H. Skilling's *Fundamentals of Electric Waves* was as early as any in this field, bravely published by Wiley in 1942. Robert I. Sarbacher and William A. Edson came along in 1943, with the resounding title *Hyper and Ultra-High Frequency Engineering*, and in the following year Simon Ramo and John R. Whinnery's *Fields and Waves in Modern Radio* appeared. Nathan Marchand's *Ultrahigh Frequency Transmission and Radiation* was published in 1947, John Thomson's *Radio Communication at Ultra High Frequency* in 1950, and *Ultra High Frequency Propagation*, by Henry R. Reed and Carl M. Russell, in 1953. The descriptive *Microwaves*, by Robert B. Muchmore (1952), is the resource of the non-mathematical, and a joy to the mathematical.

In 1954 a magnificent pair of books by Arthur R. von Hippel—*Dielectrics and Waves* and *Dielectric Materials*—marked a high point of careful authorship and publication.

In the year 1948 another group of books grew out of wartime research, among which *Principles of Servomechanisms*, by Gordon S. Brown and Donald P. Campbell, was the leader. Three years later Harold Chestnut and Robert W. Mayer brought out Volume I of their *Servomechanisms and Regulating System Design*, followed by Volume II in 1955. Joseph M. Pesterini's *Metadyne Statics* of 1952 is a related monograph. Other books on control systems will doubtless be written in the next few years. They are part of the general sub-

Examples of current book jackets

ject of systems engineering, which is, at this moment, an exciting new field, still a little nebulous, but unquestionably important.

Even now another field of electrical engineering is developing in which Richard F. Shea's *Principles of Transistor Circuits* (1953) and *Transistor Audio Amplifiers* (1955) are the first books. It requires no prophet to predict that transistor theory will be one of the greater fields of interest through the coming years.

This brief account does nothing more than indicate some major trends that have swept through electrical engineering publishing as it relates to one house. A number of specific books have been mentioned by way of illustration. That dozens of other books, as good or better, have not been mentioned, though published by Wiley in these same decades, means nothing. This is not a catalogue; it is a story. Indeed, it is only part of a story, for there was no clear beginning to electrical engineering publishing, and certainly there is as yet no thought of an end.

H. H. SKILLING

Engineering Processes and Progress

Books on Chemical Engineering and Industrial Chemistry

Engineering as we know it today is scarcely more than a hundred years old, and chemical engineering has been recognized for not much more than half that period. The chemical industry, of course, antedates the development of chemical engineering, just as the mill and factory antedate the mechanical engineer. The coal-tar dye industry, to name a fairly recent segment, dates from Perkin's mauve, discovered in 1856, twelve years before Wiley published a book, based presumably on the then authoritative German sources, on aniline and its derivatives. Other books, on cement, on gas manufacture, and on explosives, appeared before the turn of the century. These were descriptive books of chemical technology and not studies of chemical engineering. It is not surprising, therefore, that books definitely classifiable under chemical engineering are not on Wiley's lists of more than fifty years ago.

Chemical engineering was fostered by the needs of the growing chemical technology. For instance, at the time (1904) of the appearance of J. Merritt Matthews' *Textile Fibers*, synthetic fibers (as represented by viscose rayon) were already twenty years old; but this early Wiley book was devoted mainly to fibers of natural origin. Science was beginning to play an important part in the textile art, however, and the appearance of the same author's *Laboratory Manual of Dyeing and Textile Chemistry* in 1909 was called "the fulfillment of a long-felt want" in a review by the late Allen Rogers. The standing of these books attracted a number of other titles in the textile field to the Wiley list.

Many other "long-felt wants" were fulfilled by Wiley books serving the various chemical industries that developed during the first quarter of this century. Alvah H. Sabin's *Industrial and Artistic Technology of Paint and Varnish* (1904) was enlivened with philosophical asides and classical allusions seldom seen in today's technical books, but it laid a solid foundation of technical knowledge in the growing paint industry. It foreshadowed also the comprehensive five-volume study, *Protective and Decorative Coatings*, edited by Joseph J. Mattiello, the first volume of which appeared in 1941. Modern practices in this industry were later presented in Verne C. Bidlack and Edgar W. Fasig's *Paint and Varnish Production Manual* (1951), and in Henry F. Payne's *Organic Coating Technology*, the first volume appearing in 1954.

The literature on explosives in industrial chemical practice was augmented by a number of works, starting with John B. Bernadou's *Smokeless Powder, Nitro-Cellulose and Theory of the Cellulose Molecule* (1901). It is significant that the preface to the translation of H. Brunswig's *Explosives* (by Charles E. Munroe and Alton L. Kibler) in 1912 states: "The days of purely empirical progress in the technique of explosives are numbered." *The Chemistry of Powder and Explosives*, by Tenney L. Davis, is the latest publication in this field (1943).

Sugar manufacture was another growing industry, and *Physical and Chemical Methods of Sugar Analysis* (1912), by Charles A. Browne, was an outstanding book in this field. The *Cane Sugar Handbook* (1945), by Guilford L. Spencer and George P. Meade, presents today's concentrated knowledge in this area.

Books on the chemistry of the papermaking process include Edwin Sutermeister's well-known *The Chemistry of Pulp and Papermaking*, first published in 1920, and Emil F. Heuser's *Chemistry of Cellulose*, 1944.

Fuel technology, as represented in Wiley titles, ranges from Augustus H. Gill's long-standard *Gas and Fuel Analysis for Engineers* (1896–1917) to the compendious two-volume *Chemistry of Coal Utilization*, edited by H. H. Lowry in 1945. Wilhelm Gumz, in *Gas Producers and Blast Furnaces* (1950), has restricted his subject to the theories and methods involved.

Plastics became an extremely important aspect of the chemical industry in the period preceding the second World War; Wiley's first publication in this area was Harry Barron's *Modern Plastics* (1946). This book was followed by Eugene G. Rochow's *Introduction to the Chemistry of the Silicones* (1946), G. S. Whitby's *Synthetic Rubber* (1954), Calvin E. Schildknecht's *Vinyl and Related Polymers* (1952), and, in an allied field, Arthur K. Doolittle's *Technology of Solvents and Plasticizers* (1954). A treatise on *Adhesion and Adhesives* (1954), by F. Clark, J. E. Rutzler, and R. L. Savage, belongs in this category. The *Fundamental Principles of Polymerization* (1952), by Gaetano F. D'Alelio, provided a comprehensive coverage of all these various fields.

The general field of industrial chemistry was encompassed in William T. Read's work of that title, first issued in 1933, and more quantitatively in *Industrial Chemicals* (1950), by William L. Faith, Donald B. Keyes, and Ronald L. Clark. The spectacular development of contact catalysis, as exemplified by the Fischer-Tropsch process, has been compiled by Henry H. Storch, Norma Golumbic, and Robert B. Anderson (1951).

Electrochemistry was treated on the Wiley list, first by a theoretical work by Heinrich Danneel (translated by Edmund S. Merriam) in 1907, and later by H. Jermain Creighton's *Principles* (1924) and Walter A. Koehler's *Applications* (1935). Modern practice has been represented in a series of monographs sponsored by the Electrochemical Society, including *Modern Electroplating* (1953), by Allen G. Gray, *Vapor-Plating* (1955), by C. F. Powell, I. E. Campbell, and B. W. Gonser, and *High Temperature Technology* (1956), by Ivor E. Campbell.

These books on industrial chemistry and descriptive technology preceded and augmented the development of chemical engineering as a formal engineering discipline. As early as 1915, Arthur D. Little described this transition, when he wrote in a report to the President of the Massachusetts Institute of Technology:

> Any chemical process, on whatever scale conducted, may be resolved into a coordinate series of what may be termed "Unit Operations," as pulverizing, drying, roasting, crystallizing, filtering, evaporating, electrolyzing, and so forth. The number of these basic unit operations is not large, and relatively few of

them are involved in any particular process. The complexity of chemical engineering results from the variety of conditions as to temperature, pressure, etc., under which the unit operation must be carried out in different processes, and from the limitations as to materials of construction and design of apparatus imposed by the physical and chemical character of the reacting substances.

The appearance of the pioneering textbook, "Principles of Chemical Engineering," by Walker, Lewis, and McAdams (McGraw-Hill, 1923) marked the beginning of this field as a distinct branch of engineering in the academic curriculum. In 1928, Wiley published a translation (and adaptation) by E. Howard Tripp of the German treatise by E. Hausbrand, *Principles and Practice of Industrial Distillation*, a book whose value has been obscured by the appearance of American textbooks more easily assimilated here and more readily applied to the rapidly expanding petroleum refining industry.

A milestone in chemical engineering education was marked by the appearance, first in 1931, under the title *Industrial Chemical Calculations*, of the work of Olaf A. Hougen and Kenneth M. Watson. The authors, whose names are used more often than the title to identify the book, modified their work later and renamed it *Chemical Process Principles*. This title has been extended to cover in three volumes *Material and Energy Balances* (1943), *Thermodynamics* (1947), and *Kinetics and Catalysis* (1947), plus a supplementary collection of charts. These authors recognized the "need for more thorough training of chemical engineers in the exact and quantitative application of fundamental physicochemical principles to industrial chemical processes," and their attempts to fill this need have met with widely acclaimed success. We can hardly find a discussion of the chemical engineering curriculum that does not make some reference to *Hougen and Watson*. Revision of these works is now under way, with the able assistance of Professor Roland A. Ragatz as co-author.

Another distinguished textbook is Harold C. Weber's *Thermodynamics for Chemical Engineers*. First published in 1939, it did much to establish the fundamental contribution of the chemical engineer to this basic engineering science. A revised and expanded version of this book, by Professor Weber and his colleague, Professor Herman P. Meissner, was published in 1957.

Unit Operations, by George G. Brown and eleven associates at the University of Michigan (1950), was a major landmark in chemical engineering literature. As the authors state in the preface, "This textbook is the first to carry the title *Unit Operations*, but it is not the first to treat the subject." By treating modern practice and equipment in a manner developed from experience with many student generations, this book quickly established itself as a standard classroom and reference book in this central core of chemical engineering knowledge.

The advent of automatic controls has profoundly affected the chemical industry, and, indeed, the automatic operation of petroleum refineries is one of the pioneering examples of successful automation. Donald P. Eckman's *Principles of Industrial Process Control* (1945) was an early treatment of the application of automatic controls to the process industries in general, and in 1956 Norman H. Ceaglske's *Automatic Process Control for Chemical Engineers* provided a quantitative introduction to these modern developments for the process engineer. In 1957 *Process Dynamics*, by Donald P. Campbell, presented a definitive statement of process control fundamentals by one of the most active leaders in the development of servomechanisms.

Another important aspect of the process plant operation was dealt with in *Project Engineering of Process Plants* (1957), by H. F. Rasé and M. H. Barrow, a book of considerable value in bringing the manifold activities of the project engineer into systematic form.

With chemical engineering books appearing twice as rapidly as fifty years ago, what will be the rate fifty years from now? One hundred, one hundred fifty years hence? To the non-expert it may seem appalling, but these textbooks are a necessity to the scientific and economic health of industry, which is becoming more and more dependent on scientific intelligence. Perhaps, as some think, there will be new modes of communication before then. But even so there must be more books, for engineering data and the interpretations of results are fundamental needs. The industry grows not only on transmitted art and practice, but also through the careful and long study and reinterpretation of described practices, art, and data. Doubtless the reader will join in the hope that, good as these books are today, they will be better tomorrow.

THOMAS H. CHILTON

Shelter for Living

Books on Architecture

As NEAR AS CAN BE DETERMINED, it was not until the year 1775 that the first architectural book was published in this country; and this was a Philadelphia reprint, by John Norman, of Abraham Swan's well-known builder's book, "The British Architect: or The Builders' Treasury of Staircases," first issued in London in 1745. Widely subscribed for and sold, this American edition exerted a spreading influence in introducing a new note of distinction into our native architecture. Actually the book covered a larger scope than its title would imply, since numerous examples of mantel and over-mantel designs were included. Specific traces of its influence survive to this day in such extant examples as the Lee Mansion, Marblehead, and the Brice House, Annapolis. Ironically the book itself has literally been "consummed" through use; and there are more surviving examples of the Gutenberg Bible in America than there are of our first published architectural book.

As the country moved from the Colonial into the Federal period, other architectural books were published here to meet a rising demand. Among them were John Norman's "The Town and Country Builder's Assistant . . . ," published in Boston in 1786, essentially a compilation from various English builder's books. In the same year the Carpenters Company of Philadelphia issued an illustrated "price book" that informs us of the nature of buildings then being executed in that area.

What is important in all this is the fact that an architecture of merit was arising in this country, adjusted to our native building needs and materials as well as meeting the social requirements of our citizens, from the small New Hampshire farmer, the New York merchant, the Virginia planter, and the whole range of a prospering citizenry. Old New York had acquired a Georgian elegance with such mansions as those belonging to the Ten Eyck, the Van Cortlandt, the Livingston, and the de Peyster families; fine churches such as St. Paul's in Trinity Parish; and worthy public buildings such as old Federal Hall and the noble President's House, built when New York was our nation's first capital. This pattern of achievement was being repeated in varying degrees in our other important cities, in most of our smaller towns, and in the settled farming regions.

Slowly the emphasis on our Roman Classic style gave way to an infusion of interest in the purity of the Classic Greek architecture. The proud Doric porticoed mansion, church, town hall, and merchandise exchange arose in the North and in the South, spread through the valleys of New York State, out into the rich grasslands of Kentucky, up and down the banks of the Mississippi—until each town and region in our country had dutifully acknowledged, in some degree, our debt to the proud buildings on the Athenian Acropolis. Architects like William Strickland, Robert Mills, Nicholas Biddle, Minard Lafever, Isaiah Rogers, Ithiel Town, and A. J. Davis built such Greek revival buildings as the Old Patent Office in Washington, the Sub-Treasury Building on Wall Street, or Girard College and the Branch Bank of the United States in Philadelphia.

Subsequently, the Gothic Revival, with its romantic overtones, claimed our attention. Although Benjamin Latrobe had prematurely introduced it in 1805 in his *alternate* design for the Baltimore Cathedral, it gained momentum in the middle of the century with Richard Upjohn's design for Trinity Church, New York. James Renwick projected it through Grace Church and St. Patrick's Cathedral in New York. A. J. Davis, Ithiel Town, A. J. Downing, Calvert Vaux, and many others picked it up and the "gothic" cottage, villa,

Brochures and catalogues, 1942–1957

castled mansion, church, college, civic building, and shop front became familiar throughout our country.

After the Civil War, the Victorian use of renaissance forms was similarly adopted, and the Mansard-roofed structure with its heavy, self-conscious ornamentation became the symbol of progress. At the same time, interest was stirred in the use of new materials like cast iron, and new facilities like the elevator, "modern" plumbing, and gas illumination. The tall building made its appearance and eventually grew into that American phenomenon —the skyscraper. H. H. Richardson, returning from a long sojourn in France, expressed his bold, monumental Romanesque Revival in Trinity Church, Boston, and this phase of Medievalism likewise took hold of American imagination on a nation-wide scale, only to be supplanted by the Imperial Roman grandeur championed by the great firm of McKim, Mead, and White. The Chicago World's Fair of 1893, in which this firm played a vital role, presented to millions of Americans a breathtaking vision of the splendors of Ancient Rome under the Caesars. Roman classicism and its renaissance derivative was once again a determinant in American architecture, this time on a monumental scale, and with full academic understanding, to signalize the vast new wealth of our country and its barons of finance.

Our engineers rose to new heights of achievement in meeting the structural demands created by this monumental architecture. Buildings of breathtaking heights, halls of incredible span, bridges that far surpassed Roman achievements, aqueducts, dams, powerhouses, factories, and harbor installations were created that called for a new technical knowledge in handling new, or newly interpreted, materials.

The spirit of eclecticism had likewise expressed itself widely at the end of the nineteenth century and continued as a sporadic current until roughly the beginning of the first World War. With the coming of peace, a charming, knowledgeable, and sensitive period of adroit architectural design became apparent, which we might term the phase of the "Architectural Encyclopedists." All the styles of the past were comprehended and available at will to the architectural client. He had but to decide whether he wanted a house in the manner of Palladio, Gabriel, Inigo Jones, or Sir Christopher Wren. Or perhaps a Cotswold cottage, an Elizabethan hunting lodge, or an antebellum porticoed mansion from our Deep South would be preferable!

Behind this serene picture, however, other forces were at work, and had been at work more or less since roughly the turn of the century. Louis Sullivan and his protégé, Frank Lloyd Wright, were championing a true, creative architecture expressive of our time. Few in America heard their prophetic message. On the other hand, it was picked up by European architects such as Adolf Loos, H. P. Berlage, Walter Gropius, Mies Van der Rohe, and Auguste Perret, who recognized that the old idiom had ceased to have validity. In the process the so-called Modern Movement was slowly conceived and grew into a kind of architectural revolution that spread to America and eventually overthrew the old order of the traditionalists, and triumphed into a phase we call vaguely the "functional style," as expressed in the architecture of the Golden Triangle in Pittsburgh, Lever House and the Manufacturer's Trust in New York, and the host of style-related buildings throughout the country. Factories, housing units, apartment groups, shopping centers, civic centers, planned communities, private houses, and office buildings are stated in the new functional manner. Walls of glass, structural skeletons of steel, reinforced concrete, prestressed concrete, mechanical air conditioning and ventilation, automatic sunlight control, plastics, stainless and colored steel, movable partitions, and electronic equipment are incorporated into the modern "space flow" approach to architectural design. Like Louis XIV, who in building Versailles did not wish to be aided even by nature, lest the grandeur of his personal achievement be minimized, so we appear to have attained a similarly vainglorious independence from nature.

The architectural development from the end of the eighteenth century to the middle of the twentieth century thus constitutes a truly marvelous achievement. How was it brought about; how did it spread from one part of the country to another; how from one country to another with such definite abruptness? The answer lies in the richly illustrated publications: books, periodicals, journals, pamphlets, and reports in an ever-increasing flow that brought the creative world of the architect and the patron ever closer together. Ideas expressed in Boston could be received simultaneously in San Francisco or El Paso.

Although only fourteen architectural books were published in this country prior to the year 1800, since that time the total has increased to tens and tens of thousands.

It is fitting, at this point, to inquire just how the firm of Wiley has contributed to the field of architectural publishing in the course of the first century and a half of its existence. Wiley's first architectural book was issued one hundred and fifteen years ago. It was then a successful venture and it remains to this day a book sought after by collectors, and is found in any architectural library worthy of the name. It is *Cottage Residences* (1842), by Andrew Jackson Downing, a book of designs for small houses in the latest fashion as practiced in England of that day but adjusted to the needs of cultivated American families of moderate means. Clearly it was intended to heighten the level of taste on a broad scale, and naturally it found ready users throughout the country. Six years later, in 1848, the success of Wiley's first publication was repeated in *Cottage Architecture*, by the noted English author-architect, J. C. Loudon, who wrote twenty-two books dealing with various aspects of this subject. In 1848 also Wiley put out another Downing book, *Country Houses*, and Robert Dale Owen's *Hints on Public Architecture* (1848), which dealt primarily with the designs of the "Gothic" Smithsonian Institution in Washington and must have contributed to promoting interest in our Gothic revival. Between 1870 and 1890 eighteen more architectural books were published by Wiley. In this group the so-called builder's-book type prevailed. They included the seventh edition of R. G. Hatfield's *American House Carpenter;* three more titles by Downing; C. B. Allen's *Cottage Building;* G. R. Burnell's *Builders and Contractors Price Book;* and Wiley's first book dealing with the principles of construction, *The Art of Building* by the Englishman, Edward Dobson. The last-named title was in a sense prophetic of the subsequent important contributions made by the firm to the literature of the engineering aspects of architecture. In this same period the needs of the rising eclecticism, referred to earlier, were recognized by the publication of an American edition of Thomas Talbot Bury's *Styles of Architecture*, an analysis of the chief historic architectural styles "from the earliest times to the present period." E. L. Garbett's *Principles of Design in Architecture*, together with the preceding book and many subsequent ones, must have been, in part at least, directed to the needs of the newly established (in the late eighteen-sixties) college or university architectural departments, for which student textbooks were sorely needed. Further engineering textbooks were published at this time, such as C. E. Greene's three technical studies on trusses and arches; and in 1884 the first edition of Frank E. Kidder's *Architect's and Builder's Pocket-Book*, which became, and remains, as indispensable to architect, draftsman, and builder as his own drawing instruments. The eighteenth edition of this book has just had its fourteenth printing, which seems to render unnecessary further comment as to its usefulness.

By 1890 Wiley's architectural program may with some certainty be regarded as definitely established. Its primary responsibility lay in the important area of technical studies in the field of construction and building services. This clearly reflected the intensified needs felt as great structures—skyscrapers, bridges, railroad stations, hospitals, apartment houses, department stores, and a host of other great buildings—were erected. In this area, it can be said that Wiley has achieved a pre-eminence almost uncontested. In the process, certain "landmark" books were issued: Charles G. Ramsey and Harold R. Sleeper's *Architectural Graphic Standards* (1932), Sleeper's *Building Planning and Design Standards* (1955), Theodore Crane's *Architectural Construction* (1947), Harry Parker's *Simplified Engineering for Architects and Builders* (1938), his *Simplified Design of Structural Steel* (1945), his *Simplified Mechanics and Strength of Materials* (1951), and, in 1954, *Simplified Site Engineering for Architects and Builders*, which Parker wrote with John W. MacGuire.

At the same time Wiley was issuing noteworthy books on other phases of architecture, such as two valuable books dealing with the design of the classic orders, a book on naval architecture, the widely used four volumes of Rexford Newcomb's *Outlines of the History of Architecture* (1922–1939), Rowland C. Hunter's *Old Houses in England* (1930), A. Thornton Bishop's *Renaissance Architecture of England* (1938), and Ernest Pickering's *Architectural Design* (1933).

Special mention needs to be made of the breadth of technical contributions sponsored by Wiley in its program of meeting the needs of architect, draftsman and professional student in a world that became more and more complex, architecturally speaking, after the early nineteen-thirties. The first volume of the Voss and Henry (later Voss and Varney) monumental two-volume book codifying architectural construction up to that time appeared in 1925, was completed in 1927, and was soon put in the libraries of most architects and professional architectural schools. The door was open for scholarly investigation of specialized problems within the broad framework of the technical

A page of modern bindings

side of architecture. The writing of specifications alone had become an area of intense specialization, requiring, as eventually was acknowledged, an almost impossible comprehension of special materials, mechanical equipment, and new structural techniques. In this particular area, Wiley's publication, in 1935, of Goldwin Goldsmith's *Architects' Specifications—How to Write Them* and, in 1940, of Harold Sleeper's *Architectural Specifications* performed a service that it would be difficult to overvalue.

In turn, as new needs were felt, Wiley promptly filled those needs. For example, the first major use of prestressed concrete as a building system was made in this country in 1952. By 1955 Wiley had the system analyzed, tested, and its approved methods clarified in T. Y. Lin's *Design of Prestressed Concrete Structures.* If much of the guesswork has been taken out of determining the acoustical potentialities of a building still in the design stage, considerable credit should go to still another Wiley publication, Vern O. Knudsen and Cyril M. Harris's *Acoustical Designing in Architecture*, which appeared in 1950.

With the sharp rise in building costs after the second World War and the recognition that low-cost housing in vast numbers was required to offset the building lag that had occurred during the depression years of the nineteen-thirties, and had been further aggravated by a necessary dearth in new housing throughout the war itself, it was apparent that low-cost housing had become a national problem. Prefabrication, standardization of parts, modular construction, pre-assembled service units were only parts of the possible solution. Vast housing developments involving multi-storied groups of apartment blocks, as well as suburban housing estates comprising hundreds of detached small houses, were constructed across the nation, often with more haste than good judgment.

The publishing implications in this housing program were enormous, and we find the job being shared by some publishers heretofore not active in this area. The Wiley approach was two-pronged. First, a scholarly study was undertaken by Burnham Kelly, director of the Bemis Foundation at the Massachusetts Institute of Technology, which resulted in *The Prefabrication of Houses* (1951), a joint publication with Technology Press. This book critically and evaluatively explored both the "manufacturer" and the product, as well as taking up questions of financing, marketing, and adjustments to building codes. Astutely timed, it exerted a "top level" influence that provided a salutary effect on the growth of the industry and its broader acceptance by planning boards and consumers. The second prong of the Wiley approach to the housing problem was addressed primarily to the often untutored layman interested in building his own home. *The House for You* (1948), by Catharine and Harold Sleeper, might be described as a guide to sensible, knowledgeable decisions by the small-home owner with respect to planning, construction and design, so that his investment would be productive in both satisfaction and security.

It is gratifying to realize that as new achievements in contemporary architecture are being accomplished, there is a concurrent interest in understanding more fully the "contemporary" architecture of our earlier periods, to understand how forward-looking architects at all times attacked problems new to their generation. This is indicative of a true historical awareness, and far from the short-sighted view of the faddist. It augurs well for the future, and indeed explains the appearance of the last Wiley publication to be mentioned here, the concise, pocket-size *Dictionary of Architecture* (1952), by Henry H. Saylor (editor of the *Journal of the American Institute of Architects*), which offers definitions of such new terms as "piloti" and such old ones as "arenatum" and states in its preface: "The past is prologue."

In reviewing Wiley's work in this field, it is perhaps worth noting that consciously or otherwise Wiley has recognized the dual aspects of architecture—structural practice and architectural design theory. In their case, however, a natural concentration of interest developed in the more technological aspects. Within that chosen field, its contributions have been of a significance that we would be glad to have identify their expanding future, so that they too may say, "The Past is Prologue."

JAMES GROTE VAN DERPOOL

The Dream of Flight

Books on Aeronautics

One of the most ancient and persistent lures to man's imagination has been the dream of flight. The myth of Daedalus and his wax-held wings and the winged feet of the Greek god Hermes are only two of the many poetic emanations of the dream; the winged creatures of nature have always been regarded by man with envious admiration. As the processes of human thought turned toward the development of rational explanations of natural phenomena, the first attempts were made to philosophize on the theory of flight. In the fourth century B.C., Aristotle stated his views on the mutual actions between a fluid and a body moving through it, and it was not until a thousand years later that Philiponus attempted to explain inconsistencies in the Aristotelian theory. With the Renaissance, the pace of research was accelerated, and we have ample evidence of the interesting speculations advanced by Leonardo da Vinci on the mechanism of bird flight, and the later work of Galileo and Huyghens on the matter of air resistance. Starting with the latter part of the seventeenth century, significant contributions were made to the knowledge of fluid mechanics through the work of Newton, Euler, the Bernoullis, and Lagrange.

By the beginning of the twentieth century an impressive array of knowledge had been amassed on the subject of theoretical aerodynamics, largely based on Euler's equations for an ideal non-viscous fluid. These classical studies, however, did not agree with the extensive experimental work under way at the turn of the century, and the science of hydraulics was evolved by engineers who were working for solutions to practical problems. This same desire for concrete accomplishment had made possible the development of the internal combustion engine. The necessary components for powered flight were now in hand.

In 1903, when the Wright brothers made the first sustained flight, formal knowledge of the basis for flight was still chaotic. Classical theories on the action of ideal fluids were not applicable to a real fluid, such as air, and the empirical developments of hydraulics had been largely concerned with the flow of water. Knowledge of air resistance was based on very crude tests, and was inaccurate and misleading. The aircraft of the decade following were built by cut-and-try methods, but during that same time important theoretical advances were being made by Prandtl, Lanchester, and others.

The first World War did much to accelerate these developments, and the spectacular achievements of the wartime builders and pilots presented the world with a glimpse of the gigantic commercial developments to come. The impetus of the war on many young flyers provided them with undiminished energy in the postwar period; some toured the country on barnstorming exhibitions, and others put their efforts into attempts to conquer the Atlantic and other major distance barriers. The early twenties also saw a serious effort being made to systematize the technical knowledge contributing to the advance of aviation and the beginnings of aeronautical engineering as a distinct discipline in engineering colleges.

In 1919, while Alcock and Brown flew non-stop from Newfoundland to Ireland, and while the Post Office Department was establishing an air mail route from New York through Cleveland to Chicago, Edwin B. Wilson of the Massachusetts Institute of Technology was preparing his manuscript, entitled *Aeronautics*, for publication. Published in 1920, Wilson's book was based on a course that he had taught for several years to enable students to bridge the gap between basic mathematics and mechanics and the complex problems encountered in the analysis of airplane motion. Although Wilson treated a wing as a flat plate and made other erroneous assumptions, his book contained many valuable statements on dynamic stability. The permanence of Wilson's contribution to aeronautical literature is attested to by Manfred Rauscher in the preface to his *Introduction to Aeronautical Dynamics*, published by Wiley in 1953. Writing thirty-three years after Wilson, after a period of revolutionary advances, Rauscher acknowledged that he had retained the fundamental plan of Wilson's work. Although Rauscher saw the need to present students of 1953 with a broader and deeper grounding in dynamical principles than had been necessary in the past, he continued: "As every teacher knows, the very bottom layer of such a grounding, next to the scraped bedrock of basic concepts and elementary formulation of ideas, is the most difficult one to lay properly." The attention to this fundamental task is the major criterion of a textbook, and this criterion was met by both Wilson in 1920 and Rauscher in 1953.

As engineering schools established separate departments of aeronautical engineering, the pattern for a growing body of technical literature became apparent. Always at the heart of the subject was the study of dynamic stability, and Wilson's book was followed on the Wiley list in 1921 by *Dynamics of the Airplane*, by Kenneth P. Williams of Indiana University. This book showed the wing as a cambered surface and clearly stated the center of pressure movement; it also contained a chapter on the rudiments of propellers for aircraft. Williams was able to encompass in one volume a major part of the aeronautical knowledge of his time, an achievement that was prevented from duplication by the growing complexity of the field. Diversification came about inevitably with the expansion of research in aerodynamics, structures, propulsion, and other specialized areas. One important literary result of this diversification was a series of books by staff members of the Guggenheim Aeronautical Laboratory at California Institute of Technology. Launched in 1941, under the editorship of Theodore von Kármán and Clark B. Millikan, the GALCIT Series is a continuing program of advanced textbooks presenting fundamental scientific and technical subjects relating to aeronautics.

Although, as early as 1904, Prandtl had presented his paper on fluid motion with small friction, and in 1914 had conducted his famous experiments on the resistance of spheres, his boundary-layer theory was so far-reaching, and

Parts of the executive floor at 440 Fourth Avenue, showing library and office of the President

involved so many implications, that some years elapsed before the importance of his work was fully appreciated. In 1936 Wiley published *Elements of Practical Aerodynamics*, by Bradley Jones, the first college textbook that outlined in a simple manner Prandtl's ideas on induced drag and explained the proper corrections of wing characteristics for varying aspect ratio. In the same year Ovid W. Eshbach's *Handbook of Engineering Fundamentals* contained an excellent up-to-date section on fluid mechanics by Paul Hemke. Clark B. Millikan's *Aerodynamics of the Airplane*, first of the GALCIT Series, appeared in 1941, to fill the need for a concise and rigorous introduction to the field.

The high speeds achieved as a result of research during the second World War brought about new problems of aerodynamics that were due to the effects of compressibility and shock waves. It is easy to forget, in the light of today's headlines, the disorganized body of literature that existed in 1947, when *The Aerodynamics of a Compressible Fluid*, by Hans W. Liepmann and Allen E. Puckett, was published as a volume in the GALCIT Series. It became almost overnight a standard textbook for instruction in high-speed aerodynamics. In 1956 *The Molecular Flow of Gases*, by Gordon N. Patterson, appeared, presenting a brief, forceful statement of the behavior of gases in terms of the kinetic theory. It was followed in 1957 by *Elements of Gasdynamics*, by Liepmann and Anatol Roshko.

With flight at sonic and supersonic speeds becoming more common, the basic undergraduate programs underwent some inevitable changes. In the area of aerodynamics the complexities of modern problems were treated from the basic point of view of fluid mechanics in *Foundations of Aerodynamics*, by Arnold M. Kuethe and Julius D. Schetzer (1950). An intermediate treatment of *Airplane Performance, Stability, and Control*, by C. D. Perkins and R. E. Hage (1949) provided the transition from theory to specific application; and Alan Pope's *Wind Tunnel Testing* (1947, revised 1954) presented an introduction to the use of an important research tool.

The refinement of the applications of fluid mechanics to actual flight had its parallel in the area of structural research. And, as the aerodynamicist poured valuable material back into the general body of knowledge in fluid mechanics, the aeronautical structural researcher has contributed immensely to the knowledge of structures in general. When the first edition of *Aircraft Structures*, by Alfred S. Niles and Joseph S. Newell, was published in 1929, it presented the applications of engineering mechanics to airplane structures; in later editions it became a truly authentic textbook on the proper stress analysis of aircraft. This standard textbook was followed by several other significant structures books on the Wiley list. Francis R. Shanley's *Basic Structures* (1944) was a fundamental approach to structural analysis and a brilliant example of the fresh thinking brought by the aeronautical engineer to old problems. *Airplane Structural Analysis and Design* (1942), by Ernest E. Sechler and Louis G. Dunn (one of the GALCIT Series), provided a concise and lucid textbook for graduate students. Both these books reflected the profound effect of the second World War on structural research.

An awareness of the importance of elasticity on the design and the behavior of aircraft led to the publication of two GALCIT Series volumes: Sechler's *Elasticity in Engineering* (1952) and *An Introduction to the Theory of Aeroelasticity*, by Yuan-Cheng Fung (1955). In *The Analysis of Structures* (1956), Nicholas J. Hoff presented structural analysis as a logical and unified theory, starting with the principle of virtual displacements and developing the minimal principles of structural theory and an understanding of buckling phenomena. In the same year Wiley laid plans for a program of monographs on aspects of aircraft structures under the editorship of Hoff.

In the field of propulsion the transition from the chapter on propeller design in Kenneth P. Williams' *Dynamics of the Airplane* (1921) to George P. Sutton's *Rocket Propulsion Elements* (1949) is one that paralleled the advances in aerodynamics and structures. Wilbur G. Nelson's *Airplane Propeller Principles* appeared in 1944, when the German V-2 bombs were being readied for launching by a radically different means of propulsion. It was only four years later that Maurice J. Zucrow's *Principles of Jet Propulsion and Gas Turbines* was published as one of the first textbooks to serve students of the jet age. This book, together with Alexander A. Nikolsky's *Helicopter Analysis* (1951), provided introductory treatments of two basic elements in future commercial and military developments.

The period between Wilson's pioneer book and Rauscher's modern classic saw the field of aeronautics develop into a major industry in peace and an indispensable factor in the conduct of wars. Experimental development has felt the impact of theoretical advances, and the intricacies of today's aeronautical industry require the highest degree of technical ability in a dozen different areas. If the first World War brought to mankind a glimmer of the possibilities of aeronautics, the second realized these expectations to a degree undreamed of by the most imaginative myth makers. The men who guided this revolution came from a variety of backgrounds, but the professional aeronautical engineer was always in the mainstream of its advance. The era of jets, guided missiles, artificial satellites, and space exploration is now upon us, and day-by-day intercontinental transport is as commonplace as a horse-drawn cab was to Wilbur and Orville Wright.

BRADLEY JONES

Trees

Books on Forestry

THE DEVELOPMENT OF FORESTRY in America long antedates establishment of the publishing house of Wiley. It is true that by the last quarter of the nineteenth century substantial beginnings had been made looking toward the conservation and development of the forest resource. For example, in 1891 the most important legislation in the history of forestry in America (according to the late Gifford Pinchot) was enacted when Congress authorized the creation of forest reserves. This legislation marked the beginning of the national forest system, but it was not until forestry schools were established in American universities (Cornell 1898, Yale 1900, and others later) that professional training of foresters was begun in America.

An urgent need for textbooks covering all phases of forestry immediately arose. Wiley was the first publisher to visualize the need and the first to provide textbooks on an adequate scale. From 1903 to 1954 fifty-two books relating to forestry have been published by Wiley.

Their first book (in 1903) was Samuel B. Green's *Principles of American Forestry*, a generalized book covering all branches of the subject, as was appropriate because of the lack at that time of any detailed American textbooks. Other books of this nature later produced and designed especially for students in agricultural schools, were Franklin F. Moon and Nelson C. Brown's *Elements of Forestry* (1914), John A. Ferguson's *Farm Forestry* (1916), and Brown's *A General Introduction to Forestry in the United States* (1935).

In the same year (1903) appeared *The Principal Species of Wood—Their Characteristic Properties*, written by Charles H. Snow, a civil engineer, and "intended for those who are not foresters or botanists but who use woods."

Very shortly textbooks on specialized branches of forestry began to come off the press. Henry S. Graves's *Forest Mensuration*, the first American textbook on the subject, was issued in 1906. It was followed by Herman H. Chapman's *Forest Mensuration* in 1921, Hugo Winkenwerder and Elias T. Clark's *Handbook of Field and Office Problems in Forest Mensuration* in 1915, and Harold C. Belyea's *Forest Measurement* in 1931.

In 1911 *Forest Physiography of the United States and Principles of Soils in Relation to Forestry*, by Isaiah Bowman, became available. It reflected a recognition of the need for textbooks on the basic sciences underlying forestry, and was written especially for students in forestry.

The Longleaf Pine in Virgin Forest, by G. Frederick Schwarz, chiefly descriptive, but nevertheless a first attempt to study the silviculture of this important tree, came out in 1907. Graves wrote the first textbook devoted to silviculture, *Principles of Handling Woodlands* (1911), followed by James W. Toumey's *Seeding and Planting in the Practice of Forestry* (1916), Ralph C. Hawley's *Practice of Silviculture* (1921), Toumey's *Foundations of Silviculture upon an Ecological Basis* (1928), and Hawley's *Forest Protection* (1937).

Hawley and Austin F. Hawes in *Forestry in New England* (1912) pioneered in discussing silviculture and management for the various forest types and forest regions of New England, and in 1939 R. H. Westveld's *Applied Silviculture in the United States* was published, covering the same field for the whole country.

As the field of wood technology developed, Wiley brought out several textbooks in addition to the early work of Snow (1903). Samuel J. Record's *Identification of the Economic Woods of the United States* appeared in 1912, and his *Mechanical Properties of Wood* in 1914.

Former Officers of the Corporation. Top left: CHARLES WILEY, *Treasurer, 1904–1916. Top right:* S. E. NORRIS, *Vice President, 1941–1943. Bottom left:* E. A. SMITH, *Vice President and Treasurer, 1942–1953. Bottom right:* R. M. TRIEST, *Vice President, 1943–1951.*

Then in 1934 Record's *Identification of the Timbers of Temperate North America* was published. Two other books with the title *Mechanical Properties of Wood* have been published (George A. Garratt, 1931, and Frederick F. Wangaard, 1950).

In 1913 the first textbook on logging appeared—Ralph C. Bryant's *Logging*, followed in 1922 by his *Lumber*. Several books by Nelson C. Brown in the same general field have been brought out: *Forest Products* (1919 and 1950), *The American Lumber Industry* (1923), *Logging* (1934, 1936, and 1949), *Timber Products and Industries* (1937), and *Lumber* (1947).

Although more books have been published on the subjects of silviculture, wood technology, lumbering, and forest products, other branches have not been overlooked. Forest law was covered in 1917 by J. P. Kinney's two books: *Development of Forest Law in America* and *Essentials of American Timber Law*. In the early days of forestry many men lacking woods and field experience entered the profession. To help such men in practical matters, Jay L. B. Taylor's *Handbook for Rangers and Woodsmen* was published in 1916. *Shade-Trees in Towns and Cities*, by William Solotaroff (1911), helped fill the need for a textbook covering arboriculture.

Two books have been issued on forest pathology: *An Outline of Forest Pathology* (Ernest E. Hubert, 1931) and *Pathology in Forest Practice* (Dow V. Baxter, 1943). Arthur W. Sampson's *Native American Forage Plants*, one of the early books intended for use in the western grazing industry, was published in 1924.

The increasing recognition of the importance of soils in the practice of forestry led to publication in 1946 of *Forest Soils*, by Harold J. Lutz and Robert F. Chandler.

Books descriptive of European theories and practice include such titles as *Theory and Practice of Working Plans—Forest Organization* (1913) and *Forest Management* (1919), both by A. B. Recknagel, and *French Forestry* (1917) and *Studies in French Forestry* (1920), by Theodore S. Woolsey.

A contribution to the comparatively new field of wildlife management was made in 1951 by Leonard W. Wing's *Practice of Wildlife Conservation*.

RALPH C. HAWLEY

Food for the Millions

Books on Agriculture

THE COMMANDING ROLE of the more than one hundred and fifty agricultural books published by Wiley began in the "fabulous forties." The period, because of the growing interest in meeting the needs of the people, came to be known as "the era of the common man." This was a time of creative thinking in America, following scientific studies in Europe. Emerson's words, penned in 1837, "Our day of dependence, our long apprenticeship to the learning of other lands, draws to a close," presaged dramatic activity. Educators believed that "students must be trained in the elements of the arts and sciences used in industry and agriculture." The *American Journal of Science*, launched in 1818, and the establishment of the American Association for the Advancement of Science in 1846 gave encouragement to the teaching of science subjects in schools and colleges. Farmers supported this movement by frequent references to Jefferson's emphasis on "agriculture as the surest basis for a Republic." So fruitful was the knowledge of the natural sciences with special reference to agriculture that it opened up visions of man's welfare never before imagined.

The first book on the Wiley list in the agricultural group was prepared by Andrew J. Downing under the title *A Treatise on the Theory and Practice of Landscape Gardening* (1841). The author brought together the traditions and the lore of the horticultural arts and the materials from natural science. The book revealed the unique possibilities of linking the empirical arts of agriculture with the creative resources of science. Within the decade Downing prepared six additional books in horticulture, including the very timely and influential *Landscape Architecture*. These textbooks set a new high standard for all agricultural books. Downing was an important man in his day. He was invited in 1851 to design the public grounds near the Capitol in Washington, and to landscape the grounds of the White House and the Smithsonian Institution, but he died in 1852 before the actual plantings were completed. The editor of "The Easy Chair" in *Harper's* wrote in 1955, "No American has built for himself a more permanent monument than Downing, the landscape gardener."

At midcentury the nation was still very much in the pioneer stage of development. The great central plains were still "new country." The knowledge that farmers had was empirical and had been handed down from one generation to the next. Practical experience was a primary asset. While farmers needed appropriate subjects of study, scientists and teachers were hampered by the conviction of the leaders in higher education that "practical" subjects were unfit for higher learning. It was inevitable that this conflict should be resolved. Indeed, it was resolved by Congress in the passage of the Morrill Act of 1862, which provided for the establishment of colleges of agriculture in the several states. But the early teaching of agriculture was an untried field, qualified teachers were scarce, and it took time to utilize the techniques of science in their application to agriculture. College leaders recognized and developed basic courses in pure science such as botany, biology, chemistry, and physics and then built "applied science" courses such as agricultural chemistry, dairy bacteriology, and soil physics. A third group of subjects appeared as rapidly as reliable source materials were available in the operations of farm production, management, and marketing. These courses included such subjects as soil technology, field crops, agronomy, pomology, animal husbandry, poultry production, vegetable growing, and farm management.

WILLIAM H. WILEY
Senior Partner, 1889–1904
President, 1904–1925

Wiley kept abreast of these trends from the outset and toward the end of the century began an active program of book publishing. Outstanding textbooks in the applied sciences were issued, including F. W. Woll's *Handbook for Farmers and Dairymen* (1897), S. T. Maynard's *Landscape Gardening as Applied to Home Decoration* (1899), H. P. Armsby's *Principles of Animal Nutrition* (1903), E. Dwight Sanderson and L. M. Peairs' *Insect Pests of Farm, Garden and Orchard* (1912), B. S. Brown's *Modern Propagation of Tree Fruits* (1916), Albert L. Whiting's *Soil Biology* (1917), F. S. Harris' *Soil Alkali* (1920), and Andrew C. McCandlish's *Feeding of Dairy Cattle* (1922). As the requirements became evident in farm production and management areas, appropriate textbooks were made available. After Downing's death, eighteen books were published in the field of horticulture alone. From 1904 to 1924 many titles were published in such categories as soil technology and management, crop and animal production, pest control, and farm buildings. During this period specialized textbooks were devoted to the principles of animal nutrition, to dairy technology, and to the economic factors in agriculture.

Agriculture in the twenties was rapidly becoming an enterprise in which the sciences of farming were widely used. Knowledge of the mysterious forces of life, functioning in an environment of soil, water, air, and sunshine in relation to the production of food and fiber products enabled farmers to grow in efficiency and to serve better the needs of the nation. The green plant was being recognized as the finest chemical factory on earth. The role of plants in the satisfaction of man's primary needs was considered to be unequaled by any other resource of nature. Gaining from the ever-growing resources of research, from expanding educational services, from mechanization and specialization in production, and from a government that provides those services that the people cannot have for themselves, American agriculture has become the wonder of the modern world. To provide suitable books in these important areas has long been a Wiley objective.

In 1924 an agricultural college series was established under the editorship of Jacob G. Lipman, dean of the New Jersey College of Agriculture. Lipman was an international authority in the field of soil microbiology. In the journal, *Soil Science*, which he founded and of which he was editor until his death, he erected an imperishable monument to himself. He showed good judgment in the choice of collaborators worthy of great responsibility and with high reputation in agricultural research. Among the twenty books that he edited prior to his death in 1939 were such important textbooks as Firman E. Bear's *Soil Management* (1924), Donald F. Jones's *Genetics in Plant and Animal Improvement* (1924), Henry F. Judkins' *Principles of Dairying* (1924), Roscoe R. Snapp's *Beef Cattle* (1925), Laurence M. Winters' *Animal Breeding* (1925), Bernard W. Hammer's *Dairy Bacteriology* (1928), and Selman A. Waksman and Robert L. Starkey's *Soil and the Microbe* (1931).

The growth of the dairy industry, with its increasing utilization of heat and refrigeration, and with its numerous mechanical processes for the production of an expanding variety of dairy products, was the impetus for a number of Wiley books. G. L. McKay and C. Larsen's *Principles and Practices of Butter-Making* in 1906 was followed in 1913 by Larsen and White's *Dairy Technology;* in 1923 by Ernest Kelly and Clarence E. Clement's *Market Milk;* in 1925 by John T. Bowen's *Dairy Engineering;* in 1928 by Atsushi Miyawaki's *Condensed Milk;* in 1928 by Grover D. Turnbow and Lloyd A. Raffetto's *Ice Cream;* in 1942 by Arthur W. Farrall's *Dairy Engineering;* and in 1948 by Everett L. Fouts and Theodore R. Freeman's *Dairy Manufacturing Processes.* A common problem of most of these authors was stated by Farrall when he wrote that his purpose was to "bring together data concerning the engineering phases of the dairy industry, in a simple and concise manner, understandable by the practical plant operator and also by the student of the dairy industry who has not had the benefit of a technical engineering training. . . . The treatment [is] from the standpoint of the operator and student rather than from that of the designer of dairy equipment."

Still another series that should be mentioned is the one that was headed until his death in 1953 by James E. Rice of Cornell, known for decades as the dean of poultry science. Five books appeared in the series. The first was Earl W. Benjamin's *Marketing Poultry Products* in 1923, a fifth edition of which is now in preparation. Two books—Morley A. Jull's *Poultry Breeding* (1932) and Gustave F. Heuser's *Feeding Poultry* (1946)—were revised in 1952 and 1955 respectively.

In 1807, when Charles Wiley started his business, ten out of every eleven people lived on farms. The farmer was concerned chiefly with feeding and clothing his family. Today each farmer feeds his family and sixteen other persons. Each farmer gets more from each unit of operation. Since 1910, the Department of Agriculture estimates, farmers have got 34 per cent more crops per acre, 54 per cent more products per animal, and an amazing 126 per cent more output per hour of work. Increased efficiency per unit and per man is the challenge of modern agriculture. Farms are growing larger, but they are fewer in number. In the last thirty-five years the percentage of persons living on farms (in relation to total population) has decreased from 30.1 to 13.8 per cent. For the same period, the farm population has decreased from 32.0 to 22.0 millions. Fewer persons produce an adequate abundance for all our people. Farm efficiency, more than ever, requires adequate training, and teachers, students, and operators need technical books geared to specific requirements.

As early as 1880 the urgent need to provide courses in agriculture in secondary schools was recognized. The next thirty-seven years marked a formative period in developing such courses in rural high schools and in separate agricultural schools. Then in 1917 Congress passed the Smith-Hughes Act, promoting and aiding a nation-wide vocational education program of less than college grade. Instruction in agriculture as an important phase of this program has increased rapidly, with the latest available records showing 10,000 high school centers with 6.5 per cent employing two or more teachers. The enrollment of high school youth in the courses is nearly 500,000, and the enrollment of adults is well over 300,000. Mindful of the needs of such an expanding group for textbooks, Wiley in 1918 organized the Wiley Farm Series, and secured as editors Arthur K. Getman and Carl E. Ladd. With an understanding of the learning requirements of farm youth, these experienced teachers believed that the study of agriculture would cultivate the minds and interests of students as effectively as other subjects in the curriculum. They helped authors to center teaching materials about management "decisions" and creative "doing" activities of students. The twenty-six textbooks of this series, covering nearly every area of interest to farm youth, were destined to play a vital role in developing effective agricultural teaching throughout the nation. As an offshoot of the series a new group of books in vocational agriculture is currently under way to serve the needs of students in the southern states. It is significant that of the six Wiley books on agriculture selected by the United States Armed Forces Institute (USAFI), four were books in the Wiley Farm Series.

Of these many agricultural books, mostly textbooks and specialized treatments, published since Downing's historic book in 1841, none have been of national interest. They are usually reviewed learnedly and modestly in journals of limited circulation; but in June of 1953 Wiley "made" the *New Yorker*, when Alexis L. Romanoff, his wife, Anastasia, and their book, *The Avian Egg*, were the subject of two profiles in that magazine. It would be pleasant to report that sales of the book immediately skyrocketed, but the fact is that the book continued to sell at its usual modest pace.

New technical knowledge, improved power equipment, better management, the increasing need for competence for farm operators, farm co-operatives and farm service agencies, and expanded opportunities and enrollments in schools and colleges for the study of agriculture, will require the continuous publication of new books in all the areas of agriculture.

ARTHUR K. GETMAN

Technology on the Farm

Books on Agricultural Engineering

THE CONTINENT-SPANNING GROWTH of the United States drew much of its strength from advances in agricultural productivity. Few developments in American history were more important than farmers' adoption, in the nineteenth century, of animal-powered implements with which hundreds of millions of acres of virgin land were put under the plow and their crops harvested by labor-saving machines. These new machines made it possible to turn out sufficient food and fiber for the rapidly growing population and a considerable surplus for export, while releasing larger and larger percentages of the total working population to manufacturing, commerce, and the professions.

These early farm machines were not derived, however, from scientific research and engineering projects commensurate with their importance. They were largely empirical developments—the products of inventors—and, frequently, the foundations of small local manufacturing enterprises. Similarly, while artistry and skill were incorporated in farm barns, these buildings, at least in the nineteenth century, had little benefit from engineering with respect to their structural elements and still less in relation to their functions.

Scientific inquiry and experimentation led American agriculture, for a century or more, from one advance to another. During that time, however, comparatively little scientific investigation was applied to the mechanical equipment and structures used in farming. The agricultural colleges and experiment stations were generally dominated by men trained in and interested in crops, fertilizers, plant pathology, livestock, and related biological and chemical fields. But in relation to the *work* of agriculture—which has always absorbed a very large percentage of the nation's workers, physical facilities, and energy resources—collegiate interests and teaching were largely practical and vocational.

The advancing biological sciences and their allied fields have been served through the years by the Wiley books discussed in the chapter on agriculture. In contrast, in the whole area, which may be broadly characterized as the province of "agricultural engineering," Wiley published nothing during the first half of its one-hundred-and-fifty-year history, but neither did other publishers. With the publication in 1874 of G. H. Andrews' *Agricultural Engineering*, Wiley foreshadowed, in title at least, a field in which it was to achieve a position of outstanding professional service three-quarters of a century later.

Animal power dominated American agriculture through the first quarter of the twentieth century. But tractors, borrowing much in development and manufacture from the automotive industry, began displacing horses and mules in significant numbers about 1910. Signalizing the growing interest in internal combustion engines as sources of farm power, C. F. Hirshfeld and T. C. Ulbricht's *Gas Engines for the Farm* was brought out in 1913. Frederick A. Wirt followed in 1917 with *A Laboratory Manual in Farm Machinery*, intended, as the author wrote, to "lead the students to draw their own conclusions as to which machines are best adapted to the various agricultural conditions . . . with emphasis on operation and adjustment rather than on construction."

The spread of vocational agricultural training in rural high schools, coinciding with the rapid adoption of power-driven machinery on American farms, created a need for suitable textbooks. The first Wiley book in this area was *Farm Machinery*, by Byron B. Robb and Frederick G. Behrends, published in 1924. Two widely used textbooks by Archie A. Stone, *Farm Machinery* (1928) and *Farm Tractors* (1932), followed a few years later. Between 1930 and 1939, Wiley developed the areas of farm mechanics and farm utilities essentially for vocational agricultural high school use in M. A. Sharp and W. M. Sharp's *Principles of Farm Mechanics*, Forrest B. Wright's *Electricity in the Home and on the Farm*, and *Rural Water Supply and Sanitation*.

On a more advanced level, but still characterized primarily by vocational and practical rather than scientific and theoretical interests, was a Wiley publication of 1931. *Agricultural Machinery*, by the eminent J. Brownlee Davidson, served well for twenty years "the needs of those who expect to use and manage agricultural machinery." Recognizing that many users of the book would not have a chance to study the subjects elsewhere, Davidson included "a survey . . . of certain phases of mechanics, mechanics of materials, materials used in the construction of machines, and the elements of machine design." With a more recent book, Ben D. Moses and Kenneth R. Frost's *Farm Power* (1952), Wiley continues to meet the needs of college students in agriculture. These authors attempt to bring to readers without engineering training an understanding of the principles involved in Diesel and Otto cycle engines by treating fundamentals relating to power, work, energy, electricity, and combustion.

W. A. Foster and Deane G. Carter produced the descriptive, non-theoretical *Farm Buildings* (1922) for the agricultural student and the worker interested in farm structures, production buildings, and farm housing. This treatment was sustained through several revisions and in the 1954 successor book, Carter's *Farm Buildings*.

In Wilbur L. Powers and Thomas A. Teeter's *Land Drainage* (1922) and Orson W. Israelsen's *Irrigation Principles and Practices* (1932) Wiley more closely approached an engineering science treatment. Nonetheless, these books, like their contemporaries, were developed primarily from the agricultural standpoint as combination textbooks for students of general agriculture and reference books for landowners and farmers.

Descriptive, non-technical treatments of the engineering phases of agriculture failed, though, to satisfy the need for books designed to meet the requirements of the growing profession of agricultural engineering. An extensive technical literature of increasingly meritorious quality had developed, but it

WILLIAM O. WILEY
President, 1925–1941
Chairman of the Board, 1941–1956

was scattered widely in engineering and scientific journals and in state and federal government bulletins. In some of the agricultural colleges, desirable curricula had been established for training *agricultural* engineers. Professional development, and even the accreditation of curricula by the Engineers' Council for Professional Development, however, were being retarded by lack of textbooks adequate for training students seeking degrees in agricultural engineering.

The need for new books had become acute and widely recognized by 1945, but little hope was seen for their development. Qualified authors were few and were generally heavily loaded with teaching or research responsibilities. Moreover, the apparent market for professional textbooks, as contrasted with the demand for the applied or vocational books, seemed too limited to induce authorship in these unexplored areas.

This situation was brought in 1945 to the attention of the Ferguson Foundation of Detroit, which responded by establishing a project for the development of the needed books. This foundation project was unique, it is believed, in its plan for preparation of a series of books, designed as a group, to provide a scholarly, rigorously scientific base for an entire profession. These books were aimed primarily at the needs and capabilities of students who, having completed their training in basic engineering and part of basic agriculture, were ready for options in agricultural engineering.

Early in this program the Foundation had determined that, through working with one publisher, the planning of all projected textbooks could develop with sufficient interrelation of subject matter to avoid undesirable duplications. As collaborators in an over-all project, authors would benefit from their mutual experiences. Wiley's leadership in other branches of engineering, coupled with their interest and encouragement in this, led the Ferguson Foundation to choose this house.

Responsibility for manuscript preparation was in two stages. After considerable investigation, the Foundation arranged with interested institutions for the preparation of satisfactory manuscripts by a senior author and one to three co-authors, the bulk of the work being done by a full-time junior author. During manuscript development, the Foundation subsidized publication of limited trial editions for use in classes and distribution to interested teachers and engineers in industry. In addition to the improvements resulting from these trial runs, updating of concepts was furthered by authors' visits to research engineers in colleges, industry, and the United States Department of Agriculture. After sufficient work had been done to determine both the quality of the manuscript and the respective contributions of the authors, and to guarantee that the Foundation's purpose had been accomplished, Wiley made contracts with the authors. Normal publisher-author relations then were established.

The books resulting from Foundation sponsorship, under the direction of H. E. Pinches, have been published by Wiley as the Ferguson Foundation Agricultural Engineering Series. In the order of their appearance, they are: H. J. Barre and L. L. Sammet's *Farm Structures* (1950); E. L. Barger, W. M. Carleton, Eugene McKibben, and Roy Bainer's *Tractors and Their Power Units* (1952); S. M. Henderson and R. L. Perry's *Agricultural Process Engineering* (1955); R. K. Frevert, G. O. Schwab, T. W. Edminster, and K. K. Barnes's *Soil and Water Conservation Engineering* (1955); Bainer, R. A. Kepner, and Barger's *Principles of Farm Machinery* (1955). At the time of this writing (in 1956), the sixth volume in this series is being prepared to cover the engineering aspects of agricultural applications of electricity.

Although these books are the personal products of the authors—and their properties and continuing responsibilities under standard author-publisher contracts—they are also the significant results of "commissions." Sponsorship by the Ferguson Foundation, its selection of authors, and acceptance of responsibility by the collaborating universities set in motion a sufficient aggregation of qualified men and adequate resources to complete the project in little more than a decade. As a result, Wiley may say, with conviction and justifiable pride: "Here at last is a series of books of high quality, all up to date, developed by recognized and carefully chosen leaders in their respective phases of agricultural engineering, suitable for professional training in that field, stressing analysis and fundamental principles rather than descriptive and vocational interests."

This "institutional" approach has demonstrated one successful solution of the problem of producing adequate textbooks for sound professional training in a developing branch of engineering—books not forthcoming from the ordinary stimuli to authors, and for lack of which the advance of the profession had been faltering.

HAROLD E. PINCHES

The Home Front

Books on Home Economics

FROM THE BEGINNING OF CIVILIZATION, man built his culture around the institution of the family. Upon this family unit he based his economy, his religion, his education, and his recreational activities. With the advent of the industrial revolution, however, came the dispersal of family-centered activities and interests. Instead of home production and consumption of the essential material goods, specialization and factory-manufactured products gained ascendancy. Although many men left the farm for the factory, of far greater importance to the home was the entrance into industry, by choice or by necessity, of many wives and mothers. In addition, changes brought to the home by industry rendered much of the mother's teaching inadequate. Home economics as a study in the curriculum dates from this period. Educators and other far-sighted citizens, realizing that girls were not learning in the home the skills needed to feed, clothe, and house a family, encouraged supplementing homemaking skills at school. With assistance gained from the physical, biological, and social sciences, home economics has developed into a science that attempts to solve some of the problems of the decentralized family.

The development of home economics to its present status began with educational programs in the elementary schools that later spread through all academic levels, from the nursery school to the graduate school. Wiley entered the home economics field several decades after the company's founding with a book aimed at instruction in elementary schools. Miss Lambert's *Handbook of Needlework* (1842) encouraged teaching of hand sewing, since the only equipment needed was a kit containing needles, thread, and a thimble.

Although Wiley had published in 1814 the *Universal Recipe Book*, by a Society Gentleman of New York, explorations into the area of food preparation were hindered by lack of equipment in the early schools. State and national legislation, however, aided the expansion of this new field, and in 1862 national legislation was passed encouraging the development of home economics in the land-grant colleges. Other colleges, both state and private, introduced programs of varying lengths, each with the purpose of preparing young women to be better homemakers. These pioneers emphasized the urgent need for pamphlets, leaflets, and books as the field expanded. To meet this demand, Wiley published *Cost of Food* (1901), by Ellen H. Richards (the founder of home economics) and John F. Norton, followed in 1902 by Richards and Louise H. Williams' *The Dietary Computer*.

A survey of the books available for home economics students in the latter part of the nineteenth and early years of the twentieth century reveals the elementary nature of much of the literature. These publications dealt mainly with recipes and skills in the preparation of food, with pattern making and skills in sewing, and with the rudiments of sanitation. With the founding in 1908 of the American Home Economics Association, however, a more concerted effort was made to raise the level of the literature. During the years from 1914 to 1956, Wiley has contributed over fifty titles in this field, encompassing food and nutrition, the economics of household production, clothing and textiles, child development, and the many facets of the home.

Perhaps the most important single activity of the home economist centers around the selection, preparation, and storage of food, and Wiley has published much in this area. In 1917 the third edition of Richards' *Cost of Food* was published, followed in 1925 by the second edition of Mary T. Dowd and Jean D. Jameson's *Food: Its Composition and Preparation.* The year 1932, however, was a landmark in the field of foods and nutrition. Marion D. Sweetman's *Food Preparation* and Belle Lowe's *Experimental Cookery*, published in that year, have recently appeared in fourth editions. Alice M. Child and Kathryn B. Niles' *Food Preparation Studies* and *Food Preparation Recipes*, the culmination of years of experience in the field of experimental cookery, were introduced in 1932. Florence B. King's *Manual for Food Preparation Study* followed in 1933, and Dowd and Alberta Dent's *Elements of Foods and Nutrition* in 1937. In 1943, *Feeding Babies and Their Families*, by Helen Monsch and Marguerite Harper, was made available. Three years later, problems and solutions were discussed in *Good Food and Nutrition* (1946) by Edna P. Amidon, Dorothy E. Bradbury, and Vivian V. Drenckhahn, followed in 1947 by the practical *Recipes for Two*, by Mary Lou Glass. The advent of the home freezer, and the rapid increase in food-storage facilities, made possible Willis A. Gortner, Frederick S. Erdman, and Nancy K. Masterman's *Principles of Food Freezing* (1948).

Since members of a typical family eat one or more meals outside the home each day, dissemination of nutritional information to public eating places and institutions has grown to great importance. In 1937 Sina F. Fowler and Bessie B. West's *Food for Fifty*, now in its third edition, provided information on carefully tested institutional formulas for food serving and cooking classes. West and Le Velle Wood followed the next year with *Food Service in Institutions*, giving information on food planning, preparation, and organization in institutions.

In the study of food preparation, Wiley did not overlook the necessity of correct and gracious serving of these dishes. *Practical Cookery* (now in its twenty-second edition), by the Home Economics Department of the Kansas State College, combines food preparation with etiquette and service of the table. Wiley had not overlooked etiquette before, however, for in 1935 Mary Perin Barker brought out two books, *Good Manners for Young Women* and *The Technique of Good Manners*.

In conjunction with the development of food and nutrition, Wiley's publications in the textile field indicate the close alliance of the home economist with other scientists. Although many of the textile books deal with textile chemistry, Wiley has published books of more general application. Early publications in the area, such as Ernest Tompkins' *The Science of Knitting* (1914), Ethel H. Traphagen's *Costume Designing* (1918), and Edith Young's *Fashion Drawing* (1919), covered methods of using textiles. Our present-day

EDWARD P. HAMILTON
Chairman of the Board

information about textiles, however, is more advanced than it was a few decades ago. After the 1937 publication of Eda A. Jacobsen and Helen E. McCullough's *Fundamentals of Textiles: A Workbook*, the basic facts relative to the intelligent selection and use of textiles were covered in Mary Evans and Ellen B. McGowan's *A Guide to Textiles* (1939). More recently, Lucy D. Taylor's *Know Your Fabrics* (1951) represents an expert's study of upholstery and drapery fabrics. In 1943 Wiley brought fashion up to date with Grace M. Morton's *The Arts of Costume and Personal Appearance* (now in its second edition), followed the next year by Marion Featherstone and Dorothy Maack's *Elementary Costume Design*. Henrietta Thompson and Lucille Rea's *Clothing for Children* (1949) emphasized the importance of clothing comfort and durability for the child's physical health and personality development.

Each of these areas is interrelated with the entire problem of housing and with equipping and furnishing the home. House plans affect the choice of equipment needed, and both direct the selection of furnishings. In 1934 Louise Peet and Lenore Sater's *Household Equipment* emphasized the fundamental principles governing the selection, operation, and care of household equipment. Now in its fourth edition, this book gives special attention to those automatic features that greatly reduce the homemaker's expenditure of time and energy. Anna Rutt's *Home Furnishing*, published in 1935, was designed to develop good judgment in the selection and arrangement of furnishings. Deane G. Carter and Keith H. Hinchcliff's *Family Housing* (1949) discusses basic plans for houses. *The House for You* (1948), by Catharine and Harold Sleeper, is aimed at the needs of those people planning to build, rent, or buy a house. For the finer touches in the home and in dress, Doris Cox and Barbara Warren's *Creative Hands* (1945), now in its second edition, stresses the use of design, color, and materials in creating beautiful and useful objects during leisure time.

As modifications in food, clothing, and housing have been reflected in Wiley's publications, so have the variations in household management been shown. The changing social order has greatly altered the responsibilities of the homemaker. Margaret Reid in *Economics of Household Production* (1934) emphasized the home as a productive unit in society, since it is an integral part of our whole economic system. Jessie V. Coles analyzed the problem of the consumer in *The Consumer-Buyer and the Market* (1938). In Margaret R. Goodyear and Mildred C. Klohr's *Managing for Effective Living* (1954), the individual approach to solving problems was stressed. Paulena Nickell and Jean M. Dorsey in *Management in Family Living* (1942), now in its second edition, centered their attention on management or decision-making factors in homemaking.

The teacher's needs in meeting these new problems are discussed by Ivol Spafford in *Fundamentals in Teaching Home Economics* (1935) and *A Functioning Program of Home Economics* (1940). Spafford's philosophy sees education as worth while only as it "promotes the growth of the individual in all areas of living." As a science that works toward solving the problems of personal and family living, home economics is of great importance. Two levels of home economics education have been discussed in L. Belle Pollard's *Adult Education in Homemaking* (1939) and Elizabeth Stevenson's *Home and Family Life Education in Elementary Schools* (1946). Catherine Landreth's *Education of the Young Child* (1942), although written for the nursery-school teacher, also helps parents to carry out their responsibilities.

In such a brief summary not all publications can be included, but it gives a sampling of the contribution that Wiley has made to the development of home economics by encouraging capable authors to meet the changing needs of teachers in this broad field. To serve the field with needed textbooks and reference books is a sizable undertaking involving a responsibility to note the changes in the duties of the homemaker as teacher, producer, consumer, and citizen in an ever-changing environment.

WYLLE B. MCNEAL

The Realm of Behavior

Books on Psychology

"WHAT IS MAN THAT THOU ART MINDFUL OF HIM?" has deep spiritual significance. Scholars, however, from early times have been very mindful of man. The early Greek writers were, indeed, occupied with what today are considered psychological problems. Anaxagoras tried to explain change in terms of mind as an agent of movement. Socrates, Plato, and Aristotle made wise statements about mental processes, but their method was rationalistic rather than observational.

In the Middle Ages there was a theological slant to the inquiries into the nature of mind, but from the beginning of the Renaissance the study of mind took on a more empirical tone. The greatest of the men of this period was Descartes, who showed that nervous and muscular action was caused by stimulation of the sense organs, and who contributed a concept of reflexes that is basic today for a physiological explanation of behavior. Leibnitz was concerned with the relation of mind and body and with the degrees of clearness of mental processes. In England there were Hobbes and the empiricists. Hobbes thought that self-interest and fear were the central points of human action.

Locke, who followed Hobbes, was concerned with perception and thought. About the middle of the eighteenth century the association of ideas was the great principle of thought among the English and Scottish philosophers, but associationism was not popular in Germany until the time of Herbart. In France, Condillac's influence was considerable, especially in the field of education.

Thus far we have been dealing principally with the philosophers, but Kepler, Galileo, and Newton had vitalized the development of scientific research, which eventually had a beneficial effect upon modern psychology. In the meantime, however, false starts had been made, an outstanding one being phrenology, as developed by Gall. Closely related to this interest was the judgment of character and personality through facial expressions, a pseudo-scientific pursuit still popular among certain sections of the public. Gall published his "Introduction to a Course in the Physiology of the Brain" in 1808, and in 1818 Charles Wiley published what could be called the first Wiley book in psychology, Johann Casper Lavater's *The Science of Physiognomy.* It was not until twenty-six years later that other so-called psychological books appeared on their list. François Fauvel-Gouraud's *Mnemotechnic Dictionary* appeared in 1844 and his *Phreno Mnemotechny*, a treatise on the mental processes of memory, in 1845. In 1848 J. S. Grimes' *Compendium of the Phreno-Philosophy of Human Nature* was published. It was a textbook on "mental philosophy," as psychology was called at that time.

Then there was a great lapse while Wiley concentrated on books in engineering and other sciences. But scientific psychology was developing rapidly, inspired by the work of some of the great physicists of the time. Thomas Young in England formulated a theory of color vision that was supported by the German physicist Helmholtz. Helmholtz himself contributed not only to color vision but also to auditory phenomena. Johannes Müller presented his theory of the specific energy of nerves, E. H. Weber made contributions to the physiology of the sense organs, Fechner started to write in the lucrative field of psycho-physics, his main purpose being to find a mathematical expression of the relation of mind and body, and M. J. P. Flourens in his work on the brains of pigeons once and for all proved that there are not clear-cut areas in the brain for its various functions. These are only a few of the great names connected with the birth of modern scientific psychology, in which Wiley eventually became interested. The development of scientific psychology, as has been seen, was gradual, but a date to remember is 1879, when Wundt founded the first psychological laboratory at Leipzig. From this time experimental psychology, both quantitative and qualitative, developed rapidly, especially in Germany and America.

For many years William James' "Principles of Psychology" was the standard textbook. Titchener's books, which were a development of Wundt's psychology, succeeded the "Principles," and when behaviorism became popular J. B. Watson's textbooks ran parallel with Titchener's. There followed many other books stressing either introspective or behavioristic theory.

In the early thirties H. P. Weld of Cornell suggested to a Wiley representative that psychology had amassed a great many data from psychological laboratories and it was time for a textbook written on a high scientific level by a group of experts and eclectic as to methods and principles. Wiley, therefore, decided to re-enter the psychological field. E. G. Boring, of Harvard, H. S. Langfeld, of Princeton, and H. P. Weld were appointed editors, and nineteen contributors, including the editors, were selected. The result was *Psychology: A Factual Textbook*, published in 1935. In 1937 *A Manual of Psychological Experiments*, by the editors and contributors, and a *Workbook*, by Carl Wedell, were published to accompany the textbook. At first there were doubts whether such an original textbook with a different author for each chapter would not seem very disjointed, to the confusion of the student. The editors, it proved, had been able to unify the text; the book read very smoothly and was a success from the beginning. In 1939 a second edition was published. It had been so thoroughly revised and so many of the contributors had been changed that it was given a new name: *Introduction to Psychology*. In 1948 a second revision was published and the title was again changed, this time to *Foundations of Psychology*. All three editions continue to be sold in spite of their being considered difficult textbooks. They are known among psychologists as BLW and are accepted as authoritative textbooks.

The BLW textbooks were directed toward the more advanced student who desired to learn the basic facts of mental processes. In 1955 Wiley published *An Introduction to Psychology*, by Harry W. Karn of Carnegie Institute of Technology and Joseph Weitz of the Life Insurance Agency Management Association. It by-passes physiology and sensory psychology, contains suggestions for application of facts, and is written on a more popular level, especially for junior colleges.

One of the oldest problems we have in psychology is motivation; what are the drives and purposes in man's activity? In 1936 Wiley published P. T. Young's *Motivation of Behavior: The Fundamental Determinants of Human and Animal Activity.* The problem has gained in importance with the development of psychological research, and Young's book has remained a classic in the field. A section of the book is devoted to the emotions, a subject that has been given much attention by philosophers and psychologists ever since Galen's exposition in the second century of his theory of the four "humors." In 1943 Wiley published Young's *Emotion in Man and Animal*, which brought up to date much of the material of his first book.

Rather closely related to the emotions and motivation is the study of personality, a subject on which psychologists have been very actively engaged. Howard Brand in 1954 edited *A Study of Personality: A Book of Readings*, which contains excerpts from the writings of thirty-one authorities. For many years there was a need for an eclectic textbook that would delineate the major theories of personality, a need that was met in 1957 by the publication of *Theories of Personality*, by Gardner Lindzey and Calvin S. Hall.

If we look at the history of social psychology, we find that the spark came from the writings of Tarde, Le Bon, Ross, whose book was the first to have the title "Social Psychology," and William McDougall, who gave the study a new direction. Wiley first entered this field in 1938 with Daniel Katz and Richard L. Schanck's *Social Psychology*, which contained, besides a section on the fundamental scientific aspects of social studies, a section on personality. This book was followed in 1941 by Hadley Cantril's *The Psychology of Social Movements*, which presented an analysis of such social phenomena as the Oxford Group and the Nazi Party. In 1947 appeared Muzafer Sherif and Cantril's *The Psychology of Ego-Involvements: Social Attitudes and Identification.* M. Brewster Smith, Jerome S. Bruner, and Robert W. White were the authors of *Opinions and Personality*, published in 1956, a book that pointed up a new and important approach to research in social and clinical psychology. It was of inherent interest to political scientists as well, an interdisciplinary study representative of a significant trend in publishing in the nineteen-fifties.

The backbone of scientific psychology has always been what is generally spoken of as physiological and experimental psychology. Wiley can feel proud of the books it has published in this fundamental field. In 1938 S. Smith Stevens' *Hearing: Its Psychology and Physiology* appeared. This book shows a new approach to the subject and a great advance from the work on audition by Helmholtz, owing in part to the development of the electronic vacuum tube, which has made possible the amplification of small potentials. Ernest G. Wever, because of his discovery (in collaboration with C. W. Bray) of the nature of the impulses of the auditory nerve and his years of experimentation on the function of the ear, has become an internationally known authority on hearing. Wiley, therefore, was glad to be able to publish in 1949 Wever's *Theory of Hearing*. In 1905 W. Nagel published the third volume of his "Handbuch der Physiologie des Menschen." This book was for many years not only useful to physiologists but was also an absolute necessity for experimental psychologists. In 1951 S. S. Stevens edited a *Handbook of Experimental Psychology*, which is composed of contributions from thirty-four of the top authorities in their respective fields. It will be even more valuable to the present-day psychologists than was Nagel's "Handbuch" to the scientists of a past era. F. A. Geldard's *The Human Senses*, published in 1953, will undoubtedly remain a classic. The great need of a book on methodology in the training of students in experimental psychology prompted T. G. Andrews to publish in 1948 his *Methods in Psychology*.

The history of child psychology might be said to go back to the Renaissance, but the first modern book on the subject was Preyer's "The Mind of the Child," which appeared in Germany in 1881. Since then an enormous amount of research has been done on the subject, and the results have been brought together in the monumental *Manual of Child Psychology*, edited by Leonard Carmichael, who is now head of the Smithsonian Institution. It was published in 1946, with a list of probably the most authoritative contributors that could be found. A second enlarged and revised edition appeared in 1954.

Clinical psychology and the psychology of adjustment have a long history. Breuer and Freud at the beginning of the century gave the study of these topics a great impetus, and the problems appearing among the soldiers of the first World War opened the eyes of scientists still more to the importance of these practical subjects. Among other interests was a growing concern for the mental health of students. In 1941 Wiley published Fred McKinney's

W. BRADFORD WILEY
President

Psychology of Personal Adjustment: Students' Introduction to Mental Hygiene. A second revised edition appeared in 1949. The application of hypnotism grew out of Mesmer's work in the middle of the eighteenth century. About the middle of the nineteenth century Charcot of Paris, the teacher of Freud, used hypnotism to cure hysteria. This was the real start of the method. In 1953 Wiley published *Hypnotism: An Objective Study in Suggestibility*, by A. M. Weitzenhoffer, in 1954, Trygve Braatoy's *Fundamentals of Psychoanalytic Technique: A Fresh Appraisal of the Methods of Psychotherapy*, and, in 1956, William E. Henry's *The Analysis of Fantasy.*

Shortly before the first World War Hugo Münsterberg was foremost in opening up the vast field of applied psychology, especially in industry. The work of psychologists during this war hastened the development of the applied aspect of psychology. In 1935 Wiley published J. G. Jenkins' *Psychology in Business and Industry: An Introduction to Psychotechnology;* in 1942 H. R. DeSilva's *Why We Have Automobile Accidents;* in 1949 *Applied Experimental Psychology: Human Factors in Engineering Design*, by Alphonse Chapanis, W. R. Garner, and C. T. Morgan, a book based in large part on the results of experiments conducted during the second World War; and in 1952 *Principles of Human Relations: Applications to Management*, by N. R. F. Maier. Additional publications in this field in 1956 were Ross Stagner's *Psychology of Industrial Conflict* and Anne Roe's *The Psychology of Occupations.*

Psychologists concerned with the practical application of the results of their research soon learned that it was necessary to develop statistics for their particular purposes. This need was especially evident in the field of tests. In 1949 Wiley published R. L. Thorndike's *Personnel Selection: Test and Measurement Technique;* in the same year *Psychological Statistics*, by Quinn McNemar, followed by a revised edition of this very useful and popular book in 1955; in 1950 Harold Gulliksen's *Theory of Mental Tests;* in 1950 *Measurement and Evaluation in Psychology and Education*, by R. L. Thorndike and Elizabeth Hagen; and in 1955 *Stochastic Models for Learning*, by R. R. Bush and Frederick Mosteller. These titles reveal Wiley's growing concern with the fields of learning and educational psychology, an interest further reflected by the publication in 1956 of Henry Clay Lindgren's *Educational Psychology in the Classroom.*

Hand in hand with experimentation must go theoretical speculation. The first strictly theoretical book in psychology published by Wiley was J. G.

Miller's *Unconsciousness*, which appeared in 1942. D. O. Hebb's inspiring and widely discussed *Organization of Behavior: A Neuropsychological Theory* was published in 1949. Distinguished scientists, among whom were a number of the foremost psychologists, took part in the Hixon Symposium in 1948. The results of this symposium were edited by L. A. Jeffress and published by Wiley in 1951 under the title *Cerebral Mechanisms in Behavior*. The results of another symposium, the Kentucky Symposium, were published in 1954 under the title *Learning Theory, Personality Theory, and Clinical Research*. The science of "Cybernetics" has become popular since Norbert Wiener's book on that subject. W. R. Ashby's *Design for a Brain*, published by Wiley in 1952, shows the influence of Wiener's writings. In 1954 Floyd H. Allport's *Theories of Perception and the Concept of Structure* was one of the most widely discussed publications of the year. Similarly, in 1956, *A Study of Thinking* by Jerome S. Bruner, Jacqueline J. Goodnow, and George A. Austin opened up new avenues for research.

Wiley, as is evident from the foregoing list of publications, has contributed greatly in recent years to the development of psychology—the type of psychology that can take its place proudly among the other natural sciences.

HERBERT S. LANGFELD

Co-operative Publishing

Books of the Technology Press

In early April, 1937, Vannevar Bush, then Vice President and Dean of Engineering of the Massachusetts Institute of Technology, and Edward P. Hamilton, then Vice President and Treasurer of John Wiley and Sons, concluded an agreement between the Technology Press of the Massachusetts Institute of Technology and the Wiley firm that is rather unusual in the relations between universities and publishers. In the ensuing years this agreement has proved most effective. The Technology Press under this arrangement places most of its books in the hands of Wiley for manufacture and sale. The plan as originally set up has been modified and supplemented to keep pace with the changing times and with the considerable expansion of the range of interests of the Technology Press.

This pattern of co-operation was brought into being when the Department of Electrical Engineering at the Massachusetts Institute of Technology, under the stimulus of Edward L. Bowles and with the active encouragement of Vannevar Bush, launched a new approach to the teaching of electrical engineering together with a series of textbooks setting a new standard. The four

MARTIN MATHESON
Senior Vice President and Secretary

volumes issued as the Principles of Electrical Engineering Series continue in active demand: that on *Applied Electronics*, having undergone a thorough revision by Truman S. Gray, appeared in a second edition in 1954. Though the Electrical Engineering Series prompted the agreement between the Technology Press and Wiley, the first title to appear under the joint imprint was the *Wavelength Tables*, edited by Professor George R. Harrison and issued in 1939.

The Technology Press, established under the aegis of the *Technology Review*, of which James R. Killian, Jr., now President of the Institute, was then editor, issued its first independent title in 1932—"Textile Research," edited under the chairmanship of Edward R. Schwarz. Noteworthy among its other independent volumes are the "Handbook of Colorimetry," which appeared in 1936, having been edited under the direction of Arthur C. Hardy, and "When M.I.T. Was 'Boston Tech,' " by Samuel C. Prescott, published in 1954.

In recent years the program of the Technology Press, which is under the general direction of the Technology Press Board, with John E. Burchard, Dean of the School of Humanities and Social Studies, chairman, and under the specific operating direction of F. G. Fassett, Jr., has substantially widened. The Technology Press Board, it should be noted, was first appointed by Karl T. Compton in October, 1938; and of its present membership, Fassett and Ernest H. Huntress were members of the original group. The expansion of the lists of the Technology Press, particularly in the social sciences, has posed new and provocative problems that the co-operative plan has been able to handle with marked success and satisfaction.

F. G. FASSETT, JR.

Engineering at Work

The General Electric Series

When Wiley was founded, and for many years thereafter, most of the scholarship that resulted in technical and scientific books was a product of the colleges and universities.

It was in 1893 that Charles Proteus Steinmetz joined the infant General Electric Company, established the year before. Soon assuming an outstanding position in electrical engineering, he recognized the need of sharing his knowledge with others, and in 1897 wrote "Alternating Current Phenomena," the first of his notable series of books published by McGraw-Hill that did much to educate an older generation of electrical engineers.

Motives such as these were doubtless responsible for the first Wiley book by a General Electric author, published in 1917. It was *Hydro-Electric Power Stations*, by David B. Rushmore and Eric A. Lof, members of what was then called the Power and Mining Department of the General Electric Company. A substantial volume of 822 pages, it provided a valuable compilation of data in an important area then developing rapidly.

At that time the techniques of providing adequate illumination were being assembled into an independent branch of engineering, with the Company's lamp works and laboratories at Nela Park, in Cleveland, contributing importantly to this new field. In 1919, with their co-operation, an undergraduate course was inaugurated at Case School of Applied Science (now Case Institute of Technology). From the material used, a book was prepared, published by Wiley in 1925 as *Illuminating Engineering*, edited by Francis E. Cady, physicist in the General Electric Lighting Research Laboratory, and Henry B. Dates, professor of electrical engineering at Case. Of the ten contributors, seven were General Electric scientists or engineers. A second edition of this useful book appeared in 1928.

Thus it came to be realized that the industrial author had appeared; that industrial laboratories and engineering departments now rivaled the academic campus as a source of technical books on both theory and practice.

This fact is further illustrated by the history of the General Electric–Wiley series, which was begun in 1932 with Arthur L. Kimball's *Vibration Prevention in Engineering*, a book that gave full information in a field where little had been available before.

The long-range plan, developed at that time, recognized that publication of books by engineers in industry would advance the whole engineering art, by placing useful theories, knowledge, and experience within reach of students and teachers, in an up-to-date, compact, and convenient form. At the same time the books would give to practicing engineers, and to industry generally, a better understanding of new and improved types of modern equipment now at their disposal, so that they could be evaluated, selected, and utilized. Moreover, it was expected that these books would collect, in permanent reference form, the accumulated knowledge of practicing engineers, thereby providing a foundation for further advances by others.

Experience with the series has shown that these objectives have been realized in full measure. Robert E. Doherty and Ernest G. Keller's *Mathematics of Modern Engineering* (Volume 1, 1936; Volume 2, 1942) was planned to make widely available the educational textbooks employed in the Advanced Engineering Program at General Electric. In the same category are James F. Young's *Materials and Processes* (1944; second edition, 1954), and Edith Clarke's *Circuit Analysis of A-C Power Systems* (Volume 1, 1943; Volume 2, 1950).

William L. Healy and Arthur H. Rau's *Simplified Drafting Practice* (1953) has been an important aid toward increasing production with limited man power, by showing that engineering drawings could give necessary information clearly and unambiguously, even though containing far less detail than an older generation of draftsmen thought necessary.

Among books directed particularly toward practicing engineers are Louis F. Blume's *Transformer Engineering* (1938; second edition, 1951), Gerhart W. Heuman's *Magnetic Control of Industrial Motors* (1947; second edition, 1954), Selden B. Crary's *Power System Stability* (Volume 1, 1945; Volume 2, 1947), Harold Chestnut and Robert W. Mayer's *Servomechanisms and Regulating System Design* (Volume 1, 1951; Volume 2, 1955), H. F. Storm's *Magnetic Amplifiers* (1955), and I. F. Kinnard's *Applied Electrical Measurements* (1956). The books in this category are intended to aid users in understanding the attributes of various types of equipment, and in securing the greatest harmony in electrical systems composed of many varied elements.

The books by Gabriel Kron—*Tensor Analysis of Networks* (1939) and *Short Course in Tensor Analysis* (1942)—form a distinctive feature of the series, since they present his wide-ranging ideas for use of tensor theory in engineering calculations, thus forming the basis for a whole new area of engineering analysis.

Wiley has published a number of books by General Electric authors outside the series, several of the most important originating in the Company's Research Laboratory. Outstanding among them is one by the late Saul Dushman, a leading scientist whose warm personality enabled him to serve as an unofficial "dean of men" for the laboratory staff. In *Scientific Foundations of Vacuum Techniques* (1949) he produced a comprehensive study of all phases of achieving, maintaining, and measuring high vacua, for the scientific investigator and the practical engineer as well.

Eugene Rochow (now professor of chemistry at Harvard) was a member of the laboratory staff when he wrote his *Introduction to the Chemistry of the Silicones* (1946), thus sharing knowledge that he had gained as a pioneer student of these increasingly important compounds. Lewis R. Koller's *Ultraviolet Radiation* (1952) provides a useful summary of a field in which the author has worked for many years.

From other components of the General Electric Company have come such invaluable works as the Power Volume, twelfth edition, of Kent's *Mechanical Engineers' Handbook* (1950), edited by J. Kenneth Salisbury. Richard F. Shea's *Principles of Transistor Circuits* (1953) and *Transistor Audio Amplifiers* (1955) have shown how to apply these useful little devices, which can perform many functions of electron tubes with considerably less current.

Such contributions show that General Electric engineers as a group, and also individually, are keenly aware of the obligation expressed in the first section of the Engineer's Canons of Ethics: "The engineer will co-operate in extending the effectiveness of the engineering profession, by interchanging information and experience with other engineers and students, and by contributing to the work of engineering societies, schools and the scientific and engineering press."

JAMES STOKLEY

Of This and That

IN SCANNING THE LIST of books published by Wiley from its beginnings, we are impressed with the number of titles that do not fit any of the categories included in the nearly thirty comprising this book. Thus mention has not been made of many titles that, we know, were quite important and interesting in their day.

Authors of a century or more ago did not seem to have the same criteria for selecting a title for their books that writers do today. A number of titles give little idea of the contents, and since many of the topics are not familiar to the modern reader, the titles of these early books are strange and often picturesque, if not completely misleading. For instance, the title page of an 1817 Wiley book reads: *A Valedictory Delivered at the Forum on the 11th day of April 1817*. Since no copy is known to be in existence today, history will perhaps never know who gave the address, what it was about, or to what audience it was given. The prize Wiley title of all times is Samuel P. Mulliken's *A Method for the Identification of Pure Organic Compounds by a Systematic Analytical Procedure Based on Physical Properties and Chemical Reactions*, Volume I (1904).

How the bibliographers must have loved that one. Another book that has a confusing title is Park Benjamin's *Wrinkles and Recipes* (1875). At that time, the word "wrinkles" had probably a greater vogue than it has today. Now it is slang for a little trick or novelty, or it may mean an ingenious gadget. The book then comes closer to what the 1957 publisher would call "A Book of Formulas and Recipes."

For ages the great mystery of the pyramid has perplexed scholars the world over, but Robert Ballard obviously had what he thought was the answer, for his book is clearly titled *The Solution of the Pyramid Problem* (1882). What his solution was is not particularly important, for it did not seem to end the constant search. This book reminds us of the amicable vendetta that existed for years between Colonel Daniel Appleton, head of the house of D. Appleton and Company, and Major W. H. Wiley. Both Civil War veterans, they loved to play pranks on one another. The story comes down to us of a pseudo-scientist who called on Major Wiley with a manuscript about two and a half feet high on some title such as "Squaring the Circle." A crackpot, he discoursed for hour after hour on how he had solved the problem and, of course, wanted Wiley to publish the book. After squirming through this boring monologue, the Major finally got a word in by affirming complete confidence in his caller's work, but stating that this sort of book was not for Wiley but for another house. He was sure that his good friend, Colonel Appleton, would be glad to publish the book, etc., etc. The man went away happy. The next day the Major had a phone call from his friend, the Colonel, and the wires fairly sizzled with the Colonel's wrath. Of course, it wasn't long before the Major had one of Appleton's cast-offs with a similar manuscript. This sort of thing continued for many years, the two veterans enjoying the situation thoroughly.

Another phase of publishing, namely bibliography, seems to have interested John Wiley. During Charles Wiley's period there was no official systematic listing of the new books published. A previous listing service had stopped publication in the early part of the century. In 1820 the "Bibliotheca Americana" began its operations and continued to 1861. This was a highly regarded publication in the trade, and many efforts were made to revive it. Orville A. Roorbach, a Charleston bookseller, had given up his store in 1848 to work for Wiley and Putnam in their wholesale department. In 1858,

J. S. SNYDER
Vice President

J. S. BARNES
Vice President

Wiley and Halsted became his backers and issued an addenda to the *Bibliotheca Americana* to include listings from May, 1855, to March, 1858. It was then called *Roorbach's Bookseller's Medium.*

Still another former Wiley employee was to emerge as a bibliographer of note. James Kelly, born in County Tipperary, Ireland, succeeded Roorbach as the editor of the "American Book Catalogue." He was in charge of the Wiley and Halsted order department for most of the seventeen years he was with the firm. It was there he acquired the bibliographical knowledge and skill that was to lead a critic of his time to say of his two volumes of *The American Book Catalogue*, "Bibliographically Kelly's work was far superior to that of his predecessors in completeness and accuracy." Volume I appeared in 1866 and Volume II in 1871. The listings covered the period from January, 1861, to January, 1871. They were published under the imprint of John Wiley and Son.

We have seen from the article on civil engineering that much of this kind of engineering derived from the military. In fact, most of the authors of the early books were teachers at West Point, or army officers who had done outstanding professional work after their graduation from the Military Academy. It was quite natural that these men exerted considerable influence on American civil engineering until the end of the nineteenth century. The outstanding name in this group was unquestionably that of Dennis H. Mahan, professor of military and civil engineering in the United States Military Academy. All but a few of the great leaders of the Civil War on both sides absorbed their military and engineering knowledge from Mahan. He was the father of the great admiral, Alfred Thayer Mahan, and it was his influence that moved the son to do for naval strategy what the father had done for land operations. He had six books on the Wiley list, the earliest being *An Elementary Treatise on Advanced Guard Outposts and Detachment of Troops* (1847). His most important work, of course, was his *Military Engineering* (Part I, 1865; Part II, 1867). In 1891 the first edition of the Academy's *Ordnance and Gunnery* was issued. Sixty-six years later this title is still on the Wiley list. Henry Metcalfe started it, but the revisions came out periodically as needed—Laurence L. Bruff (1895); O. M. Lissak (1907); William H. Tschappat (1917); Earl McFarland (1929); and Thomas J. Hayes (1938). Second World War experience in ordnance is reflected in Theodore C. Ohart's *Elements of Ammunition* (1946), a book not in the West Point series mentioned above.

A number of Wiley books similarly came from the United States Naval Academy, beginning with Augustus P. Cooke's *Textbook of Naval Ordnance and Gunnery* (1875). However, one of the most distinguished books in this area was written by William F. Durand, then at Cornell. His book, *Resistance and Propulsion of Ships* (1898), was acclaimed as "a classic . . . a volume of brilliant analysis which for the first time rationalized design procedure, and affected the correlation of speed trial data with model test results by the use of non-dimensional parameters." Durand later went on to do notable work in hydrodynamic and aerodynamic theory. It seems a little like stretching the definition of the word classic, but that term has been applied many times to David W. Taylor's *The Speed and Power of Ships*, Volumes I and II (1910). Of interest is the fact that the David W. Taylor Model Basin, Carderock, Maryland, was named for this distinguished engineer. And while we are on the subject of service academies, it might be well to point out that Paul J. Kiefer was attached to the Postgraduate School of the United States Naval Academy when Kiefer and Milton C. Stuart's *Thermodynamics* was first published in 1930.

The record shows that Wiley published in its career over eighty books in religion, beginning in 1817 and ending in 1929. Books on this subject had a great vogue in Charles Wiley's day, and from the best-seller lists of today it would appear that interest still runs high. We know that John Wiley was a very religious man, who conducted evening devotions with his family up to the day of his death, so it is not surprising that during his regime he added some very important titles in this area. Leopold Ranke's *History of the Popes* is considered one of the standard publications of its kind and is still consulted for critical purposes. In the earlier years of the *Bibliotheca Sacra and Theological Review* this periodical formed one of the important, if not the most important, American periodicals for theological expression. William J. Conybeare's *Life and Epistles of St. Paul*, though now old, is considered standard and is frequently consulted by scholars. It is to be noted that it now sells in second-hand book dealers' lists for as much as ten and twelve dollars a set. Perhaps the tool that has had the most abiding worth is the *Englishman's Greek Concordance of the New Testament* and the *Englishman's Hebrew and Chaldee Concordance of the Old Testament*. These two titles, together with *Gesenius*, form a permanent contribution. The *Englishman's Greek Concordance of the New Testament* was used by the Committee that recently issued the revised standard version of the Bible. There is really no tool that quite takes its place. Perhaps among the titles listed, the one that had the most popular reception was J. P. Smyth's *How We Got Our Bible*, a small book that had great appeal. Two other titles on the list are conspicuous because of their distinguished authorship—François R. de Chateaubriand's *The Martyrs* (1815) and John Greenleaf Whittier's *The Supernaturalism of New England* (1847). Of interest to students of the Bible and of rare books is the part that John Wiley took in the most epoch-making single book purchase of his time. This was the Mazarin Bible (1450–1455), which he purchased for James Lenox, well-known rare book collector in 1847. As an expert in this field writes us, "All in all I would characterize the list which you sent me as fairly representative of American religious publications for the period indicated. While you have changed your field of interest for publication, I think that you need not have any misgivings about what your predecessors have done in the matter of publishing religious books."

At this stage in Wiley's career, it is difficult to realize that the firm once published a number of medical titles, some of which attained considerable success and prestige. The earliest one goes back to 1814, and the title, characteristic of the times, is a long one: *Syllabus of the Several Courses of Physicians and Surgeons of the University of the State of New York*. More than a century later, three important titles bore our imprint: Charles V. Chapin's *Sources and Modes of Infection* (1910); Martin H. Fischer's *Nephritis* (1911); and J. Rogues De-Fursac and Aaron J. Rosanoff's *Manual of Psychiatry* (1905). The last was revised from time to time by Rosanoff and is now in its seventh edition, having enjoyed a long and honorable career.

Of passing interest is the fact that in 1844 Wiley published a book by Bull called *Hints to Mothers during Pregnancy;* one hundred and two years later Wiley published its modern counterpart, but with the more imaginative title, *Modeling for Motherhood*, the work of Doris Heinz and Katherine Bolt.

In the mid-nineteenth century Wiley must have been in the midst of a current medical fad because in a span of only five years it published ten books on various phases of hydropathy. For moderns who think that psychosomatic medicine is something new, let it be recalled that in 1816 Charles Wiley published Peter S. Townsend's *Dissertation on the Influence of the Passion in the Production and Modification of Disease.*

Although the firm published a number of books on pharmacy, beginning with Green's *Selection from Favorite Prescriptions of Living American Practitioners*, the ones we recall best were Edsel A. Ruddiman's *Incompatibilities in Prescriptions* (1897) and *Whys in Pharmacy* (1906). The latter went out of print only a short time ago; the former is still doing well in its sixth edition. Dean Hugh Muldoon's *Lessons in Pharmaceutical Latin and Prescription Writing* (1916), now in its fourth edition (1946), is an example of longevity dear to the heart of a publisher.

It would appear that Charles Wiley was as much interested in the field of law as he was in medicine and religion. His very good friend, Chancellor James Kent, undoubtedly had a part in helping him to map out a program in this field—a fact that may explain the high quality of the few books he published in this area. William Ballentine's *Treatise on the Statute of Limitations* (1812) was well known in its time. An old standard, it ran into several editions. It was sufficiently important to be part of the library of the famous diplomat, lawyer, and chief justice of the United States, John Jay. *The New York Term Reports* (1813) are still a standard item necessary in a law library that aspires to reasonable completeness. *The Johnson Digest* (1815) was also a standard of its time that had several supplements. Joseph D. Fay's *A Disquisition on Imprisonment for Debt* (1818) is interesting because relatively little has been written on the subject. After the publication of George B. Cheever's books on *Capital Punishment* in 1846–1849, in their time standard books on this topic, Wiley published little or nothing on law until 1897, when the firm had definitely launched on its career in technical book publishing. An 1892 publication, Winthrop's *An Abridgement of Military Law*, was an exception. Through this book, a standard in the army for many years, Winthrop exerted an important influence in the development of military justice. Thereafter a number of books definitely related to the laws of technology were published, beginning with J. C. Wait's *Engineering and Architectural Jurisprudence* (1897), and running into the current period with Walter C. Sadler's *Legal Aspects of Engineering* (1940) and Melvin Nord's *Legal Problems in Engineering* (1956). Chester H. Biesterfeld's *Patent Law* of 1943, now in a second edition, is well regarded by the profession.

Vocational training has become a vital part of American life during the last fifty years. As early as 1848, Wiley was publishing books of a vocational nature. Some of the early books bear quaint titles, such as *Dyeing and Calico Printing* (1876), by F. Crace-Calvert. Several books on this subject parallel the development of the American clothing industry. Most of the Wiley books in this period were guides to efficiency or skill in a particular field like Stevens' *Art of House Painting* (1877), M. A. Gessert's *Glass Staining* (1874), Robert Grimshaw's *Saw Filing* (1882), and Svedelius' *Handbook for Charcoal Burners* (1874).

Early in the twentieth century, J. M. Jameson, at that time associated with Pratt Institute, became editor of a series of vocational books that dominated the field for several decades. It was Jameson who first interested William H. Timbie in writing his books on electricity. As noted elsewhere, these books were widely used, the total circulation passing the three-quarter million mark. Many of his books, regularly revised, are still on the Wiley list, notably *The Elements of Electricity* (1910), and *Essentials of Electricity* (1913). In Jameson's Wiley Technical Series were such long-lived titles as Joseph M. Jameson's *Elementary Practical Mechanics* (1909), Joseph C. Chase's *Decorative Design* (1915), C. F. Hirshfeld and T. C. Ulbricht's *Steam Power* (1916), Ernest Schwarzkopf's *Plain and Ornamental Forging* (1916), Frank S. Henry's *Printing for School and Shop* (1917), Ethel H. Traphagen's *Costume Design and Costume Illustration* (1918), Walter H. James and Malcolm C. Mackenzie's *Principles of Mechanism* (1918), Henry L. Nachman's *Elements of Machine Design* (1918), Mary T. Dowd and Jean D. Jameson's *Food: Its Composition and Preparation* (1918), Harry M. Keal and Clarence J. Leonard's *Mathematics for Electrical Students* (1921), Keal and Leonard's *Mathematics for Shop and Drawing Students* (1921), and Samuel Slade and Louis Margolis' *Mathematics for Technical and Vocational Schools* (1922).

After the first World War, with changed conditions and new requirements, John C. Wright, director of the Federal Board of Vocational Education, edited The Wiley Trade Series, a series of books that had an important part in the training of veterans, among which might be mentioned Wright's *Automotive Repair*, in four volumes, published between 1921 and 1923, Wright and Fred C. Smith's *Automotive Construction and Operation* (1924), Harrison C. Givens' *Blue Print Reading* (1924), Frank Cushman's *Mathematics and the Machinist's Job* (1925), and J. W. Barritt's *Care and Operation of Machine Tools* (1927).

The advent of the second World War led to a quickening of books in this area; in fact, it was difficult to keep up with the demand of the military services. Many books were published, a number solely because they were

FRANCIS LOBDELL

Vice President and Treasurer

WARREN SULLIVAN

Vice President

greatly needed and not because they were particularly good books that could meet normal peacetime publishing standards. During this period (1942–1944), of the more important titles published we should mention the following: James H. Suddeth's *Aircraft Engine Maintenance* (1942), John C. Butler's *Sheet Metal Theory and Practice* (1943), James V. Frost's *Fundamentals of Automotive Mechanics* (1943), Hubert G. Lesley's *Basic Airplane Mechanics* (1944), Roy W. Toliver's *Care and Use of Hand Tools* (1944), and John T. Shuman and Lewis H. Bardo's *How to Operate a Lathe* (1944).

The rapid growth and development of industrial arts and vocational education were reflected not only by the vast number of books of the kind mentioned above, but in the books published that were designed to orient teachers in the field and to teach them how to teach. In this area John C. Wright and Charles R. Allen's three books, particularly *Supervision of Vocational Education* (1926), F. Theodore Struck's *Creative Teaching* (1938), and *Vocational Education for a Changing World* (1945) were considered useful aids to teachers.

A number of language dictionaries have been published by Wiley. Dictionaries of English, French, Italian, Spanish, German, Latin, Hebrew, and Greek languages have been issued, as well as many dictionaries in specialized fields. Alfred Ewle's dictionaries of the English, Italian, and French languages, and Hamilton's dictionaries of the German, French, and English languages were well known during the latter part of the nineteenth century.

In the twentieth century, Wiley has confined itself in this area for the most part to technical subjects, thus publishing Austin M. Patterson's *German-English Dictionary for Chemists* (1917), and *French-English Dictionary for Chemists* (1921), Ludmilla Callaham's *Russian-English Technical and Chemical Dictionary* (1947), and Louis A. Robb's Spanish-English, English-Spanish *Engineers' Dictionary* (1944), *Dictionary of Business Terms* (1950), and *Dictionary of Legal Terms* (1955).

The field of astronomy and navigation has been explored by Wiley, and, although the number of books published is not large, several have received widespread recognition. Some of the older books are now out of date, and therefore it is difficult to measure their influence at the time they were written. But books on astronomy were being printed from 1839 on. The earliest book that is known to have received acclaim is John F. Hayford's *Textbook of*

Geodetic Astronomy, published in 1898. This is not only one of the standard books on this subject, and written by a man of great eminence in the field, but also it is one of the last on this topic published in this country. The field has since been taken over by experts in other countries. George L. Hosmer's books, *Textbook of Practical Astronomy* (1910) and *Navigation* (1918), were widely used, and George C. Comstock's *Sumner Line* (1919) had a high reputation in its time. Of the more recent publications, Clyde Fisher and Marian Lockwood's *Astronomy* (1940), the first of five short books in the Survey of Science Series, and Bernard Lovell and J. A. Clegg's *Radio Astronomy* (1952) enjoyed a modest distribution. The latter was actually the first one of its kind published in this field; the section on meteor radio astronomy is considered exceptionally good. Leiv Harang's *The Aurorae* (1951) and J. G. Porter's *Comets and Meteor Streams* (1952) are other important books in a specialized field.

From this point of vantage, we cannot imagine that Wiley's 1815 publication by Lazare Nicholas Carnot, *An Exposition of the Political Conduct of Lieut. Carnot since the First of July, 1814*, could have sold more than one hundred copies. Neither can we get very enthusiastic about the prospect for J. Allen's *Autocracy in Poland and Russia* (1854). When we get down to more modern times in the area of political science, we can speak with somewhat greater enthusiasm about the reception accorded Charles Hodges' *The Background of International Relations* (1931), which the London *Times* pronounced "a remarkable book." This book sold well, but not any better than several later titles in the field of political science.

The earliest book on the Wiley list that might properly be called sociological is the one by George Catlin called *North American Indian Portfolio* (1848). Catlin, following in the footsteps of H. R. Schoolcraft, depicted the plight of the Indian in a series of books, and demanded that something should be done by the government to ease his difficulties. Of the thirty-eight books on sociology published by the firm, the important titles in fairly recent years included Maurice R. Davie's *Problems of City Life* (1932) and Joseph Folsom's *The Family* (1934). E. Dwight Sanderson, an entomologist by training, having written a good book on insects that, regularly revised, is still on our list, changed his interests, becoming an authority on rural sociology. His book, *Rural Sociology and Rural Social Organization* (1942), was an important book in its time. Ellsworth Huntington, a geographer, a prolific writer in his field, and author of many good textbooks, probably will be better known for his *Mainsprings of Civilization* (1945), which students in this area have given high praise. Of more recent publications, August B. Hollingshead's *Elmtown's Youth* (1949), a study in adolescence, has attracted much favorable attention.

A separate article might well have been written about Wiley's publications in the field of business and economics. More than one hundred titles were published in this area, of which twenty-five were devoted to books on accounting. Most of the recent books in this field are part of the Wiley Publications in Accounting, under the editorship of H. T. Scovill and C. A. Moyer—books like Charles F. Schlatter's two volumes, *Cost Accounting* (1927 and 1939), Lloyd Morey's *Introduction to Government Accounting* (1927), Harry H. Wade's *Fundamentals of Accounting* (1934), H. Heaton Baily's *Specialized Accounting Systems* (1941), and R. K. Mautz's *Fundamentals of Auditing* (1954). We are constantly amazed at the titles that Charles and John Wiley published in the early days of the firm's existence, and it would be most enlightening to have sales figures available to determine how well they guessed in choosing some of them, for guessing it must have been. Today, we could do little with an 1817 publication called *Auctions Inconsistent with Regular Trade and Injurious to the City—Address to the People of New York.* Fortunately, as the years went along, practical books on accounting, investments, and manufacturing filled the lists and undoubtedly brought some money into the company coffers. With the turn of the century, we can spot titles that must have had a ready sale. With the publication in 1916 of Carl E. Grunsky's *Valuation, Depreciation and the Rate Base*, the modern era began. We can then point to books of the quality of O. B. Goldman's *Financial Engineering* (1920), Simon Litman's *Essentials of International Trade* (1923), Warren M. Persons' *Forecasting Business Cycles* (1931), George F. Warren and Frank A. Pearson's *Prices* (1933), George W. Dowrie and Douglas R. Fuller's *Investments* (1941), Wilson Wright's *Forecasting for Profit* (1947), Kenneth E. Boulding's *Reconstruction of Economics* (1950), and Abraham Charnes, William W. Cooper, and Alexander Henderson's *An Introduction to Linear Programming* (1951). This brief account cannot be concluded without mention of the Cowles Commission Monographs that Wiley now publishes, a series of books concerned with the various phases of econometrics. There are now fifteen volumes in the series.

In 1948, when the company embarked on a visual aids program of providing slides and film strip to complement new editions of books in the various sciences, it prided itself on up-to-dateness in embarking on an entirely new venture. A little research showed that Wiley was only ninety years off, for a full page advertisement for 1858 in *Roorbach's Bookseller's Medium*, published by John Wiley, informed us of a series of stereopticon views featuring slides of France, Italy, Switzerland, and other European countries.

For many years during the nineteenth century, Wiley's business in Europe was conducted through a number of publishers acting as distributors. In 1895 an agreement was made with Chapman and Hall, the English firm famous as publishers of Dickens, Trollope, Meredith, and other great writers of the times. This agreement, a very informal document, made Chapman and Hall Wiley's sole agents for Great Britain. This was a fortunate move for both companies, as the cordial relationship established then has continued through the years. Moreover, Chapman and Hall, then known primarily as a trade house, has moved steadily forward in its technical and scientific business so that today the trade department represents the smaller part of its business. In his book, "A Hundred Years of Publishing," Arthur Waugh, managing director of Chapman and Hall, observed, "By this time [1895], the firm [Wiley] had attained the recognized position of the leading American house for books on engineering and the allied sciences."

Today all Wiley books carry on the title page: New York: John Wiley & Sons, Inc.; London: Chapman & Hall, Ltd. Under the successive direction of Oswald Crawfurd, Arthur Waugh, John Bale, and now John McDougall, this informal partnership has greatly prospered.

MARTIN MATHESON

Up to Now

LOOKING BACK OVER WHAT HAS BEEN WRITTEN in these pages, we see clearly that the House of Wiley has enjoyed a diversified history. It is difficult to find a single phase of publishing untouched in these one hundred and fifty years. Fiction, poetry, travel, juveniles, books in the specialized areas of law, medicine and religion, science, technology, and brief sorties into literary, biographic, and medical magazine publishing—these areas occupied the attention of the several generations of Wileys.

We have seen the firm emerge from the printer-bookseller-publisher stage of the early literary period of Charles Wiley. At best it was a small business, almost a one-man operation despite the many combinations on the title page —Charles Wiley; Van Winkle and Wiley; Wiley and Halsted; Wiley and Long. Cooper's *The Spy* and three additional Cooper titles, and the popular *Fanny* by Fitz-Greene Halleck, were among the important books of the Charles Wiley period (1807–1826). Then came the more affluent international period in partnership with the alert and far-sighted George Putnam, and the publication of books by such distinguished writers as Hawthorne, Margaret Fuller, Melville, Poe, Carlyle, and Ruskin.

Junior Officers of the Corporation. Upper left: W. G. STONE. *Upper right:* G. S. IERARDI. *Bottom left:* W. H. GRIMSHAW. *Bottom right:* A. H. NEILLY, JR.

When the Wiley and Putnam partnership was dissolved in 1848, John Wiley, continuing under his own name, began to publish more books in the scientific and technical fields, which since have become the firm's dominant interest. This was not a sudden change, for as early as 1815 Charles Wiley was bringing out technical books. *The American Practical Brewer and Tanner*, by Joseph Coppinger, appeared in that year, and in 1819 *A View of the Lead Mines of Missouri*, by Henry R. Schoolcraft, was published. Charles Davies, a professor of mathematics at West Point, wrote *Elements of Surveying*, printed in 1835, and nine years later Wiley and Putnam published the second edition of James Dwight Dana's famous *System of Mineralogy*.

John Wiley had two sons, Charles and William. Charles joined his father in business in 1850 and William in 1876, after he had completed ten years in the practice of engineering. The firm name then became known as John Wiley and Sons. Charles, the older of the sons, devoted himself to the sales and financial aspects of the business throughout his career. To the younger son, Major William H. Wiley, a Civil War veteran and civil engineering graduate, belongs much of the credit for carrying the Wiley name to the front rank in technical publishing at such an early date. Unlike his grandfather, Charles, and his father, John, who were by all accounts cautious and conservative men, content to make progress slowly, Major Wiley possessed a bold temperament. Perhaps his Civil War experience had something to do with it, for he demanded action, and plenty of it. He had vision, ambition, and a willingness to take risks. He was gregarious, a member or officer of the leading engineering societies, and a personal friend of the many famous engineers and educators whose works he published—such men as DeVolson Wood, Henry S. Drinker, August J. DuBois, and Robert Thurston. It was during this period that the firm began publication of the condensed engineering pocket books that over the years have evolved into the comprehensive technical handbooks of today.

By the time John Wiley and Sons was incorporated in 1904, with Major Wiley as the corporation's first president, the publication of general literature had been virtually abandoned. In the years since 1904 and the present, as the Wiley imprint became more and more closely associated with works of a scientific and educational nature, extensive coverage has been achieved in all the major branches of engineering, the pure and applied sciences, the social sciences, and in many collateral fields.

During Major Wiley's three terms in Congress beginning in 1903, Mr. William O. Wiley, who had come into the firm in 1890, took over the main responsibility for the company's editorial program. "W.O.," as he was called by his associates, was a Greek and Latin scholar of some distinction, and it was no surprise to anyone to note how well he grasped the needs of the times and how ably he persuaded some of the best scientific and technical minds of the day to write books, many of which turned out to be standard books in their fields. The listing of the authors of this period is literally a roster of the ranking men in engineering and science, men of the calibre of Charles Breed, Herman Diederichs, C. E. Fuller, G. F. Gebhardt, Dexter Kimball, W. A. Johnston, Emil Chamot, Edward Dana, Louis Pirrson, Charles Schuchert, James Toumey, and many others.

Major William H. Wiley died in 1925, and was succeeded in the presidency of the company by William O. Wiley, who was a nephew of Major Wiley, a grandson of John Wiley, and a great-grandson of the founder, Charles Wiley. In 1941 he became chairman of the board and was succeeded in the presidency by Edward P. Hamilton, also a grandson of John Wiley. On his retirement in 1956 Mr. Hamilton became chairman of the board, and W. Bradford Wiley became president. Mr. Wiley is the fifth generation of his family to serve the business.

Although Wiley is by most business standards a venerable institution with an excellent record of achievement, the outstanding fact is that its greatest growth has taken place in the last forty years. The most spectacular growth, as one would expect, occurred after the second World War. There is, of course, some satisfaction in having survived wars, depressions, and stiff competition for over a century and a half; there may even be some justification for a mild bit of self-congratulation and complacency. Many publishers have come and gone, flourished for a time, and then disappeared or been absorbed by a more prosperous rival. But what happened to this firm in these many decades is, after all, history. It represents the past, whereas the all-important consideration of the present group of officers is the present, as well as the future. The current healthy state of the company is ample testimony that the philosophy of constantly looking to an even better future has permeated the entire organization.

Martin Matheson

Index